Brief Contents with Listing of Writing Projects

W9-BXG-593

An Insider's Guide to Academic Writing

A Brief Rhetoric

An Insider's Guide to Academic Writing

A Brief Rhetoric

Susan Miller-Cochran

University of Arizona

Roy Stamper

North Carolina State University

Stacey Cochran

University of Arizona

Bedford/St. Martin's

A Macmillan Education Imprint

Boston • New York

For Bedford/St. Martin's

Vice President, Editorial, Macmillan Higher Education Humanities: Edwin Hill
Editorial Director, English and Music: Karen S. Henry
Publisher for Composition, Business and Technical Writing, and Developmental Writing:
    Leasa Burton
Senior Executive Editor: Stephen A. Scipione
Executive Editor: Molly Parke
Developmental Editor: Sherry Mooney
Senior Production Editor: Ryan Sullivan
Assistant Production Supervisor: Victoria Anzalone
Marketing Manager: Emily Rowin
Copy Editor: Alice Vigliani
Indexer: Schroeder Indexing Services
Director of Rights and Permissions: Hilary Newman
Senior Art Director: Anna Palchik
Text Design: Claire Seng-Niemoeller
Cover Design: William Boardman
Cover Art: Andrea Tsurumi
Composition: Jouve
Printing and Binding: RR Donnelley and Sons

Manufactured in the United States of America.

0 9 8 7 6

f e d c

For information, write: Bedford/St. Martin's, 75 Arlington Street, Boston, MA 02116
(617-399-4000)

ISBN 978-1-319-02030-9

Acknowledgments

Text acknowledgments and copyrights appear at the back of the book on page 323, which constitutes an extension of the copyright page. Art acknowledgments and copyrights appear on the same page as the art selections they cover. It is a violation of the law to reproduce these selections by any means whatsoever without the written permission of the copyright holder.

Preface for Instructors

What is an "insider"? In all walks of life, insiders are the ones who know the territory, speak the language, have the skills, understand the codes, keep the secrets. With *An Insider's Guide to Academic Writing*, we want to help college students, new to the world of higher education, learn the territory, language, skills, codes, and secrets of academic writing in disciplinary contexts. While no single book, or course, or teacher could train all students in all the details of scholarly writing in all disciplines, *An Insider's Guide* offers a flexible, rhetoric-based pedagogy that has helped our students navigate the reading and writing expectations of academic discourse communities across the curriculum. We have found that because the pedagogy is grounded in rhetorical principles and concepts, writing instructors who might otherwise be wary of teaching outside their scholarly expertise feel confident about the approach. Moreover, students quickly grasp the transferable benefits of the approach to their future courses, so their level of enthusiasm and personal investment is high.

As a unique enhancement to its rhetoric-based pedagogy, *An Insider's Guide to Academic Writing* integrates, through video and print interviews, the writing advice of scholars and undergraduates from many disciplines; they speak from and about their own experiences as academic writers. (We conducted, filmed, and curated the interviews ourselves, and they are available as part of the LaunchPad Solo package with the book.) Whether professor or student, these credible and compelling experts humanize and demystify disciplinary discourse, sharing their insider knowledge with academic novices.

An Insider's Guide to Academic Writing derives from the research and teaching that went into transitioning the first-year writing program at North Carolina State University to a writing-in-the-disciplines (WID) approach. This approach is gaining wider currency nationwide as calls for instruction in transferable college writing skills increase. At that time, more than a decade ago, faculty in the program (including the authors of this book) immersed themselves in scholarship on WID and WID pedagogy. We also began to seek supporting instructional materials, but did not find any existing textbooks that met our needs. While several texts focused, to varying degrees, on introducing students to writing in the academic disciplines, few texts employed a rhetorical approach to explore these kinds of writing. Fewer still employed a rhetorical approach to understanding the conventions of writing that characterize those disciplinary texts while also providing support for students' own production of disciplinary genres.

The book that emerged from these years of teaching and research, *An Insider's Guide to Academic Writing*, is a composition rhetoric with readings that distills much of the writing-in-the-disciplines approach that we and our colleagues have used with success for many years. This approach begins by applying rhetorical principles to the understanding of texts, and then shows those principles at work in various domains of academic inquiry, including the humanities, the social sciences, the natural sciences, and the applied fields. It does so mainly by (1) introducing students to rhetorical lenses through which they can view the genres and conventions they will be expected to read and produce in other courses, (2) providing examples of those genres and conventions to analyze and discuss, and (3) including carefully scaffolded writing activities and projects designed to help students explore and guide their production of those genres.

We believe that composition programs pursuing a WID-oriented approach to academic writing will find that *An Insider's Guide* provides a foundation of instruction in disciplinary thinking and writing but is flexible enough to accommodate the diverse teaching interests of individual instructors. Some faculty, for instance, use this approach to support themed courses; they examine how a particular topic or issue is explored by scholars across a range of disciplines. Other faculty situate principles of argument at the center of their course designs and explore disciplinary perspectives and writing in light of those principles. Still others organize their courses as step-by-step journeys through academic domains while attending to the similarities and distinctions in writing practices (rhetorical conventions and genres) of various fields.

The goal of each of these approaches is to foster students' understanding of the various academic communities they participate in as part of the typical undergraduate experience. With the support of *An Insider's Guide to Academic Writing*, these approaches can also foster a deepening rhetorical sensitivity in our students while providing opportunities for them to analyze and practice the kinds of genres they often encounter in college. The book encourages students to exercise rhetorical skills that are transferable from one writing situation to another and supports a rhetorical approach to understanding writing that should be at the core of any first-year writing experience.

A Closer Look at What's in the Book

An Insider's Guide to Academic Writing takes students inside the worlds of higher education, academic writing and research, and disciplinary writing.

- Part One, "A Guide to College and College Writing," begins by introducing students to colleges and universities, as well as to the kinds of writing expectations they will likely face in college. It introduces students to core principles of rhetoric and explores a number of frameworks for rhetorical analysis. This part of the book also reviews basic principles of argument and strategies for conducting library research.

- Part Two, "Inside Academic Writing," is an exploration of the research practices, rhetorical conventions, and genres that characterize the major academic disciplinary domains—the humanities, the social sciences, the natural sciences, as well as a number of applied fields. The first chapter in Part Two (Chapter 5) explores the role of the core principles from Part One—rhetoric, argument, and research—in the various academic disciplines. Each of the remaining chapters in Part Two focuses on a different domain, but they all begin with an exploration of research practices specific to those academic communities. Each chapter also employs a practical, three-part framework (SLR, or "structure, language, and reference")* for identifying and analyzing the conventions that characterize writing in each discipline. In addition, these chapters provide scaffolded support for students' production of discipline-appropriate genres. In the social sciences, for example, we offer support for students' production of theory-response position papers as well as for the literature review.

"INSIDER" FEATURES

The chapters in this book provide a number of features that help facilitate instruction and student learning:

"Insider's View" Sidebars and Videos Linked to LaunchPad Solo Students hear directly from scholars in various academic fields who explore disciplinary writing expectations and reflect on their own writing practices. These unique features provide a form of personal access to the academic world that students sometimes find alien, uninviting, or intimidating. Each video is accompanied by a pair of activities within LaunchPad Solo, one to confirm students' understanding of the content and the second inviting them to make larger connections and provide thoughtful written responses.

Sidebars and video links

*For the concept of the SLR framework, we are indebted to Patricia Linton, Robert Madigan, and Susan Johnson ("Introducing Students to Disciplinary Genres: The Role of the General Composition Course," *Language and Learning across the Disciplines* 1.2 [October 1994]: 63–78).

Insider Example
Professional Research Report in Nursing

As you read the following research report, pay particular attention to the structure, language, and reference parallels between the form of the report and those you've encountered already in the fields of the natural sciences and the social sciences. Keep in mind that the text presented here is made up of a series of excerpts from a much lengthier and more substantial research report.

Rural African-American Mothers Parenting Prematurely Born Infants: An Ecological Systems Perspective

MARGARET SHANDOR MILES, PhD, FAAN; DIANE HOLDITCH-DAVIS, PhD, FAAN; SUZANNE THOYRE, PhD; LINDA BEEBER, PhD

"Insider Example" reading

"Insider Example" Readings   These readings appear throughout the chapters, providing models of writing by scholars and students. Most of the readings exemplify important genres of academic and disciplinary writing; many are annotated with marginal commentary that identifies writers' rhetorical moves and/or poses questions for students' further consideration. These annotations take students "inside" the production of various disciplinary texts and, by extension, inside the academy itself.

"Inside Work" and "Writing Project" Activities   These activities appear strategically throughout the book's chapters. They are designed to provide opportunities for students to put their learning into action, to analyze and

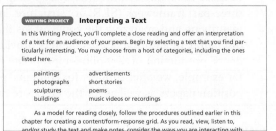

INSIDE WORK   **Reflecting on a Discipline**

In his Insider's View, "Scientists must write all sorts of things," Mike Brotherton makes several generalizations about science, scientists, and scientific writing. Which of these comments, if any, surprised you, and which ones didn't? Explain why. ▶

"Inside Work" and "Writing Project" activities

WRITING PROJECT   **Interpreting a Text**

In this Writing Project, you'll complete a close reading and offer an interpretation of a text for an audience of your peers. Begin by selecting a text that you find particularly interesting. You may choose from a host of categories, including the ones listed here.

paintings	advertisements
photographs	short stories
sculptures	poems
buildings	music videos or recordings

As a model for reading closely, follow the procedures outlined earlier in this chapter for creating a content/form-response grid. As you read, view, listen to, and/or study the text and make notes, consider the ways you are interacting with

---

tip sheet

Reading and Writing in Academic Disciplines

- **You should not expect to master the writing of every academic discipline by reading one book,** even this one.

- It's important to become familiar with key concepts of disciplinary writing in academic discourse communities: *research* expectations; *conventions* (expectations) of writing; *genres* (types) of writing.

- Genres are not always bound by discipline, although their conventions may vary somewhat from discipline to discipline. For example, you can expect to write literature reviews in many different courses across the curriculum.

- **Analyzing academic writing is a multistep process.** (1) Understand the rhetorical context (author, audience, topic, purpose for writing); (2) identify the disciplinary area and what you know about it; (3) consider how expectations for features of *structure, language,* and *reference* govern the writing situation; (4) identify the genre of writing and the conventions that apply; (5) analyze the persuasive strategies if the writer is developing an argument.

- **Remember SLR.** The acronym for *structure, language,* and *reference* offers categories that can help you determine conventions and choices appropriate for most academic writing situations.
  - *Structure* concerns how texts are organized. *Example:* IMRAD—signifying Introduction, Methods, Results, and Discussion—is a common format in both the social and natural sciences.
  - *Language* encompasses conventions of style or word choice. *Example:* Active voice is typically favored in the humanities, and passive voice is more characteristic of writing in the social and natural sciences.
  - *Reference* concerns the ways writers engage source material, including their use of conventions of citation and documentation.

"Tip Sheet"

practice the skills and moves taught in the chapters. These activities function throughout the chapters to build a scaffold that supports students' mastery of skills needed to produce the various "Writing Projects" explored throughout the book, from rhetorical analyses and interpretations (in the humanities), theory-response papers and literature reviews (in the social sciences), research proposals and formal observation reports (in the natural sciences), to lesson plans and memoranda (in the applied fields).

Summary "Tip Sheets"   Every chapter concludes with a "Tip Sheet" that underscores critical concepts and insights for students as they move from novices to academic insiders.

Finally, the appendix, "Introduction to Documentation Styles," discusses how specific citation styles reflect disciplinary concerns and emphases while concisely explaining and exemplifying the basics of MLA, APA, and CSE documentation.

In all walks of life, not all who are invited inside become insiders. Students taking your course in writing are there because they have accepted the invitation to higher education; they've crossed the first threshold. But to become insiders, they'll need the wisdom and counsel of other insiders. We have prepared this book, with its supporting videos and ancillary materials (detailed on p. xiii) to help them learn the territory, language, skills, codes, and secrets of academic writing. But a guidebook can only do so much. Students need insiders such as yourself and your colleagues to guide their understanding. We hope our *Insider's Guide* proves to be a resource you rely on as you start them on their journeys.

Acknowledgments

Writing this textbook has been a journey for all three of us as we have experimented with various pedagogical approaches, assignments, and content with students and faculty colleagues. We have had tremendous support from the team at Bedford, first and foremost from Steve Scipione, our editor, who has helped us see this project through to completion while providing insightful suggestions that have guided our approach. We are also indebted to composition publisher Leasa Burton, who understood our goals and championed this project from the beginning, and executive editor Molly Parke, whose creative thinking about the book's potential has been encouraging and invigorating. We have also received outstanding support and guidance from developmental editor Sherry Mooney, who has helped us successfully incorporate the voices of many scholars and students into this project, and Ryan Sullivan, who guided the book through the production process with great care and good humor. Claire Seng-Niemoeller created the superb design of the book, and Christine Voboril cleared the permissions. We thank Emily Rowin and Melissa Famiglietti for their marketing and market development efforts. We remain grateful to other contributors who helped in so many ways behind the scenes, including Edwin Hill, Karen Henry, Elise Kaiser, Anna Palchik, Kalina Ingham, Lindsey Jaroszewicz, Alyssa Demirjian, and Sophia Snyder, who made her mark during the earliest stages of the project.

We are also indebted to the students who were willing to try this approach and, in many cases, share their writing in this book. Their examples provide essential scaffolding for the book's approach, and their honest feedback helped us refine our explanation of various genres and disciplines.

We are also grateful to our colleagues in the First-Year Writing Program at North Carolina State University, who have shared their expertise and ideas about teaching writing in and about disciplines over the years. Without their support and their innovation, we would not have been able to complete this project. Specifically, we want to thank David Gruber, who helped us solicit responses from professionals in a range of fields early in the project. We also want to thank Brent Simoneaux, who provided outstanding feedback on early drafts of the chapters. We are also indebted to Kate Lavia-Bagley, whose experience and success with teaching this approach is showcased in the outstanding Instructor's Manual she has written to accompany the book.

We also appreciate the outstanding comments and suggestions we received from reviewers throughout the development of this first edition: Steven Alvarez, Queens College of CUNY; Sonia Apgar Begert, Olympic College; JoAnn Buck, Guilford Technical Community College; Diana Kaye Campbell, Forsyth Technical Community College; Jennifer Cellio, Northern Kentucky University; Jill Channing, Mitchell Community College; Polina Chemishanova, University of North Carolina at Pembroke; Jason DePolo, North Carolina Agricultural and Technical State University; Brock Dethier, Utah State University; Anthony Edgington, University of Toledo; Stephanie Franco, Texas Tech; Sarah Hallenbeck, University of North Carolina at Chapel Hill; Michael Harker, Georgia State University; Kimberly Harrison, Florida International University; Jonathan Hartmann, University of New Haven; Elizabeth Finch Hedengren, Brigham Young University; Lisa Hirsch, Hostos Community College of CUNY; Karen Keaton Jackson, North Carolina Central University; Patricia Lynne, Framingham State University; Janel Mays, Durham Technical Community College; Jessie L. Moore, Elon University; Tracy Morse, East Carolina University; Alice J. Myatt, University of Mississippi; Carroll Ferguson Nardone, Sam Houston State University; Kristin Redfield, Forsyth Technical Community College; Georgia Rhoades, Appalachian State University; Kevin Roozen, Auburn University; Kathleen Ryan, University of Montana; Jessica Saxon, Craven Community College; Loreen Smith, Isothermal Community College; Donna Strickland, University of Missouri, Columbia; Elizabeth West, Central Piedmont Community College; Carl Whithaus, University of California, Davis; and Hui Wu, University of Texas at Tyler.

And finally, we are indebted to our friends and families, who provided a great deal of support as we worked on this project over several years. Without their patience and encouragement, we would not have been able to make this idea into a reality.

Susan Miller-Cochran
Roy Stamper
Stacey Cochran

Get the Most Out of Your Course with *An Insider's Guide to Academic Writing*

Bedford/St. Martin's offers resources and format choices that help you and your students get even more out of your book and course. To learn more about or to order any of the following products, contact your Bedford/St. Martin's sales representative, e-mail sales support (**sales_support@bfwpub.com**), or visit the website at **macmillanhighered.com/insidersguide/catalog**.

LaunchPad Solo for *An Insider's Guide to Academic Writing*: Where Students Learn LaunchPad Solo for *An Insider's Guide to Academic Writing* provides unique content and new ways to get the most out of your book. For students, "Insider's View" videos feature advice from scholars and students about thinking and writing in different academic fields, with accompanying questions and activities. A special set of "Insider Videos" for instructors gives tips and strategies for introducing students to a wide range of disciplines, including the social sciences and the sciences. You'll also find additional interactive exercises and tutorials for reading, writing, and research, as well as LearningCurve, adaptive, game-like practice that helps students focus on the topics where they need the most help.

To get the most out of your book, order LaunchPad Solo for *An Insider's Guide to Academic Writing* packaged with the print book. (LaunchPad Solo for *An Insider's Guide to Academic Writing* can also be purchased on its own.) An activation code is required. To order LaunchPad Solo for *An Insider's Guide to Academic Writing* with the print book, use ISBN 978-1-319-05355-0.

Alternative versions of *An Insider's Guide to Academic Writing* are available. *An Insider's Guide to Academic Writing: A Brief Rhetoric* is available in both print and value-priced e-book versions. Additionally, you may want to examine a copy of *An Insider's Guide to Academic Writing: A Rhetoric and Reader,* a print text combining the contents of the brief rhetoric with an extensive thematic reader that foregrounds real scholarly writing in the humanities, the social sciences, the natural sciences, and the applied fields. For details on all these options, visit **macmillanhighered.com/insidersguide/catalog**.

Bedford/St. Martin's offers a range of affordable formats, so students can choose what works best for them. For details, visit **macmillanhighered .com/insidersguide/catalog**.

Select value packages. Add value to your text by packaging one of the following resources with *An Insider's Guide to Academic Writing.* To learn more about package options for any of the following products, contact your Bedford/St. Martin's sales representative or visit **macmillanhighered.com/insidersguide /catalog**.

Writer's Help 2.0 is a powerful online writing resource that helps students find answers, whether they are searching for writing advice on their own or as part of an assignment.

- **Smart Search**   Built on research with more than 1,600 student writers, the smart search in *Writer's Help 2.0* provides reliable results even when students use novice terms, such as *flow* and *unstuck*.

- **Trusted Content from Our Best-Selling Handbooks**   Choose *Writer's Help 2.0 for Hacker Handbooks* or *Writer's Help 2.0 for Lunsford Handbooks* and ensure that students have clear advice and examples for all of their writing questions.

- **Adaptive Exercises That Engage Students**   *Writer's Help 2.0* includes LearningCurve, game-like online quizzing that adapts to what students already know and helps them focus on what they need to learn.

Student access is packaged with *An Insider's Guide to Academic Writing* at a significant discount. Contact your Bedford/St. Martin's sales representative to ensure that your students have easy access to online writing support with *Writer's Help 2.0 for Hacker Handbooks* or *Writer's Help 2.0 for Lunsford Handbooks*. Students who rent a book or buy a used book can purchase access to *Writer's Help 2.0* at **macmillanhighered.com/writershelp2**.

Instructors may request free access by registering as an instructor at **macmillanhighered.com/writershelp2**. For technical support, visit **macmillanhighered.com/getsupport**.

***Portfolio Keeping*, Third Edition, by Nedra Reynolds and Elizabeth Davis**, provides all the information students need to use the portfolio method successfully in a writing course. *Portfolio Teaching*, a companion guide for instructors, provides the practical information instructors and writing program administrators need to use the portfolio method successfully in a writing course. To order *Portfolio Keeping* packaged with this text, contact your sales representative for a package ISBN.

Instructor Resources
macmillanhighered.com/insidersguide/catalog
You have a lot to do in your course. Bedford/St. Martin's wants to make it easy for you to find the support you need — and to get it quickly.

Resources for Teaching An Insider's Guide to Academic Writing is available as a PDF that can be downloaded from the Bedford/St. Martin's online catalog at the URL above. In addition to chapter overviews and teaching tips, the instructor's manual includes sample syllabi, proposed answers or responses to the questions and activities throughout the text, and classroom activities.

Resources for Teaching North Carolina English 112 with An Insider's Guide to Academic Writing is available as a PDF that can be downloaded from the Bedford/St. Martin's online catalog at the URL above. This brief resource complements *Resources for Teaching An Insider's Guide to Academic Writing*, with teaching attention to specific course outcomes and transfer requirements articulated in the 2014 Comprehensive Articulation

Agreement between the University of North Carolina and the North Carolina Community College System.

Teaching Central offers the entire list of Bedford/St. Martin's print and online professional resources. You'll find landmark reference works, sourcebooks on pedagogical issues, award-winning collections, and practical advice for the classroom—all free for instructors. Visit **macmillanhighered .com/teachingcentral**.

Join Our Community! The Macmillan English Community is now Bedford/St. Martin's home for professional resources, featuring *Bits*, our popular blog site offering new ideas for the composition classroom and composition teachers. Connect and converse with a growing team of Bedford authors and top scholars who blog on *Bits*: Andrea Lunsford, Nancy Sommers, Steve Bernhardt, Traci Gardner, Barclay Barrios, Jack Solomon, Susan Bernstein, Elizabeth Wardle, Doug Downs, Elizabeth Losh, Jonathan Alexander, and Donna Winchell.

In addition, you'll find an expanding collection of resources that support your teaching:

- Sign up for webinars.
- Download resources from our professional resource series.
- Start a discussion.
- Ask a question.
- Follow your favorite members.
- Review projects in the pipeline.

Visit **community.macmillan.com** to join the conversation with your fellow teachers.

How This Book Supports WPA Outcomes for First-Year Composition

Note: This chart aligns with the latest WPA Outcomes Statement, ratified in July 2014.

WPA Outcomes	Relevant Features of *An Insider's Guide to Academic Writing*
Rhetorical Knowledge	
Learn and use key rhetorical concepts through analyzing and composing a variety of texts.	*An Insider's Guide to Academic Writing* is built on a foundation of rhetorical analysis and production that commences in Chapter 2, "Reading and Writing Rhetorically" (pp. 20–36), and is extended through the rest of the book. The book uses a variety of "rhetorical lenses" to help students become academic insiders who know what conventions to expect and adapt in disciplinary writing. And it brings in, via print and video, the insights of real academic professionals to help students become insiders.
Gain experience reading and composing in several genres to understand how genre conventions shape and are shaped by readers' and writers' practices and purposes.	Each of the nine chapters in Parts One and Two provide instruction in reading and composing a variety of key academic and disciplinary genres, from a rhetorical analysis (Chapter 2, "Reading and Writing Rhetorically," pp. 30–34) to a literature review (Chapter 7, "Reading and Writing in the Social Sciences," pp. 180–95) to a research proposal (Chapter 8, "Reading and Writing in the Natural Sciences," pp. 240–48).
Develop facility in responding to a variety of situations and contexts, calling for purposeful shifts in voice, tone, level of formality, design, medium, and/or structure.	*An Insider's Guide* is predicated on the practice of situational and contextual composition, where rhetorical context and attention to conventions of structure, language, and reference determine a writer's approach to material. For example, in Chapter 5, "Reading and Writing in Academic Disciplines" (pp. 94–99), an astronomer explains how he writes for different audiences, with examples of the same scientific research written up for two different audiences. The chapter introduces the "Structure/Language/Reference" heuristic.
Understand and use a variety of technologies to address a range of audiences.	The use of "Insider's View" videos, available in LaunchPad Solo for *An Insider's Guide to Academic Writing*, models and reinforces the principle of using different technologies to communicate to a range of audiences. The videos of academics explaining how and why they write represent a different channel of explanation, to students and instructors, than the pedagogy in the print book. See astronomer Mike Brotherton's interviews (Chapter 5, "Reading and Writing in Academic Disciplines," pp. 93, 96, 100) and "Insider's View" videos, for example.

WPA Outcomes	Relevant Features of *An Insider's Guide to Academic Writing*
Match the capacities of different environments (e.g., print and electronic) to varying rhetorical situations.	See the previous entry, and also the various discussions of genre and genre awareness throughout the book—for example, the opening pages of Chapter 2, "Reading and Writing Rhetorically" (pp. 20–24). See also the cluster of material in Chapter 6, "Reading and Writing in the Humanities," on interpreting images (pp. 109–12) and the Dale Jacobs essay on multimodality (pp. 114–23).
Critical Thinking, Reading, and Composing	
Use composing and reading for inquiry, learning, thinking, and communicating in various rhetorical contexts.	All of the discipline-specific chapters include detailed information about research and inquiry in their academic domains. See Chapter 6, "Reading and Writing in the Humanities" (pp. 111–29); Chapter 7, "Reading and Writing in the Social Sciences" (pp. 154–65); Chapter 8, "Reading and Writing in the Natural Sciences" (pp. 212–21); and Chapter 9, "Reading and Writing in the Applied Fields" (pp. 261–64).
Read a diverse range of texts, attending especially to relationships between assertion and evidence, to patterns of organization, to interplay between verbal and nonverbal elements, and how these features function for different audiences and situations.	Chapter 3, "Developing Arguments" (pp. 37–58), offers instruction in identifying claims and assertions and relating them to evidence. The genres sections of all the disciplinary chapters in Part Two, "Inside Academic Writing" (Chapters 5–9), help students pay attention to patterns of organization (e.g., the IMRAD format), with particular attention to the Structure, Language, and Reference systems in play. See, for example, "Genres of Writing in the Natural Sciences" (pp. 227–59).
Locate and evaluate primary and secondary research materials, including journal articles, essays, books, databases, and informal Internet sources.	See in particular Chapter 4, "Academic Research" (pp. 59–85), where information on locating and evaluating primary and secondary research materials—including journal articles, essays, books, databases, and informal Internet sources—can be found.
Use strategies—such as interpretation, synthesis, response, critique, and design/redesign—to compose texts that integrate the writer's ideas with those from appropriate sources.	Chapter 4, "Academic Research" (pp. 59–85), discusses working with sources. Furthermore, Chapter 6, "Reading and Writing in the Humanities" (pp. 108–51), explores textual interpretation, response, and critique; and Chapter 7, "Reading and Writing in the Social Sciences," pays particular attention to strategies of synthesis (pp. 183–95).
Processes	
Develop a writing project through multiple drafts.	*An Insider's Guide to Academic Writing* presents an overview of the writing process in Chapter 2 (the "Rhetorical Writing Processes" section, pp. 27–30), and many chapters include "Inside Work" activities that ask students to build on the previous activities to develop a paper. For example, Chapter 3, "Developing Arguments," includes a sequence of such activities on pp. 39, 42, 45, 46, and 48.

(continued)

WPA Outcomes	Relevant Features of *An Insider's Guide to Academic Writing*
Processes (continued)	
Develop flexible strategies for reading, drafting, reviewing, collaboration, revising, rewriting, rereading, and editing.	See the previous entry. Additionally, the "Writing Project" activities that generally close each chapter are sequenced and scaffolded to support process writing. Throughout the book and in LaunchPad Solo interviews, academic insiders discuss both the nature of collaborative writing and working with editors.
Use composing processes and tools as a means to discover and reconsider ideas.	All of the discipline-specific chapters include detailed information about research and inquiry in their academic domains, and pay attention to the notion of testing ideas with audiences. See in particular Chapter 8, "Reading and Writing in the Natural Sciences," which traces how the process of developing observation and research inevitably leads to a modification of ideas (contrast the two papers by student Kedric Lemon on pp. 230–39 and pp. 250–59).
Experience the collaborative and social aspects of writing processes.	Many of the "Inside Work" activities require collaborative work, and the ethos of collaboration comes through strongly in the chapters on social sciences (Chapter 7) and natural sciences (Chapter 8). The chapter on writing in the natural sciences explicitly discusses the importance of cooperation and collaboration in the conventions section (p. 226).
Learn to give and act on productive feedback to works in progress.	See the previous rubric. Many of the articles reprinted in the book were written by teams of researchers.
Adapt composing processes for a variety of technologies and modalities.	*An Insider's Guide to Academic Writing*'s start-to-finish emphasis on rhetorically situated, genre-aware, and convention-informed writing makes this point.
Reflect on the development of composing practices and how those practices influence their work.	Many of the "Inside Work" activities throughout the book have students reflect on what they know, what they think they know, and what they learn. For example, see the "Inside Work" activities throughout Chapter 1, "Inside Colleges and Universities" (pp. 3–19).
Knowledge of Conventions	
Develop knowledge of linguistic structures, including grammar, punctuation, and spelling, through practice in composing and revising.	The distinctive SLR framework (Structure/Language/Reference) introduced in Part Two ("Inside Academic Writing," Chapters 5–9; see the introduction to SLR in Chapter 5, pp. 96–98) has a Language category that emphasizes the linguistic choices and conventions in disciplinary writing, and the Reference feature puts emphasis on formatting issues that include spelling and punctuation. Bedford/St. Martin's also offers a variety of writing handbooks that can be packaged inexpensively with *An Insider's Guide*. See the preface for information.

WPA Outcomes	Relevant Features of *An Insider's Guide to Academic Writing*
Understand why genre conventions for structure, paragraphing, tone, and mechanics vary.	Genre conventions across and within disciplines are emphasized throughout Part Two of the book. Beyond that, the Appendix on documentation styles (pp. 307–21) discusses disciplinary conventions in referencing, with implications for structure and mechanics.
Gain experience negotiating variations in genre conventions.	*An Insider's Guide* provides many opportunities for students to experiment and negotiate variations in disciplinary conventions. See, for example, the "Writing Projects" in Chapter 5, "Reading and Writing in Academic Disciplines," which include "Comparing Scholarly and Popular Articles" (p. 102) and "Translating a Scholarly Article for a Public Audience" (p. 106). In particular, some of the "Inside Work" activities in Chapter 9, "Reading and Writing in the Applied Fields" (pp. 272, 282, 294, 304), ask students to become professionals "for a day" and try writing important genres by extrapolating from models in the chapter.
Learn common formats and/or design features for different kinds of texts.	The design features of key genres, such as IMRAD, are highlighted (especially in Chapters 7 and 8, on the social sciences and natural sciences respectively). Chapter 4, "Academic Research," introduces different documentation formats (MLA, APA, CSE—pp. 76–77), which is expanded upon in the Appendix on documentation styles (pp. 307–21).
Explore the concepts of intellectual property (such as fair use and copyright) that motivate documentation conventions.	The Appendix on documentation styles (MLA, APA, CSE formats) raises issues of different documentation conventions (pp. 307–21), and the discussion of plagiarism in Chapter 4, "Academic Research," raises concerns about intellectual property (pp. 75–76).
Practice applying citation conventions systematically in their own work.	The Appendix (pp. 307–21) enables students to apply citation conventions of MLA, APA, and CSE styles systematically in their own work.

Contents

LaunchPadSolo *Additional video material may be found online in LaunchPad Solo when the ⏵ icon appears.*

An Insider's Guide to
Academic Writing
A Brief Rhetoric

PART ONE

A Guide to College and College Writing

Inside Colleges and Universities

What Is Higher Education?

This book introduces the expectations about writing you'll likely encounter in college and gives you a set of tools to complete writing tasks successfully. To understand those expectations, you must first understand how colleges and universities are structured; how your other writing experiences in high school, college, and work might compare; and what expectations about writing you might encounter in your particular college or university classes. These expectations will likely differ according to the type of college or university you attend.

As you read through the chapters in this book, certain recurring features will help expand your knowledge of college writing:

- *Insider's View* boxes contain excerpts of comments by scholars and students discussing academic writing. Many of these are gleaned from video interviews that complement the instruction in this book. The videos, which are further referenced in the page margins, can be viewed for greater insight into the processes and productions of academic writers. Video content and other great resources are available on the LaunchPad Solo designed to accompany this text.

- *Inside Work* activities prompt you to reflect on what you have learned while trying out new insights and techniques.

- *Writing Projects* offer sequences of activities that will help you develop your own compositions.

- *Tip Sheets* summarize key lessons of the chapters.

Before we turn to college writing, however, we ask you to read about and reflect on some of the wider contexts of higher education—in particular, your place in it.

ANDREA TSURUMI

HOW DO COLLEGES AND UNIVERSITIES DIFFER FROM ONE ANOTHER?

As we discuss the expectations you might encounter related to writing in college, you should consider the specific context of the school you're attending. What kind of school is it? What types of students does it serve? What are the school's mission and focus? It's important to realize that different schools have differing missions and values that influence their faculty members' expectations for students.

How did you determine where to attend college? Some prospective students send out applications to multiple schools, while others know exactly where they want to start their college careers. Some students transfer from one school to another, and they do so for a variety of reasons. If you researched potential schools, and especially if you visited different campuses as part of your decision-making process, you likely realized that there are many different kinds of schools in the United States (not to mention the variety of institutions of higher education elsewhere in the world). If we just focus on the range of higher education options in the United States, we find:

- **Community Colleges:** schools that typically offer associate's degrees. Some community colleges prepare students to enter careers directly following graduation; others specialize in helping students transfer to bachelor's-granting institutions after completing most of their general education requirements or an associate's degree.

- **Liberal Arts Colleges/Universities:** schools that introduce students to a broad variety of disciplines as they pursue their bachelor's degrees. Liberal arts schools generally focus on undergraduate education, although some offer graduate degrees as well.

- **Doctoral-Granting/Research-Intensive Universities:** schools with an emphasis on research and a focus on both undergraduate and graduate education. Doctoral-granting universities, especially those that are research-intensive, can often be quite large, and they generally have higher expectations for faculty members' research activities than other types of institutions do. As a result, students may have more opportunities for collaborative research with faculty members, and graduate students might teach some undergraduate classes.

- **Master's-Granting Institutions:** schools that offer bachelor's degrees in addition to a selection of master's degrees. Such schools usually have a dual focus on undergraduate and graduate education, but they might not emphasize research expectations for their faculty as intensely as doctoral-granting institutions do.

- **Schools with a Specific Focus:** schools that serve specific populations or prepare students for particular careers. Such schools might be single-sex institutions, historically black colleges and universities, Hispanic-serving institutions, religious-affiliated schools, or agricultural, technical, and vocational schools.

- **For-Profit Institutions:** schools that operate on a business model and are privately held or publicly traded companies. Some are regionally accredited institutions; many focus on meeting the needs of students whose schedules or other commitments require a different approach from what a typical non-profit college or university provides.

What kind of school is the institution that you currently attend? Knowing how your particular college or university is structured, and how it fits into the larger context of higher education, can help you understand its institutional values and the emphasis it places on particular kinds of academic preparation. If you know these important factors, you'll be able to anticipate the expectations for your academic work and understand the reasoning behind the requirements for your degree.

INSIDE WORK) **Choosing a College**

Write brief responses to the following questions, and be prepared to discuss them with your classmates.

- What kind of institution do you attend? What characteristics of your school seem to match that category?
- What degree program or major are you most interested in? Why?
- Was your interest in a particular degree program or major a factor when you decided to go to college? Did it draw you to your particular college? Why or why not?
- What classes are you taking, and how did you choose them?
- What kinds of factors do you consider when choosing your classes? What guidance, requirements, or other influences help you make those choices? ❯

WHAT IS THE PURPOSE OF COLLEGE?

People's reasons for pursuing an undergraduate degree can differ, depending on the school and the individual student. Some schools and degree programs focus on preparing students for particular vocations that they can pursue directly after graduation. Others focus more broadly on developing well-rounded, informed graduates who will be active in their communities regardless of which careers they pursue. Still others emphasize different, and sometimes quite specific, outcomes for their graduates. If you have never done so, consider taking a look at the mission or values statements for your university, college, or department. What do the faculty members and administrators value? What are their expectations of you as a student?

For example, the mission statement of Texas A&M University begins by stating:

> Texas A&M University is dedicated to the discovery, development, communication, and application of knowledge in a wide range of academic and professional fields.

This statement shows a broad commitment to a range of academic interests and professions; therefore, students at Texas A&M can expect to find a wide range of majors represented at the university. The mission statement also emphasizes that knowledge discovery is important at Texas A&M, highlighting the school's role as a research-intensive university.

As another example, the mission statement of San Juan College in New Mexico reads:

> The mission of San Juan College is to improve the quality of life of the citizens it serves by meeting the educational and human needs of the entire community in concert with community agencies, businesses, industries, and other groups.

This statement illustrates San Juan College's emphasis on connection to the community and the agencies, businesses, and industries surrounding and connected to the college. San Juan's mission is connected intricately to the community it serves.

A third example is the mission statement of Endicott College in Massachusetts, which begins by stating:

> The mission of Endicott College is to instill in students an understanding of and an appreciation for professional and liberal studies. Deeply woven within this philosophy is the concept of applied learning, which has been the hallmark of Endicott. Linking classroom and off-campus work experience through required internships remains the most distinguishing feature of the College.

Endicott's mission mentions an emphasis on applied learning, which is evident through its requirement of internships to extend classroom learning. Students who enroll at Endicott College should expect to make practical, hands-on application of their learning throughout their coursework.

Of course, different students have different goals and reasons for pursuing undergraduate degrees. Sometimes those goals match the institution's mission fairly closely, but not always. What is your purpose in attending your college or university? How do your personal and professional goals fit within the school's goals and values? What will you need to do while in college to achieve your goals? What have you already accomplished, and what do you still need to know and do?

Read the following questions, and write a brief response to each.

- What goals do you hope to achieve by attending college?

- What steps should you take to maximize your opportunity to achieve your academic goals?

Next, find your college or university's mission statement (usually available on the school's website), and write a brief description that compares your goals for college to the mission statement. How does the mission of your school fit your goals? How might the strengths and mission of your college or university help you achieve your goals? ▶

What Are Academic Disciplines?

Another structural feature of colleges and universities is the way they are divided into academic disciplines. Depending on the school, this might take the form of departments, divisions, colleges, or other groupings. **Academic disciplines** are, broadly defined, areas of teaching, research, and inquiry that academics pursue. Sometimes these disciplines are listed in broad categories, such as psychology, English, biology, physics, and engineering.

At other times, disciplines are listed in more specialized categories that demonstrate the diversity of areas encompassed within higher education: for example, adolescent psychology, abnormal psychology, sociolinguistics, second language acquisition, molecular biology, physiology, astrophysics, quantum mechanics, civil engineering, mechanical engineering, computer science, Victorian poetry, and medieval literature.

While the specific divisions may differ according to the institution, most college and university faculties are grouped into departments. Larger schools are often further divided into colleges

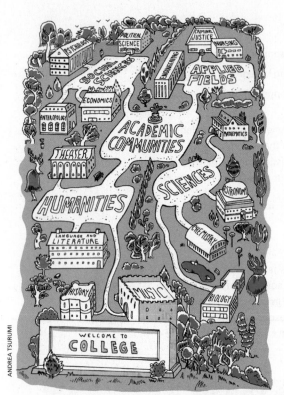

or divisions, which usually cluster departments together that are related in some way to one another. These divisions often, but not always, fall along common lines that divide departments into broader disciplinary areas of the humanities, social sciences, natural sciences, and applied fields. We describe these broad categories in more detail in the next section.

HOW MANY DIFFERENT ACADEMIC DISCIPLINES ARE THERE?

You might find that different faculty members give varying answers to the question, "How many different academic disciplines are there?" And those answers differ for good reason. Sometimes academic disciplines are seen as equivalent to departments. Faculty in the history department study history, right? But the subject of history can be divided into many different categories, too: ante-bellum U.S. history, Middle Eastern history, and African American history, for example. In addition, people in other departments might study and teach topics that are related to history, such as American religious history, medieval literature and culture, and ancient rhetoric. You can probably imagine how categorizing all these different areas of study and research would be difficult.

For the purposes of this text, we're going to explore writing in different disciplinary areas that are grouped together according to (1) the kinds of questions that scholars ask in those disciplines and (2) the research strategies, or methods of inquiry, that they use to answer those questions. As mentioned earlier, we've divided various academic disciplines into four broad disciplinary categories: humanities, social sciences, natural sciences, and applied fields. As we talk about these four areas of study and the disciplines associated with them, both here and in Part Two of the book, you'll notice some similarities and differences within the categories:

- Scholars in the **humanities** usually ask questions about the human condition. To answer these questions, they often employ methods of inquiry that are based on analysis, interpretation, and speculation. Examples of academic disciplines that are generally considered part of the humanities are history, literature, philosophy, foreign languages, religious studies, and the visual arts. For examples of the kinds of questions humanists ask, see Chapter 6.

- Scholars in the **social sciences** usually ask questions about human behavior and society. To answer these questions, they often employ methods of inquiry that are based on theory building or empirical research. Examples of academic disciplines that are generally considered part of the social sciences are communication, psychology, sociology, political science, economics, and anthropology. For examples of the kinds of questions social scientists ask, see Chapter 7.

- Scholars in the **natural sciences** usually ask questions about the natural world and the universe. To answer these questions, they often employ methods of inquiry that are based on experimentation and quantifiable data. Examples of academic disciplines that are generally considered part of the natural sciences are chemistry, biology, physics, astronomy, and mathematics. For examples of the kinds of questions natural scientists ask, see Chapter 8.

- Scholars in **applied fields** might have their foundation in any one (or more) of the disciplinary categories, but their work is generally focused on practical application. Some disciplines that could fall under the category of applied fields are criminal justice, medicine, nursing, education, business, agriculture, and engineering. Each of these fields has elements that are closely aligned with the humanities, social sciences, and/or natural sciences, but each also focuses on application of that knowledge in specific contexts. For examples of the kinds of questions scholars in applied fields ask, see Chapter 9.

These categories are not perfectly distinct, though; they sometimes overlap with one another. You'll see examples of overlap in the chapters in Part Two, in the student writing examples there, and when you undertake your own research in academic journals. However, the disciplinary categories of humanities, social sciences, natural sciences, and applied fields are useful for understanding some of the distinctions in the ways academics think and do research.

INSIDE WORK) **Understanding Disciplinarity**

In your own words, write a brief description of the four academic disciplines mentioned in the previous section.

- humanities

- social sciences

- natural sciences

- applied fields

Next, list your current course schedule. How might you classify the classes you're taking in terms of these four categories? For each class, write for a few minutes about what characteristics of the class cause it to fit into the category you've chosen. Finally, compare your answers with a classmate's. ❯

WHY DO ACADEMICS WRITE?

As you think about the writing you will do in college, keep in mind that you are learning how to participate in the kinds of discussions that scholars and faculty members engage in about topics and issues of mutual interest. In other words, you're entering into academic conversations that have been going on for a while. As you are writing, you will need to think about who your audience is (other students? teachers? an audience outside of the academic setting?), who has already been participating in the conversations of interest to you (and perhaps who hasn't), and what expectations for your writing you'll need to follow in order to contribute to those conversations. (We'll have much more to say about the concept of audience in Chapter 2.)

As we explore the kinds of writing done in various disciplinary areas, you'll notice that different disciplines have different expectations for writing. In other words, faculty members in a particular discipline might expect a piece of writing to be structured in a particular way, or they might use specific kinds of language, or they might expect you to be familiar with certain research by others and refer to it in prescribed ways. Each of these expectations is an aspect of the writing *conventions* of a particular discipline. **Conventions** are the customs that scholars in a particular discipline follow in their writing. Sometimes those conventions take the form of repeated patterns in structure or certain choices in language use, just to name a few. As students learn these conventions, we sometimes say that they are developing *literacy* in the conventions of a discipline. **Literacy** generally refers to the ability to read and write, but it can also refer to the development of familiarity with the conventions and expectations of different situations. As a student, you will be developing academic literacy—or literacies, since you'll be navigating the expectations of several disciplinary contexts.

To prepare for writing in varied academic contexts, it might be helpful to think about why academics write. Most faculty members at institutions of higher education explain their responsibilities to the institution and their discipline in terms of three categories: their teaching, their research (which generates much of their writing), and their service (what they do outside of their research and teaching that contributes both to the school and to their discipline). Many academics' writing is related to communicating the results of their research, and it might be published or shared with academic audiences or more general audiences. In fact, a scholar might conduct a research project and then find that he or she needs to communicate the results of that project to a variety of audiences.

Imagine that a physiologist who studies diabetes has discovered a new therapy that could potentially benefit diabetic individuals. The researcher might want to publish the results of her study in an academic journal so that other scientists can read about the results, perhaps replicate the study (repeat it to confirm that the results are the same), and maybe expand on the research findings. She might also want to communicate the results of her research to doctors who work with diabetic patients but who don't necessarily read academic journals in physiology. They might read medical journals, though, so in this case the researcher would need to tailor her results to an audience that is primarily interested in the application of research results to patients. In addition, she might want to report the results of her research to the general public, in which case she might write a press release so that newspapers and magazines can develop news stories about her findings. Each of these writing situations involves reporting the same research results, but to different audiences and for different purposes. The physiologist would need to tailor her writing to meet the needs of each writing situation.

INSIDE WORK **Thinking about What Academics Write**

Look for a published piece that has been written by one of the professors that you have for another class. Try to find something that you can access in full, either online or through your school's library. Some colleges and universities have lists of recent publications by faculty on their websites. Additionally, some faculty members list their publications on personal websites. You might also seek help from librarians at your institution if you aren't familiar with the library's resources. Then write your responses to the following questions.

- What does the professor write about?

- Where was that work published?

- Who is the audience for your professor's work?

- What surprised you most about your professor's published work? ▶

Insider's View
Undergraduate students on academic writing
SAM STOUT, GENA LAMBRECHT, ALEXANDRIA WOODS, STUDENTS

Left to right: Sam, engineering; Gena, design; Alexandria, biology

QUESTION: How does the writing you did in high school compare to the writing you've done in college so far?

SAM: Well, in high school [teachers] mainly chose what we wrote about. And here in college they allow you to write about what you're going to be focusing on and choose something that's actually going to benefit you in the future instead of writing for an assignment grade.

GENA: Well, I thought I would be doing a lot more writing like in my AP English classes, which was analyzing literature and poems and plays and writing to a prompt that talked a lot about specific conventions for that type of literature.

ALEXANDRIA: I expected my college writing to be science-related—doing lab reports and research proposals—rather than what I did before college, in middle school and high school, which was just doing definition papers, analysis of books, and things like that.

 LaunchPadSolo
Hear more from students about college writing.

How Does Writing in College Compare with Writing in Other Contexts?

Some students find that writing in college focuses less on personal experience and more on academic research than writing they've done in other contexts. Many of your expectations for writing in college might be based on prior experiences, such as the writing you did in high school or in a work setting. Some students are surprised to find that writing instruction in college is not always paired with discussion of literature, as it often is in high school. While some colleges and universities use literature as a starting point for teaching writing, many other schools offer writing instruction that is focused on principles of **rhetoric**—the study of how language is used to communicate—apart from the study of literature. (Rhetoric will be discussed in detail in subsequent chapters throughout this book.) If you are used to thinking about English courses, and the writing assigned in those courses, as being primarily about literature and literary analysis, you might find that the expectations in your college-level writing courses are somewhat different. Many writing courses at the college level will require you to write about different topics, in different forms, and for different audiences. Depending on your school, writing program, and instructor, the study of literature might be part of that approach, but you might also need to learn about the expectations of instructors in other disciplines.

When we compare the writing expectations in college with what you might have experienced in other contexts, we're making some general assumptions about your experience that may or may not be true. We're also making generalizations about colleges and universities that might differ from the school you're currently attending. One of the most important concepts we'll discuss in this book is the importance of context (see Chapter 2), so you'll need to balance the principles we talk about in this text with your firsthand experience of the context of your particular college or university. You might find that some of our assumptions are true to your particular experience and some are not. When possible, make note of the principles we discuss that are similar to your experience and the ones that are different. As you do so, you'll be learning about and applying these principles in a way that is much more useful than just memorizing information.

Although the approaches toward teaching writing at various colleges and universities differ, we can talk about some common expectations for college-level writing. The Council of Writing Program Administrators (CWPA), a professional organization of hundreds of writing program directors from across the country, published a list of common outcomes for first-year writing courses that has been adapted for use by many schools. The first list of common outcomes was published in 2000, and it has been revised twice since then, most recently in 2014. The purpose of the statement is to provide common expectations for what college students should be able to accomplish in terms of their writing after finishing a first-year course, but the details of those expectations are often revised to fit a specific institution's context. For example, the third outcome deals with "Processes" and states that:

By the end of first-year composition, students should
- Develop a writing project through multiple drafts
- Develop flexible strategies for reading, drafting, reviewing, collaborating, revising, rewriting, rereading, and editing
- Use composing processes and tools as a means to discover and reconsider ideas
- Experience the collaborative and social aspects of writing processes
- Learn to give and act on productive feedback to works in progress
- Adapt composing processes for a variety of technologies and modalities
- Reflect on the development of composing practices and how those practices influence their work

http://wpacouncil.org/positions/outcomes.html

The statement doesn't specify which steps or strategies in a writing process students should practice, or what kinds of writing they should be doing. It is left up to individual schools to determine what will be most helpful for their students.

Some institutions follow the guidelines from the Council of Writing Program Administrators explicitly, while others do not. Even at institutions that use these outcomes as a foundation for the writing curriculum, however, it's often possible to find many different approaches to teaching writing that help students achieve academic literacy. How do your institution's outcomes for writing compare and contrast with your experience in high school English classes? How do the outcomes for writing compare and contrast with your writing experience outside of school (perhaps in work-related or personal settings)?

INSIDE WORK **Understanding the Goals of Your Writing Course**

Take a look at the goals, objectives, or outcomes listed for the writing course you are currently taking. You might look for a course description on the school's website or in a course catalog, or you might find goals or learning objectives listed in the course syllabus.

- What surprised you about the goals or objectives for your writing course?
- What is similar to or different from the writing courses you have taken before?
- What is similar to or different from the expectations you had for this course?
- How do the outcomes for the course align with your goals for writing and for college?
- What does the list of goals for your course tell you about what is valued at your institution? ◗

WHAT DO YOU ALREADY KNOW ABOUT WRITING IN DIFFERENT CONTEXTS?

The culminating writing projects in this chapter ask you to explore your own writing and literacy experiences in more detail. Thinking about the experience and skills that you already bring to your college writing will help you to build on them and expand your abilities.

WRITING PROJECT **Composing a Literacy Narrative**

A *literacy narrative* is an essay that reflects on how someone has developed literacy over time. Literacy is sometimes defined as the ability to read and write, but in this context we'd like you to use a broader definition. Think of literacy not only as the ability to read and write, but also as the ability to successfully function in a specific context or contexts. Your instructor may give you more direction about how to define literacy for the purpose of this assignment, but you could focus on the following questions.

Academic Literacy

- What are your first memories of writing in school?
- How did you learn about the expectations for writing in school?
- Can you think of a time when you struggled to meet the requirements of a school writing assignment? What happened?

Technological Literacy

- What early memories do you have of using technology?
- How do you use technology now to communicate in your daily life? What technologies are most important to you for work, for school, and/or for personal commitments?

Workplace Literacy

- What writing and communication skills are expected in the occupation you aspire to when you graduate? How will you develop those skills?
- Can you think of a time when you encountered a task at work that you didn't know how to accomplish? What did you do? How did you address the challenge?

Social and/or Cultural Literacy

- Have you ever been in a social situation where you didn't know how to act? What did you do?

- What groups do you identify with, and what expectations and shared beliefs make that group cohesive?

A literacy narrative should do three things: (1) make a point about the author's literacy development, (2) read as a story and use narrative strategies to tell the story, and (3) provide specific details that support the point of the narrative.

In a narrative essay, explore the development of your own literacy. You might do this chronologically, at least as you start writing. Be specific in identifying how you define literacy and how you developed your abilities. In your narrative and analysis, provide examples from your experience, and show how they contribute to the development of that literacy. Ultimately, your narrative should be directed to a particular audience for a particular purpose, so think of a context in which you might tell this story. For example, a student who is studying to be a teacher might write about his early literacy experiences and how they led to an interest in teaching other children to read and write. Or an applicant for a job requiring specific technological ability might include a section in an application letter that discusses her development of expertise in technological areas relevant to the job. Be imaginative if you like, but make sure that your narrative provides specific examples and makes a point about your literacy development that you believe is important.

WRITING PROJECT   **Interviewing a Scholar**

Under the guidance of your instructor, find a professor at your college or university who teaches in a discipline that is of interest to you. You might choose a faculty member with whom you already have a connection, either through taking a class, having a mutual acquaintance, or enjoying a shared interest. Ask the scholar if you can interview him or her, either in person or through e-mail. Consider the descriptions of different disciplinary areas in this chapter, and write a profile of the faculty member that addresses questions about his or her writing, such as the following.

- What kinds of writing do scholars in your field do?

- What writing conventions are specific to and important to your field? How did you learn those conventions?

- What was your first experience of writing a scholarly article like? What did you learn through that experience?

- What kinds of writing do you do most often in your work?

- What expectations do you have for students who are learning to write in your field?

Be sure to follow up your questions by asking for specific examples if you need more information to understand the scholar's responses. In addition, you might ask to see an example of his or her academic writing to use as an illustration in your narrative. Above all, be sure to thank the faculty member for taking the time to respond to your questions.

A profile of a faculty member's writing should do two things: (1) make a point about the person being interviewed (in this case, your point should focus on the person's writing), and (2) include details about the person that help develop the point. You might write the questions and answers in an interview format, or you might incorporate the scholar's responses into an essay that uses the interview to make a specific point about his or her development and experience as a writer.

Insider Example
Student Interview with a Faculty Member

Kaitie Gay, a first-year student at North Carolina State University, conducted an interview via e-mail with Marvin Malecha, who is a professor of architecture and dean of the College of Design. Kaitie conducted her interview after reading a selection from one of Malecha's books, *Reconfiguration in the Study and Practice of Design Architecture* (2002). Her interview questions, and Malecha's responses, could lay the foundation for a writing profile.

COURTESY OF KAITIE GAY

KAITIE: In your article, you talk about the different ways that individuals learn about the field of architecture. Which do you find more beneficial to students studying architecture, learning by experience or learning in a classroom setting?

MALECHA: I believe both settings are important, as one complements the other. However, it is also true that certain individuals will have their epiphany on a construction site while others will gain insight from theoretical discourse. But in the end, both are important because each gives perspective to the other. For those interested in theory and classroom investigation, the construction site makes real what otherwise would be disconnected ideas. For the individual who is most likely to be inclined to build and ask questions later, the theoretical discussion forces them to be more reflective. It is for this reason that we maintain a close relationship with the architectural profession at NC State. We want students to work in offices as they progress through school. It is also the reason we offer design build experiences during the summer sessions. But the desire to balance a student's experience also justifies our desire to have students study abroad and to participate in scholarship and research. These experiences exercise the mind.

KAITIE: In the article you said, "Technology will reduce the need for a studio-based culture." Is it important that we balance technology and studio, or do you find it a good thing that the field is becoming more technology-driven?

MALECHA: It is easy to forget the rather primitive state of technology in the field of architecture when I wrote this article. The social media and the many tools at our discretion today really amplify my comments. I was speaking to a traditional studio-based culture where students sat at their desks almost solely dependent on the direction and handouts of their instructor. I believed that this sole relationship would be significantly changed by the ability to have incredible amounts of information at hand, including case studies, new materials, programming insights to push along scholarship, and plan development. I believed that it would be possible to check in with a studio instructor from anywhere in the world, blurring the difference between the virtual and the real. It was already true when I wrote this article that joint studios were conducted between schools on different continents utilizing the telephone and fax technology. Given this, I believed that new technologies would enhance such possibilities. I also believed that schools could conduct studios in professional offices, thereby making the bond between practice and education even stronger.

I have never been intimidated by new tools, only concerned that the tools might overwhelm our intentions. The new technologies have brought many wonderful possibilities to the conduct of the design professions. In architecture, ideas such as integrated project delivery would not be possible without the tools. We can build better with fewer errors using new technologies, we can communicate among a diverse set of users and clients using new technologies, and we can archive our work more effectively using new technologies.

It is important, however, that we teach students to control the technology, so as not to be overwhelmed by it.

KAITIE: Later in your piece you talk about the architecture field becoming more competitive, individual, and sometimes arrogant as opposed to cooperative. Throughout your career, have you found that the field is really more individual, or is there a sense of collaboration with other designers when working on a project?

MALECHA: I have found it to be both. There is a very strong culture of the individual within the architecture profession. At times, it will show itself in ugly ways. The prominent celebrity architects are referred to by some as the Black Cape Architects. This reveals the tension between those who take the lead in the concept phase of a project and those who see to the realization of a project through complex phases of design development, construction documents, and construction administration. It is true that great buildings have a personality that is derived most often from the personality of an individual or at least from an office working with a singular mind. It is equally true that the profession is wholly dependent on collaboration to realize even the smallest project.

When I wrote this particular section of the article, I was specifically addressing educators, because in the schools the teaching of collaborative practices was absent for the most part. The school experience had become focused on producing the next great cadre of superstar architects. Of course, this is a flawed strategy, since on a major project such as a hospital or skyscraper there may be a small team of designers led by a strong individual to bring about a design concept and then hundreds within the architectural office and related consultant offices to realize the project. It was my intention to advocate that educators face this dilemma and cause them to teach collaborative methods even as individual design skills were heightened. In addition, it is important to remember that there are many roles architects assume, complementing the obvious role of principal designer. There are those who manage the specification process, those who oversee construction document preparation, those who specialize in construction administration, and those who serve as the primary contact to the clients and users. Each of these roles serves an incredibly important purpose. Again, educators must make students aware of these many roles, give credence to their importance, and encourage students to seek their best place in an interesting and diverse professional culture.

Buildings need the bold ideas of individuals who are strong conceptually. Buildings also need individuals who can put a building together in the most effective way.

KAITIE: What audience were you trying to reach with this article, and what pushed you to write it?

MALECHA: At the time I was writing this article, I was primarily speaking to other educators. However, it is also true that the magazine had a broad audience, and therefore students and practicing architects were very much on my mind. I was trying to get the readers to think differently about the study and practice of architecture.

Discussion Questions

1. Read through Kaitie Gay's questions for Dr. Malecha. What was her purpose in interviewing Dr. Malecha? What did she want to understand?

2. Was there anything that surprised you in Dr. Malecha's responses? If so, what was it?

3. If you were going to add a question to Kaitie's interview, what would it be? Why would you add that question?

4. If Kaitie were to use this interview as the basis for a writing profile of Dr. Malecha, what other information would she need to find? What steps would she need to take?

tip sheet — Inside Colleges and Universities

- **Colleges and universities are not all the same.** Different kinds of colleges and universities have varying purposes, majors, and degrees, and they appeal to a variety of potential students.

- **The institution you attend has a specific focus.** You may find it helpful to identify this focus and understand how it fits with your academic and career goals.

- **Colleges and universities are divided into disciplinary areas.** You might see these areas at your school as departments, divisions, and/or colleges. In this book, we talk about four broad disciplinary areas: humanities, social sciences, natural sciences, and applied fields.

- **Academic writing follows unique conventions.** When academics write, they often follow conventions specific to their writing situations and to their disciplinary areas.

- **Writing in college is not always the same as writing in other contexts.** In college writing courses, we focus on principles of rhetoric, or how language is used to communicate.

CHAPTER

2

Reading and Writing Rhetorically

You read and write in many different situations: at school, at home, with your friends, and maybe at work. Perhaps there are other situations in which you read and write, too, likely through a variety of different media. You might read and write in a journal, in a status update on Facebook, in a photo caption on Instagram, in a word processor as you prepare a paper for school, in a text message, or in a note to a friend. You could probably name many other situations in which you read and write on a daily basis.

Have you ever considered how different the processes of reading and writing are in these situations? You're performing the same act (reading or writing a text) in many ways, but several features might change from one situation to another:

- the way the text looks
- the medium or technology you use
- the tone you use
- the words you use (or avoid using)
- the grammar and mechanics that are appropriate

ANDREA TSURUMI

Even within the more specific category of "academic writing" that we address in this book, some of these features might shift depending on the context. In some disciplines, the structure, vocabulary, style, and documentation expectations are different from those in other disciplines. If you've ever written a lab report for a physics class and a literary analysis for a literature class, then you've likely experienced some of those differences. The differences arise because of the specific demands of each of the differing writing situations.

Understanding Rhetorical Context

As you read and write, we want you to consider closely the specific situation for which you are writing. In other words, you should always think about the **rhetorical context** in which your writing takes place. In this text, we'll define rhetorical context through four elements:

- who the author is, and what background and experience he or she brings to the text
- who the intended audience is for the text
- what issue or topic the author is addressing
- what the author's purpose is for writing

Each of these elements has an impact on the way a text is written and interpreted. Consider how you might write about your last job in a text message to a friend in comparison with how you might write about it in an application letter for a new job. Even though the author is the same (you) and the topic is the same (your last job), the audience and your purpose for writing are vastly different. These differences thus affect how you characterize your job and your choice in medium for writing the message.

Sometimes writing situations call for more than one audience as well. You might address a **primary audience**, the explicitly addressed audience for the text, but you might also have a **secondary audience**, an implied audience who also might read your text or be interested in it. Imagine you wrote a job application letter as an assignment for a business writing class. Your primary audience would likely be your instructor, but you might also write the letter as a template to use when actually sending out a job application letter in the future. So your future prospective employer might be a secondary audience.

In academic settings, also, these elements of rhetorical context shift depending on the disciplinary context within which you're writing. Consider another example: Imagine a student has decided to research the last presidential election for a school assignment. If the research assignment were given in a history class, then the student might research and write about other political elections that provide a precedent for the outcome of the recent election and the events surrounding it. The student would be approaching the topic from a historical perspective, which would be appropriate for the context of the discipline and audience (a history professor). If the student were writing for an economics class, he or she might focus on the economic impact of elections

See more on considering audience as you write.

and how campaign finance laws, voter identification laws, and voters' socioeconomic statuses affected the election. Even though the author, audience, topic, and purpose seem similar at first glance (they're all academic research assignments, right?), the student would focus on different questions and aspects of the topic when examining the election from different disciplinary perspectives and for different audiences. Other elements of the student's writing would likely shift, too, and we'll discuss those differences in Part Two of this book.

Why might it be important to consider the rhetorical context when reading or writing? As you read, noticing the rhetorical context of a text can help you understand choices that the author makes in writing that might at first seem confusing or inconsistent, even in academic writing. For example, writers might use the passive voice in an experimental study report ("the data were collected by...") but not in an essay on the poetry of John Donne. Or the same scholar might write in the first person in one kind of academic text (like this textbook) but not in another (perhaps a scholarly article). In all these writing situations, the author makes choices based on the rhetorical context. In this textbook, the first person ("I" or "We") helps to establish a personal tone that might not be appropriate for an academic journal article. We (first person) made this choice specifically because of our audience for the textbook—students who are learning to navigate academic writing. We wanted the text to have a friendlier and less academically distant tone. Such a conversational tone wouldn't always be appropriate in other rhetorical contexts, though. When you write, understanding the rhetorical context can help you be more effective in achieving your purpose and communicating with your audience because you make choices that are appropriate to the situation.

As you notice the kinds of choices a writer makes, you are analyzing the rhetorical context of the writing: that is, you are taking elements of the writing apart to understand how they work together. Analyzing rhetorical context is a key strategy we'll use throughout this book to understand how different forms of writing work and what the similarities and differences are in writing across various disciplines.

INSIDE WORK   Identifying Rhetorical Context

Think about a specific situation in the past that required you to write something. It could be any kind of text; it doesn't have to be something academic. Then create a map—by drawing a diagram, a chart, or some other visual image—of the rhetorical context of that piece of writing. Consider the following questions as you draw.

- What was your background and role as the author?
- Who was the audience?
- What was the topic?
- What was your purpose for writing? ❭

Understanding Genres

As you learn to analyze the rhetorical context of writing, keep in mind that much writing takes place within communities of people who are interested in similar subjects. They might use similar vocabulary, formats for writing, and grammatical and stylistic rules. In a sense, they speak the same "language." The common practices that they typically employ in their writing are called *conventions*, as we discussed in Chapter 1. As you read and analyze the writing of academic writers, we'll ask you to notice and comment on the conventions that different disciplines use in various rhetorical contexts. When you write, you'll want to keep those conventions in mind, paying attention to the ways you should shape your own writing to meet the expectations of the academic community you are participating in. We'll go into more detail about how to analyze the specific conventions of disciplinary writing in Part Two.

In addition to paying close attention to the conventions that writers employ, we'll ask you to consider the *genre* through which writers communicate their information. **Genres** are approaches to writing situations that share some common features, or conventions. You already write in many genres in your daily life: If you've sent or read e-mail messages, text messages, personal letters, and thank-you notes, then you've written and read examples of four different genres that are all associated with personal writing. If you like to cook, you've probably noticed that recipes in cookbooks follow similar patterns by presenting the ingredients first and then providing step-by-step directions for preparation. The ingredients usually appear in a list, and the instructions generally read as directives (e.g., "Add the eggs one at a time and mix well"), often in more of a prose style. Recipes are a genre. If you've looked for an office job before, you've probably encountered at least three different genres in the job application process: job advertisements, application letters, and résumés. How well you follow the expected conventions of the latter two genres often affects whether or not you get a job.

You've also likely had experience producing academic genres. If you've ever written a business letter, an abstract, a mathematical proof, a poem, a book review, a research proposal, or a lab report, then you might have noticed that these kinds of academic writing tasks have certain conventions that make them unique. Lab reports, for example, typically have specific expectations for the organization of information and for the kind of language used to communicate that information. Throughout Part Two of the book, we offer examples of a number of other academic genres—a literature review, an interpretation of an artistic text, as well as a theory response, just to name a few.

Because different writing situations, or rhetorical contexts, call for different approaches, we ask you to think about the genre, as well as associated conventions, that you might be reading or writing in any particular situation. Our goal is not to have you identify a formula to follow for every type of academic

LaunchPadSolo

See what writing studies instructor Moriah McCracken has to say about genres.

writing, but rather to understand the expectations of a writing situation—and how much flexibility you have in meeting those expectations—so that you can make choices appropriate to the genre.

Reading Rhetorically

Since we're talking about paying attention to rhetorical context, we want to explain the difference between the reading you do with an eye toward rhetorical context and the reading you might do in other circumstances. Whenever you read during a typical day, you probably do so for a variety of reasons. You might read:

- **To Communicate:** reading a text message, a letter from a friend, an e-mail, a birthday card, or a post on Instagram
- **To Learn:** reading instructions, a textbook, street signs while you drive, dosage instructions on a medication bottle, or the instructor's comments at the end of a paper that you turned in for a class
- **To Be Entertained:** reading novels, stories, comics, a joke forwarded in e-mail, or a favorite website

The details that you pay attention to, and the level at which you notice those details, vary according to your purpose in reading.

In this text, however, we will ask you to read in a way that is different from reading just to communicate, learn, or be entertained. We want you to *read rhetorically*, paying close attention to the rhetorical context of whatever you are reading. When you read rhetorically, you make note of the different elements of rhetorical context that help to shape the text. You'll notice who the **author** is (or, if there are multiple authors, who each one is) and what background, experience, knowledge, and potential biases the author brings to the text. In addition, you'll notice who the intended **audience** is for the text. Is the author writing to a group of peers? To other scholars in the field? How much prior knowledge does that audience have, and how does the intended audience shape the author's approach in the text? Are there multiple audiences (primary and secondary)? You'll also notice what the **topic** is and how it influences the text. Does the author use a specific approach related to the topic choice? Additionally, you'll notice the author's **purpose** for writing. Sometimes the purpose is stated explicitly, and sometimes it is implied. Why does the author choose to write about this topic at this point? What does the author hope to achieve? Finally, you'll want to notice how these four elements work together to shape the text. How is the choice of audience related to the author's background, topic, and purpose for writing?

Reading Visuals Rhetorically

We should stress that the strategies for understanding rhetorical context and for reading rhetorically are applicable to both verbal and visual texts. In fact, any rhetorical event, or any occasion that requires the production of a text, establishes a writing situation with a specific rhetorical context. Consider the places you might encounter visual advertisements, as one form of visual texts, over the course of a single day: in a magazine, on a website, in stores, on bill-boards, on television, and so on. Each encounter provides an opportunity to read the visual text rhetorically, or to consider how the four elements of author, audience, topic, and purpose work together to shape the text itself (in this case, an advertisement). This process is called **rhetorical analysis**.

In fact, noticing these elements when you read will help you become a careful and critical reader of all kinds of texts. When we use the term *critical*, we don't use it with any negative connotations. We use it in the way it works in the term *critical thinking*, meaning that you will begin to understand the relationships among author, audience, topic, and purpose by paying close attention to context.

INSIDE WORK   **Reading Rhetorically**

With the direction of your instructor, choose a text (either verbal or visual) to read and analyze. As you read the text, consider the elements of rhetorical context. Write about who the author is, who the intended audience is, what the topic is, and what the author's purpose is for writing or for creating the text. Finally, consider how these elements work together to influence the way the text is written or designed. In future chapters, we'll ask you to engage in this kind of *rhetorical analysis* to understand the different kinds of texts produced by students and scholars in various academic contexts. ▶

Writing Rhetorically

Writing is about choices. Writing is not a firm set of rules to follow. There are multiple choices available to you anytime you take on a writing task, and the choices you make will help determine how effectively you communicate with your intended audience, about your topic, for your intended purpose. Some choices, of course, are more effective than others, based on the conventions expected for certain situations. And yet, sometimes you might break conventions in order to make a point or draw attention to what you are writing. In both cases, though, it's important to understand the expectations of the rhetorical context for which you are writing so that your choices will have the effect you intend.

When you write rhetorically, you'll analyze the four elements of rhetorical context, examining how those elements shape your text through the choices that you make as a writer. You'll think about the following elements:

- **What You, as the *Author*, Bring to the Writing Situation** How do your background, experience, and relative position to the audience shape the way you write?

- **Who Your Intended *Audience* Is** Is there a specific audience you should address? Has the audience already been determined for you (e.g., by your instructor)? What do you know about your audience? What does your audience value?

- **What Your *Topic* Is** What are you writing about? Has the topic been determined for you, or do you have the freedom to focus your topic according to your interests? What is your relationship to the topic? What is your audience's relationship to it?

- **What Your *Purpose* Is for Writing** Why are you writing about this topic, at this time? For example, are you writing to inform? To persuade? To entertain?

Outside of school contexts, we often write because we encounter a situation that calls for us to write. Imagine a parent who wants to write a note to thank her son's teacher for inviting her to assist in a class project. The audience is very specific, and the topic is determined by the occasion for writing. Depending on the relationship between the parent and the teacher, the note might be rather informal. But if the parent wants to commend the teacher and copy the school's principal, she might write a longer, more formal note that could be included in the teacher's personnel file. Understanding the rhetorical context would help the parent decide what choices to make in this writing situation.

For school assignments, thinking about the topic is typically the first step because students are often assigned to write about something specific. If your English professor asks you to write a literary interpretation of Toni Morrison's *Song of Solomon*, your topic choice is limited. Even in this situation, though, you have the freedom to determine what aspect of the text you'll focus on. Do you want to look at imagery in the novel? Would you like to examine Morrison's use of language? Would you like to analyze recurring themes, or perhaps interpret the text in the historical and cultural context in which it was written?

In this text, we would like you also to consider the other elements of rhetorical context—author, audience, and purpose—to see how they influence your topic. Considering your purpose in writing can often shape your audience and topic. Are you writing to communicate with a friend? If so, about what? Are you completing an assignment for a class? Are you writing to persuade someone to act on an issue that's important to you? If you are writing to argue for a change in a policy, to whom do you need to write in order to achieve your purpose? How will you reach that audience, and what would the audience's expectations be for your text? What information will you need to provide? Your understanding of the rhetorical context for writing will shape your writing and help you to communicate more effectively with your audience, about your topic, to meet your purpose.

INSIDE WORK) **Analyzing Rhetorical Context**

Think back to the rhetorical situation you identified in the "Inside Work: Identifying Rhetorical Context" activity on page 22. Consider that situation more analytically now, using the questions from that activity and slightly revised here as a guide. Write your responses to the following questions.

- As the *author*, how did your background, experience, and relative position to the audience shape the way you created your text?

- Were you addressing a specific *audience*? Was the audience already determined for you? What did you know about your audience? What did your audience value or desire?

- What was your text about? Was the *topic* determined for you, or did you have the freedom to focus your topic according to your interests? What was your relationship to the topic? What was your audience's relationship to it?

- What was your *purpose* for creating a text about that topic, at that time? For example, were you writing to inform? To persuade? To entertain? ❱

Rhetorical Writing Processes

In addition to making choices related to the context of a writing situation, writers make choices about their own process of writing. Writers follow different processes, sometimes being influenced by their own writing preferences, their experience with writing, and the specific writing tasks they have to accomplish. Writing can be a messy process that involves lots of drafting, revising, researching, thinking, and sometimes even throwing things out, especially for longer writing tasks. With that said, though, there are several steps in the process that experienced writers often find useful, and each step can be adapted to the specific writing situation in which they find themselves.

You might already be familiar with some of the commonly discussed steps of the writing process from other classes you've taken. Often, writing teachers talk about some variation of the following elements of the writing process:

- **Prewriting/Invention** The point at which you gather ideas for your writing. There are a number of useful brainstorming strategies that students find helpful to the processes of gathering their thoughts and arranging them for writing. A few of the most widely used strategies are *freewriting*, *listing*, and *idea mapping*.

    Freewriting As the term implies, **freewriting** involves writing down your thoughts in a free-flow form, typically for a set amount of time. There's no judgment or evaluation of these ideas as they occur to you.

MORRIS: So often it's not about "I need to write this page." It's that "I have to spend hours and hours and hours doing the analysis. And even once I've done the analysis, taking the statistics and putting them in a way that the reader can understand and is relevant to the story will take days." Now, what I've adjusted to in this *writing process* is "Okay, I don't need to get a page a day. But I've got to have these sets of tasks for today." And it may be doing a series of statistics and then putting them into an Excel to make a nice, pretty chart that'll support the story.

BAUMGARTNER: Well, sure.

MORRIS: So it's about tasks.

You simply write down whatever comes to mind as you consider a topic or idea. Later, of course, you revisit what you've written to see if it contains ideas or information worth examining further.

Listing   **Listing** is a way of quickly highlighting important information for yourself. The writer starts with a main idea and then just lists whatever comes to mind. These lists are typically done quickly the first time, but you can return to them and rework or refine them at any point in the writing process.

Idea Mapping   This brainstorming technique is a favorite among students because it allows you to represent your ideas in an easy-to-follow map. **Idea mapping** is sometimes referred to as cluster mapping because as you brainstorm, you use clusters of ideas and lines to keep track of the ideas and the relationships among them.

- **Research**   Sometimes research is considered a separate step in the writing process, and sometimes it is part of prewriting/invention. Of course, depending on the nature of your project, there might be a considerable amount of research or very little research involved. We explore some strategies for conducting research in more detail in Chapter 4.

- **Drafting**   At the drafting stage, you get ideas down on paper or screen. You might already realize that these stages don't happen in isolation in most cases; drafting might occur while you're doing prewriting/invention and research, and you might go back and forth between different stages as you work.

- **Peer Review**   Writers often benefit from seeking the feedback of others before considering a project complete. **Peer review** is the process of having other students, classmates, or audience members read your work and provide feedback. Later in this text, we'll use the term *peer review* to refer to the specific process that scholars go through when they submit academic writing for publication. It's similar: they submit work for publication, then peers in their discipline read and comment on it (they may or may not recommend it for publication), and then the scholars often revise it again prior to publication.

- **Revising**   At the revision stage, a writer takes another look at his or her writing and makes content-level and organizational changes. This is different from the final step of editing/proofreading.
- **Editing/Proofreading**   Finally, the writer focuses on correcting grammatical, mechanical, stylistic, and referential problems in the text.

Depending on the rhetorical context of a writing task, these processes might shift in importance and in the order in which you do them. Imagine you get a last-minute writing assignment at work. You would progress through these stages rather quickly, and you might not have time for more than a cursory peer review. If you're writing a term paper for a class, however, you might be able to do initial prewriting, research, and drafting well before the project's deadline. As we discuss different types of scholarly writing in this text, you might also consider how the writing process for each of these types of writing can vary. When conducting an experimental study, the research stage of the process will take a significant portion of the time allocated to the project.

You might be able to think of examples from your own experience when you wrote in different ways for different projects because the rhetorical context was not the same. We want to encourage you to plan your writing process deliberately and avoid the mistake that many inexperienced writers make—waiting until the last minute and quickly writing a first draft and then turning it in because there is no time left for anything else. The most effective writers carefully plan out their writing and take the time they need to work through different parts of the writing process.

As you consider the influence of rhetorical context on your writing process, also think about the specific preferences you have as a writer. In order to do your best writing, be aware of where and how you write best. Consider these questions: What physical space do you like to write in? Where are you most productive? At what time of day do you write best? If you have a pressing deadline, what environmental factors help you to meet the deadline? Do you need to work someplace quiet? Do you like to have noise in the background? What

kind of work space works best for you? Do you usually keep coffee or another favorite drink nearby? An awareness of preferences such as these will help you meet the challenges of different writing situations as you encounter them.

We'll ask you to practice different parts of your writing process throughout this book, both through the exercises you'll participate in and the larger writing assignments that you'll complete. As you work through the exercises, think about what part of the writing process you're addressing.

Writing a Rhetorical Analysis

When you read rhetorically, you analyze a text through a particular lens. Examining a text through the formal framework of author, audience, topic, and purpose can be a way of analyzing a text in a written assignment as well. Such an examination is called a *rhetorical analysis*, a genre of writing that explores elements of a text's rhetorical context. We'll provide several opportunities for you to conduct rhetorical analyses in this book, since it is one of the ways you will begin to discover the features of writing across different academic contexts.

In a rhetorical analysis, the writer uses a rhetorical framework to understand how the context of the text helps to create meaning. One framework you might use involves walking through the different elements of rhetorical context to examine the piece of writing in detail:

Rhetorical Context

Author	What does the author bring to the writing situation?
Audience	Who is the author addressing, and what do they know or think about this topic?
Topic	What is the author writing about, and why did he or she choose it?
Purpose	Why is the author writing about this topic, at this time?

These four components of the rhetorical context function together dynamically. You might analyze the author's background and experience and how he or she develops credibility in the text. Or you could make assertions about the author's primary and secondary audiences based on the author's choices regarding style and language. But in reality, all four of the rhetorical context components function together to shape how someone writes or speaks.

The following text is a letter that George H. W. Bush, the forty-first president of the United States (and father of the forty-third president, George W. Bush), sent to Iraqi president Saddam Hussein on January 9, 1991, shortly before the United States, in cooperation with over thirty other countries, launched an assault to expel Iraqi forces from Kuwait. This action came in response to Iraq's invasion and annexation of Kuwait in 1990, and it became a part of the history that is now referred to as the First Gulf War. While the events that precipitated this letter occurred a long time ago, it is a helpful artifact for understanding the complicated power dynamics at play in the United States' involvement in ongoing events in the Middle East. As you read the letter, pay close attention to the rhetorical moves that President Bush makes. Who are his primary and secondary audiences? Is his audience only Saddam Hussein? If not, then who else is his audience, and what in his letter suggests who the secondary audience is? What is the letter's purpose? Does Bush seem to think Saddam will leave Kuwait? How do you know?

Letter to Saddam Hussein

GEORGE H. W. BUSH

© AP PHOTO/DENNIS COOK

Mr. President,

We stand today at the brink of war between Iraq and the world. This is a war that began with your invasion of Kuwait; this is a war that can be ended only by Iraq's full and unconditional compliance with UN Security Council resolution 678.

I am writing to you now, directly, because what is at stake demands that no opportunity be lost to avoid what would be a certain calamity for the people of Iraq. I am writing, as well, because it is said by some that you do not understand just how isolated Iraq is and what Iraq faces as a result.

I am not in a position to judge whether this impression is correct; what I can do, though, is try in this letter to reinforce what Secretary of State James A. Baker told your foreign minister and eliminate any uncertainty or ambiguity that might exist in your mind about where we stand and what we are prepared to do.

The international community is united in its call for Iraq to leave all of Kuwait without condition and without further delay. This is not simply the policy of the United States; it is the position of the world community as expressed in no less than twelve Security Council resolutions.

We prefer a peaceful outcome. However, anything less than full compliance with UN Security Council resolution 678 and its predecessors is unacceptable. There can be no reward for aggression.

Nor will there be any negotiation. Principles cannot be compromised. However, by its full compliance, Iraq will gain the opportunity to rejoin the international community. More immediately, the Iraqi military establishment will escape destruction. But unless you withdraw from Kuwait completely and without condition, you will lose more than Kuwait. What is at issue here is not the future of Kuwait—it will be free, its government restored—but rather the future of Iraq. This choice is yours to make.

The United States will not be separated from its coalition partners. Twelve Security Council resolutions, twenty-eight countries providing military units to enforce them, more than one hundred governments complying with sanctions—all highlight the fact that it is not Iraq against the United States, but Iraq against the world. That most Arab and Muslim countries are arrayed against you as well should reinforce what I am saying. Iraq cannot and will not be able to hold on to Kuwait or exact a price for leaving. You may be tempted to find solace in the diversity of opinion that is American democracy. You should resist any such temptation. Diversity ought not to be confused with division. Nor should you underestimate, as others have before you, America's will.

Iraq is already feeling the effects of the sanctions mandated by the United Nations. Should war come, it will be a far greater tragedy for you and your country. Let me state, too, that the United States will not tolerate the use of chemical or biological weapons or the destruction of Kuwait's oil fields and installations. Further, you will be held directly responsible for terrorist actions against any member of the coalition. The American people would demand the strongest possible response. You and your country will pay a terrible price if you order unconscionable acts of this sort.

I write this letter not to threaten, but to inform. I do so with no sense of satisfaction, for the people of the United States have no quarrel with the people of Iraq. Mr. President, UN Security Council resolution 678 establishes the period before January 15 of this year as a "pause of good will" so that this crisis may end without further violence. Whether this pause is used as intended, or merely becomes a prelude to further violence, is in your hands, and yours alone.

I hope you weigh your choice carefully and choose wisely, for much will depend upon it.

Discussion Questions

1. For what purpose(s) does President Bush write this letter?
2. How does Bush establish his credibility, honesty, and resolve in the letter?
3. Who is the primary audience? Who are the secondary audiences?
4. What conventional features for this form of writing (genre) does Bush's letter exhibit?

Insider Example
Student Rhetorical Analysis

The following is a student rhetorical analysis of the letter written from George H. W. Bush to Saddam Hussein. As you read this analysis, consider how the student, Sofia Lopez, uses audience, topic, and purpose to construct meaning from Bush's letter. Additionally, pay attention to how Sofia uses evidence from the letter to support her assertions. These moves will become more important when we discuss using evidence to support claims in Chapter 3 (see pp. 43–45).

Sofia Lopez

Mr. Harris

English 100

January 201-

The Multiple Audiences of George H. W. Bush's Letter to Saddam Hussein

President George H. W. Bush's 1991 letter to Saddam Hussein, then the president of Iraq, is anything but a simple piece of political rhetoric. The topic of the letter is direct and confrontational. On the surface, Bush directly calls upon Hussein to withdraw from Kuwait, and he lays out the potential impact should Hussein choose not to withdraw. But when analyzed according to the rhetorical choices Bush makes in the letter, a complex rhetorical situation emerges. Bush writes to a dual audience in his letter and establishes credibility by developing a complex author position. By the conclusion of the letter, Bush accomplishes multiple purposes by creating a complex rhetorical situation.

> The introduction outlines the writer's approach to analyzing Bush's letter. Based on the introduction, what do you see as the writer's overall purpose for this rhetorical analysis?

While Bush's direct and primary audience is Saddam Hussein, Bush also calls upon a much larger secondary audience in the first sentence of the letter by identifying "the world" as the second party involved in the imminent war that the letter is written to prevent. Bush continues to write the letter directly to Hussein, using second person to address him and describe the choices before him. Bush also continues, however, to engage his secondary audience throughout the letter by referring to resolutions from the UN Security Council in five separate paragraphs (1, 4, 5, 7, and 9). The letter can even be interpreted to have tertiary audiences of the Iraqi and the American people because the letter serves to justify military action should Hussein not comply with the conditions of the letter.

> In this paragraph, the writer outlines potential audiences for Bush's letter in more detail. Who are those audiences?

Because Bush is addressing multiple audiences, he establishes a complex author position as well. He is the primary author of the letter, and he uses first person to refer to himself, arguably to emphasize the direct, personal confrontation in the letter. He constructs a more complex author position, however, by speaking for other groups in his letter and, in a sense, writing "for" them. In paragraph 4, he speaks for the international community when he writes, "The international community is united in its call for Iraq to leave all of Kuwait. . . ." He draws on the international community again in

> In this paragraph, the writer explores the ways Bush is able to align himself with multiple audiences. What evidence does the writer use to demonstrate Bush's associations with his various audiences?

paragraph 6 and refers to his coalition partners in paragraph 7, aligning his position with the larger community. Additionally, in paragraph 7, he builds his credibility as an author by emphasizing that he is aligned with other Arab and Muslim countries in their opposition to Hussein's actions. Writing for and aligning himself with such a diverse group of political partners helps him address the multiple audiences of his letter to accomplish his purposes.

The writer frequently refers to Bush's "complex author position." What do you think the writer means by this?

While the primary and literal purpose of the letter is to call upon Iraq to withdraw from Kuwait and to outline the consequences of noncompliance, Bush accomplishes additional purposes directly related to his additional audiences and the complex author position he has established. The primary purpose of his letter, naturally, is addressed to his primary audience, Saddam Hussein. The construction of the letter, however, including the repeated mention of UN Security Council resolutions, the invocation of support from other Arab and Muslim countries, and the reference to other coalition partners and the international community, serves to call upon the world (and specifically the United Nations) to support military action should Hussein not comply with the conditions of the letter. The construction of a letter with a complex audience and author allows Bush to address multiple purposes that support future action.

What other elements of the rhetorical situation might the writer explore to further analyze Bush's letter?

Discussion Questions

1. What does Sofia Lopez identify as Bush's purpose? How does she support that interpretation of Bush's purpose?

2. Whom does Sofia see as Bush's audience? How does she support that reading of the letter?

3. What might you add to the analysis, from a rhetorical perspective?

WRITING PROJECT **Analyzing the Rhetorical Features of a Text**

In this paper, you will analyze the rhetorical situation of a text of your choosing. You might want to choose something publicly available (already published) that represents a piece of polished writing so that you know that the author(s) has finished making revisions and has had time to think through important rhetorical choices. Alternatively, you might choose something written for an academic, personal, work, or other context. Start by reading the text carefully and rhetorically. Use the elements of rhetorical context to analyze and understand the choices the writer has made in the text.

Rhetorical Context

- author
- audience

- topic
- purpose

In addition to describing the rhetorical features of the article, you will also explore why you believe the author made certain choices. For example, if you're analyzing a blog entry on a political website, you might discuss who the author is and review his or her background. Then you could speculate about the writing choices the author has made and how his or her background might have influenced those choices.

Consider what conclusion you can draw about the text, and highlight that as an assertion you can make in the introduction to your analysis. The body of your paper should be organized around the rhetorical features you are analyzing, demonstrating how you came to your conclusion about the text.

In your conclusion, reflect on what you have found. Are there other issues still to be addressed? What other rhetorical strategies could be explored to analyze the work further? Are there surprises in the choices the writer makes that you should mention?

Keep in mind that your essential aim is to analyze, not to evaluate.

tip sheet — Reading and Writing Rhetorically

- **It is important to consider rhetorical context as you read and write.** Think about how the following four elements have shaped or might shape a text:
  - who the *author* is, and what background and experience he or she brings to the text
  - who the intended *audience* is
  - what issue or *topic* the author is addressing
  - what the author's *purpose* is for writing

- **Genres are approaches to writing situations that share some common features, or conventional expectations.** As you read and write texts, consider the form of writing you're asked to read or produce: Is it a recognizable genre? What kinds of conventional expectations are associated with the genre? How should you shape your text in response to those expectations?

- **Reading rhetorically means reading with an eye toward how the four elements of author, audience, topic, and purpose work together** to influence the way an author shapes a text, verbal or visual or otherwise.

Continued

- **Writing rhetorically means crafting your own text based on an understanding of the four elements of your rhetorical context.** Specifically, you consider how your understanding of the rhetorical context should affect the choices you make as a writer, or how your understanding should ultimately shape your text.

- **A rhetorical writing process involves a set of steps that include prewriting, researching, drafting, revising, and editing/proofreading.** The order of the steps and their importance to any writer can be altered or repeated as needed.

- **A rhetorical analysis is a formal piece of writing that examines the different elements of the rhetorical context of a text.** It also often considers how these elements work together to explain the shape of a text targeted for analysis.

CHAPTER 3

Developing Arguments

Many writing situations, both academic and non-academic, require authors to persuade audiences on a particular topic—in other words, to develop an *argument*. When we refer to arguments, we don't mean heated, emotional sparring matches that are often supported by little else than opinion. Rather, we use **argument** to refer to the process of making a logical case for a particular position, interpretation, or conclusion. You experience and participate in these kinds of arguments around you every day as you decide what to eat for a meal, choose certain classes to take, determine what movie to see with a group of friends, or read (or perhaps choose to ignore) online advertisements about products to purchase.

In academic settings, arguments are frequently research-oriented because the authors are presenting and arguing for a particular interpretation or conclusion from the results of their research. To make such an argument effectively, academics must develop clear, persuasive texts through which to present their research. These arguments make **claims**—arguable assertions—that are supported with evidence from research. The unifying element of any academic argument is its primary or central claim, and although most sustained arguments make a series of claims, there is usually one central claim that makes an argument a coherent whole. Our goal in this chapter is to introduce you to some of the basic principles of argumentation and to help you write clear central claims and develop successful arguments, especially in your academic writing.

ANDREA TSURUMI

If arguments are persuasive and effective, they are likely well reasoned and well supported, and they draw on evidence that is chosen for a specific rhetorical context. All writers must pay attention to the audience and purpose of their argument. Often, they do this by developing, either implicitly or explicitly, *proofs* of their arguments and *appeals* that are appropriate to their audience. Proofs and appeals are elements specific to arguments that you'll need to pay attention to in addition to rhetorical context, which is relevant for all writing situations.

Understanding Proofs and Appeals

Aristotle, a rhetorician in ancient Greece, developed a method of analyzing arguments that can be useful to us in our own reading and writing today. He explained that arguments are based on a set of proofs that are used as evidence to support a claim. He identified two kinds of proofs: inartistic and artistic. **Inartistic proofs** are based on factual evidence, such as statistics, raw data, or contracts. **Artistic proofs**, by contrast, are created by the writer or speaker to support an argument. Many arguments contain a combination of inartistic and artistic proofs, depending on what facts are available for support. Aristotle divided the complex category of artistic proofs into three kinds of **rhetorical appeals** that speakers and writers can rely on to develop artistic proofs in support of an argument:

- Appeals to **ethos** are based on the author's or speaker's credibility or character. An example might be a brand of motor oil that is endorsed by a celebrity NASCAR driver. Another example could be a proposal for grant money to conduct a research study that discusses the grant writer's experience in successfully completing similar research studies in the past. In both examples, the speaker's or writer's experiences (as a NASCAR driver or as an established researcher) are persuasive elements in the argument. We might be more inclined to buy a certain brand of motor oil if our favorite driver says it's the best kind, and a grant-funding agency will likely feel more comfortable giving a large sum of money to a researcher who has demonstrated successful completion of research projects in the past.

- Appeals to **logos** are based on elements of logic and reason. An example might be an argument for change in an attendance policy that outlines the negative effects and potential repercussions of maintaining the current policy. The argument relies on logic and reason because it presents the negative effects and draws a connection to the policy, emphasizing how a change in the policy might reverse those effects.

- Appeals to **pathos** are based on the anticipated emotional response of the audience. Emotion can be a powerful motivator to convince an audience to hear an argument. An example might include telling the story of a particular community affected by current gun control regulation when arguing for a shift in policy. If a politician uses this strategy when arguing for passage of an important bill in Congress, for example, the emotional impact might influence other legislators to vote in favor of the bill.

These types of appeals are present in arguments in both academic and non-academic settings. Many arguments, and often the most effective ones, include elements of more than one kind of appeal, using several strategies to persuade an audience. In the example above of a politician arguing before Congress, the argument would be much stronger and likely more persuasive if other appeals were used in addition to an emotional appeal. The politician might develop an argument that includes raw data and statistics (an inartistic proof), the advice of experts in the field (ethos), a cause and effect relationship that points to a particular cause of the problem (logos), along with the story of a community affected by current gun control regulation (pathos). Understanding the structure of arguments, and knowing the potential ways you can develop your own arguments to persuade an audience, will help you to write more effectively and persuasively.

INSIDE WORK) **Writing about Arguments**

Choose a text to read that makes either an explicit or an implicit claim. Consider something that interests you—perhaps an advertisement, or even your college's or university's website. Write about the kinds of rhetorical appeals you notice. Do you see evidence of ethos? Logos? Pathos? Is the argument drawing on statistics or raw data, an inartistic proof? Why do you think the author(s) or designer(s) structured the argument in this way? To answer this question, you'll also need to consider the rhetorical context. Who is the author, and who is the intended audience? What is the topic, and what is the purpose of the argument? In other words, what is the ultimate goal of the argument? ▶

Making Claims

As we mentioned earlier, the unifying element of any academic argument is its primary or central claim. In American academic settings, the central claim is often (but not always) presented near the beginning of a piece so that it can tie the elements of the argument together. A form of the central claim that you might be familiar with is the **thesis statement**. Thesis statements, whether revealed in an argument's introduction or delayed and presented later in an argument (perhaps even in the conclusion), are central claims of arguments that are typical of writing that is centrally focused on civic concerns, as well as writing in some academic fields such as those in the humanities (see Chapter 6).

Imagine for a moment that you've been asked to write an argument taking a position on a current social topic like cell phone usage, and you must decide whether or not to support legislation to limit cell phone use while driving. In this instance, the statement of your position is your claim. It might read something like this: "We should support legislation to limit the use of cell phones while driving," or "We should not support legislation to limit the use of cell phones while driving." There are many types of claims. The statement "We should pass legislation to limit the use of cell phones" is a claim of proposal or policy, indicating that the writer will propose some action or solution to a problem. We could also explore claims of definition ("Cheerleading is a sport") or claims of value ("Supporting a charity is a good thing to do"), just to name a few.

Literary analyses, a genre commonly taught in high school English classes, usually present a thesis statement as part of their introductions. You may be familiar with a thesis statement that reads something like this: "Nathaniel Hawthorne's 'The Birthmark' is a complex tale that cautions us against believing that science is capable of perfecting our natures." This thesis statement makes a claim in support of a specific interpretation of the story. Regardless of the specific type of claim offered, the argument that follows it provides evidence to demonstrate why an audience should find the claim persuasive.

THESIS VERSUS HYPOTHESIS

In an academic setting, thesis statements like those typical of arguments in the humanities are not the only kind of unifying claim you might encounter. In fact, arguments in the natural and social sciences are often organized around a statement of hypothesis, which is different from a thesis statement. Unlike a thesis statement, which serves to convey a final position or conclusion on a topic or issue that a researcher has arrived at based on study, a **hypothesis** is a proposed explanation or conclusion that is usually either confirmed or denied on the basis of rigorous examination or experimentation later in a paper. This means that hypothesis statements are, in a sense, still under consideration by a writer or researcher. A hypothesis is a proposed answer to a research question. Thesis statements, in contrast, represent a writer or researcher's conclusion(s) after much consideration of the issue or topic.

Consider the following examples of a hypothesis and a thesis about the same topic:

Hypothesis	Thesis
Decreased levels of sleep will lead to decreased levels of academic performance for college freshmen.	College freshmen should get at least seven hours of sleep per night because insufficient sleep has been linked to emotional instability and poor academic performance.

The hypothesis example above includes several elements that distinguish it from the thesis statement. First, the hypothesis is written as a prediction, which indicates that the researcher will conduct a study to test the claim. Additionally, it is written in the future tense, indicating that an experiment or study will take place to prove or disprove the hypothesis. The thesis statement, however, makes a claim that indicates it is already supported by evidence gathered by the researcher. A reader would expect to find persuasive evidence from sources later in the essay.

We highlight this distinction in types of claims to underscore that there is no single formula for constructing a good argument in all academic contexts. Instead, expectations for strong arguments are bound up with the expectations of particular writing communities. If you write a lab report with the kind of thesis statement that usually appears in a literary analysis, your work would likely convey the sense that you're a novice to the community of writers and researchers who expect a hypothesis statement instead of a thesis statement. One of the goals of this text is to help you develop awareness of how the expectations for good argumentation change from one academic context to the next.

Developing Reasons

When writing an academic argument that requires a thesis statement, you can choose how detailed to make that thesis statement. When we introduced thesis statements as a type of claim, we asked you to consider two possible statements on the topic of cell phone use while driving: "We should/should not support legislation to limit the use of cell phones while driving." We can also refer to these two possible forms as **simple thesis statements** because they reveal a writer's central position on a topic but do not include any reasoning as support for that position. When reasons are included as logical support, then we can think about the thesis statement as a **complex thesis statement**:

Simple Thesis:	We should support legislation to limit the use of cell phones while driving.
Reasons:	They are an unnecessary distraction.
	They increase the incidence of accidents and deaths.

When we combine the simple statement of position or belief with the reasons that support it, then we have a more complex, and fuller, thesis statement:

Complex Thesis:	We should support legislation to limit the use of cell phones because they are an unnecessary distraction for drivers and because they increase needless accidents and deaths on our roadways.

Although constructing complex thesis statements allows you to combine your statement of position with the reasons you'll use to defend that position, you may frequently encounter arguments that do not provide the reasons as part of the thesis. That is, some writers, depending on their rhetorical context, prefer to present a simple thesis and then reveal the reasons for their position throughout their argument. Others choose to write a thesis that both establishes their position and provides the reasoning for it early on. An advantage of providing a complex thesis statement is that it offers a road map to the reader for the argument that you will develop. A disadvantage is that it might provide more information about your argument than you want to or should reveal up front.

INSIDE WORK Constructing Thesis Statements

Generate a list of six to eight current social issues that require you to take a position. Consider especially issues that are important to your local community. Choose one or two to focus on for the other parts of this activity.

Next, explore multiple positions. Consider competing positions you can take for each of the issues you identified. Write out a simple thesis statement for those positions. Be careful not to limit your positions to pros and cons, especially if you can think of alternative positions that might be reasonable for someone to argue. Often, there are multiple sides to an issue, and we miss the complexity of the issue if we only acknowledge two sides. Then, list as many reasons as you can think of to support each of those positions. It might be helpful to connect your simple statement of thesis to your reasons using the word *because*. This activity can help you to strengthen your argument by anticipating rebuttals or counterarguments. We'll take these issues up later in the chapter.

For example:

Claim: **The U.S. Congress should support federal legislation that allows same-sex couples to marry.**

Reasons:

because _____.

because _____.

because _____.

Alternate Claim: **The U.S. Congress should not support federal legislation that allows same-sex couples to marry.**

Reasons:

because _____.

because _____.

because _____.

Alternate Claim: **The decision to develop legislation allowing same-sex couples to marry should be made at the state level and not by the federal government.**

Reasons:

because _____.

because _____.

because _____.

Finally, combine your simple thesis with your reasoning to construct a complex thesis for each potential position. Write out your thesis statements. ▶

Supporting Reasons with Evidence

Reasons that support a claim are not particularly powerful unless there is **evidence** to back them up. Evidence that supports an argument can take the form of any of the rhetorical appeals. Let's look again at the complex thesis from the previous section: "We should support legislation to limit the use of cell phones because they are an unnecessary distraction for drivers and because they increase needless accidents and deaths on our roadways." In order to generate the reasons, the writer relied on what he already knew about the dangers of cell phone use. Perhaps the writer had recently read a newspaper article that cited statistics concerning the number of people injured or killed in accidents as a direct result of drivers using their phones instead of paying attention to the roadways. Or perhaps the writer had read an academic study that examined attention rates and variables affecting them in people using cell phones. Maybe the writer even had some personal knowledge or experience to draw upon as evidence for her or his position. Strong, persuasive arguments typically spend a great deal of time unpacking the logic that enables a writer to generate reasons in support of a particular claim, and that evidence can take many forms.

Personal Experience You may have direct experience with a particular issue or topic that allows you to speak in support of a position on that topic. Your personal experience can be a rich resource for evidence. Additionally, you may know others who can provide evidence based on their experiences with an issue. Stories of personal experience often appeal to either ethos (drawing on the credibility of the writer's personal experience) or pathos (drawing on readers' emotions for impact). Sometimes these stories appeal to both ethos and pathos at the same time.

Imagine the power of telling the story of someone who has been needlessly injured in an accident because another driver was distracted by talking on the phone.

"When you jump into a scholarly text, the conversation is so implicit.... For me, the biggest thing that can be kind of disconcerting is that you have to figure out, what are people even talking about? And then you have to figure out, who are the voices that are most popular? Who are the voices that people turn to when they're trying to resolve this issue?"

LaunchPadSolo

Learn more about entering academic conversations.

Expert Testimony   Establishing an individual as an expert on a topic and using that person's words or ideas in support of your own position can be an effective way of bolstering your own ethos while supporting your central claim. However, the use of expert testimony can be tricky, as you need to carefully establish what makes the person you're relying on for evidence an actual expert on the topic or issue at hand. You must also consider your audience—whom would your audience consider to be an expert? How would you determine the expert's reputation within that community? The use of expert testimony is very common in academic argumentation. Researchers often summarize, paraphrase, or cite experts in their own discipline, as well as from others, to support their reasoning. If you've ever taken a class in which your instructor asked you to use reputable sources to support your argument, then you've probably relied on expert testimony to support a claim or reason already.

Imagine the effectiveness of citing experts who work for the National Transportation and Safety Board about their experiences investigating accidents that resulted from inattentive driving due to cell phone use.

Statistical Data and Research Findings   Statistics frequently serve as support in both popular and academic argumentation. Readers tend to like numbers, partly because they seem so absolute and scientific. However, it is important, as with all evidence, to evaluate statistical data for bias. Consider where statistics come from and how they are produced, if you plan to use them in support of an argument. Additionally, and perhaps most important, consider how those statistics were interpreted in the context of the original research reported. What were the study's conclusions?

Writers also often present the findings, or conclusions, of a research study as support for their reasons and claims. These findings may sometimes appear as qualitative, rather than just statistical, results or outcomes.

Imagine the effectiveness of citing recently produced statistics (rates of accidents) on the highways in your state from materials provided by your state's Department of Transportation.

When selecting the types and amounts of evidence to use in support of your reasons, be sure to study your rhetorical context and pay particular attention to the expectations of your intended audience. Some audiences, especially academic ones, are less likely to be convinced if you only provide evidence that draws on their emotions. Other audiences may be completely turned off by an argument that relies only on statistical data for support.

So far, we've discussed several types of evidence that are typically used in the construction of arguments—personal experience, expert testimony, statistical data and research findings. Collecting the data you need to make a strong argument can seem like a daunting task at times. It's important to keep in mind, though, that the amount of evidence you provide and the types of data your argument requires will depend entirely on the kind of argument you are constructing, as well as on the potential audience you want to persuade. Therefore, it's essential that you analyze and understand your audience's expectations when selecting support for your argument. Above all, select support that your audience will find credible, reliable, and relevant to your argument.

LaunchPadSolo

Hear criminologist Michelle Richter comment on types of research in her field.

INSIDE WORK **Analyzing Audience Expectations**

Choose any one of the complex thesis statements you constructed in the "Inside Work" activity on pages 42–43. Then identify two potential target audiences for your arguments. Freewrite for five to ten minutes in response to the following questions about these audiences' likely expectations for evidence.

- What does each audience already know about your topic? That is, what aspects of it can you assume they already have knowledge about?

- What does each audience need to know? What information do you need to make sure to include?

- What does each audience value in relation to your topic? What kinds of information will motivate them, interest them, or persuade them? How do you know?

- What sources of information about your topic might your audiences find questionably reliable? Why? ◗

Understanding Assumptions

Anytime you stake a claim and provide a reason, or provide evidence to support a reason, you are assuming something about your audience's beliefs and values, and it is important to examine your own assumptions very carefully as you construct arguments. Though assumptions are often unstated, they function to link together the ideas of two claims.

Let's consider a version of the claim and reason we've been looking at throughout this section to examine the role of assumptions: "We should support legislation to limit the use of cell phones while driving because they increase needless accidents and deaths on our roadways." In this instance, the claim and the reason appear logically connected, but let's identify the implied assumptions that the reader must accept in order to be persuaded by the argument:

Claim: We should support legislation to limit the use of cell phones while driving.

Reason: They increase needless accidents and deaths on our highways.

Implied Assumptions: We should do whatever we can to limit accidents and deaths.

Legislation can reduce accidents and deaths.

Many audiences would agree with these implied assumptions. As a result, it would likely be unnecessary to make the assumptions explicit or provide support for them. However, you can probably imagine an instance when a given audience would argue that legislating peoples' behavior does not affect how people actually behave. To such an audience, passing laws to regulate the use of cell phones while driving might seem ineffective. As a result, the audience might actually challenge the assumption(s) upon which your argument rests, and you may need to provide evidence to support the implied assumption that "legislation can reduce accidents and deaths."

A writer who is concerned that an audience may attack his argument by pointing to problematic assumptions might choose to explicitly state the assumption and provide support for it. In this instance, he might consider whether precedents exist (e.g., the effect of implementing seat belt laws, or statistical data from other states that have passed cell phone use laws) that could support his assumption that "legislation can reduce accidents and deaths."

INSIDE WORK **Considering Assumptions and Audience**

In the previous activity, you considered the most appropriate kinds of evidence for supporting thesis statements for differing audiences. This time, we ask you to identify the assumptions in your arguments and to consider whether or not those assumptions would require backing or additional support for varying audiences.

Begin by identifying the assumption(s) for each of your thesis statements. Then consider whether or not those assumptions need backing as the intended audience for your argument changes to the following:

- a friend or relative

- a state legislator

- an opinion news column editor

- a professional academic in a field related to your topic ▶

Anticipating Counterarguments

Initially, it may strike you as odd to think of counterarguments as a strategy to consider when constructing an argument. However, anticipating the objections of those who might disagree with you may actually strengthen your argument by forcing you to consider competing chains of reasoning and evidence. In fact, many writers actually choose to present **counterarguments**, or rebuttals of their own arguments, as part of the design of their arguments.

Why would anyone do this? Consider for a moment that your argument is like a debate. If you are able to adopt your opponent's position and then explain why that position is wrong, or why her reasoning is flawed, or in what ways her evidence is insufficient to support her own claim, then you support your own position. This is what it means to offer a **rebuttal** to potential counterarguments. Of course, when you provide rebuttals, you must have appropriate evidence to justify dismissing part or all of the entire counterargument. By anticipating and responding to counterarguments, you also strengthen your own ethos as a writer on the topic. Engaging counterarguments demonstrates that you have considered multiple positions and are knowledgeable about your subject.

You can also address possible counterarguments by actually conceding to an opposing position on a particular point or in a limited instance. Now you're probably wondering: Why would anyone do this? Doesn't this mean losing your argument? Not necessarily. Often, such a concession reveals that you're developing a more complex argument and moving past the pro/con positions that can limit productive debate.

Imagine that you're debating an opponent on a highly controversial issue like fracking (hydraulic fracturing). You're arguing a pro-fracking position, and your opponent makes the point that some people have experienced health issues as a result of the fracking in areas local to their homes. You might choose to concede this point by acknowledging that fracking could be a root cause of some individuals' illnesses. Though you still support fracking, you might now choose to limit the scope of your original position. That is, you could qualify your position by supporting fracking as long as it occurs, say, outside of a five-mile radius of any residence. In this case, your opponents' points are used to adjust or to **qualify** your own position, but this doesn't negate your entire argument. Your position may appear even stronger precisely because you've acknowledged the

opponents' points and refined the scope of your claim as a result, or because you've identified instances when your position might not hold true.

INSIDE WORK **Dealing with Counterarguments**

Throughout this section, you've been working with a series of claims that you constructed. You've linked those claims to reasons as support, and you've considered the kinds of evidence most appropriate for your theses in light of particular audiences. You've also considered the likely acceptability of your assumptions, according to various potential audiences. This time, consider possible counterarguments for your thesis statements.

- Who might argue against you?
- What will their arguments be based on?
- What might their arguments be?
- How might you use a counterargument to actually support your own claim?

Brainstorm a list of instances in which you might want to concede a point or two as a means of strengthening your own position. ▶

Analyzing Arguments

One way to understand the process of developing a persuasive argument is to study how others structure theirs. If you'll recall, in Chapter 2 we discussed how visual texts, like verbal ones, construct rhetorical situations. In the same way, visual texts may also seek to persuade an audience, and they may use many of the techniques explored throughout this chapter.

The following papers present arguments about visual texts. In the first, Jack Solomon, a professional writer, explores how advertisements reflect what he sees as contradictory impulses in the American character. In the second, Timothy Holtzhauser, a student writer, examines the argument strategies employed in a 1943 American war bonds ad. As you engage with their arguments, keep in mind that each writer is both making an argument and analyzing an argument simultaneously, so you'll want to consider their texts from both perspectives. Also keep in mind that their arguments are supported by evidence found in their own research. We'll explore how to conduct research in more detail in Chapter 4.

Insider Example
Professional Analysis of an Advertisement

In the following passage from "Masters of Desire: The Culture of American Advertising," Jack Solomon uses *semiotics*—a method for studying and interpreting cultural signs and symbols—to analyze the arguments made in two advertisements. As you read Solomon's argument, try to identify which elements of argument discussed in this chapter he uses in his analysis.

Excerpt from **"Masters of Desire: The Culture of American Advertising"**

JACK SOLOMON

COURTESY OF JACK SOLOMON

The American dream ... has two faces: the one communally egalitarian and the other competitively elitist. This contradiction is no accident; it is fundamental to the structure of American society. Even as America's great myth of equality celebrates the virtues of mom, apple pie, and the girl or boy next door, it also lures us to achieve social distinction, to rise above the crowd and bask alone in the glory. This land is your land and this land is my land, Woody Guthrie's populist anthem tells us, but we keep trying to increase the "my" at the expense of the "your." Rather than fostering contentment, the American dream breeds desire, a longing for a greater share of the pie. It is as if our society were a vast high-school football game, with the bulk of the participants noisily rooting in the stands while, deep down, each of them is wishing he or she could be the star quarterback or head cheerleader.

For the semiotician, the contradictory nature of the American myth of equality is nowhere written so clearly as in the signs that American advertisers use to manipulate us into buying their wares. "Manipulate" is the word here, not "persuade"; for advertising campaigns are not sources of product information, they are exercises in behavior modification. Appealing to our subconscious emotions rather than to our conscious intellects, advertisements are designed to exploit the discontentments fostered by the American dream, the constant desire for social success and the material rewards that accompany it. America's consumer economy runs on desire, and advertising stokes the engines by transforming common objects—from peanut butter to political candidates—into signs of all the things that Americans covet most.

But by semiotically reading the signs that advertising agencies manufacture to stimulate consumption, we can plot the precise state of desire in the audiences to which they are addressed. In this chapter, we'll look at a representative sample of ads and what they say about the emotional climate of the country and the fast-changing trends of American life. Because ours is a highly diverse, pluralistic society, various advertisements may say different things depending on their intended audiences, but in every case they say something about America, about the status of our hopes, fears, desires, and beliefs.

Let's begin with two ad campaigns conducted by the same company that bear out Alexis de Tocqueville's observations about the contradictory nature of American society: General Motors' campaigns for its Cadillac and Chevrolet lines. First, consider an early magazine ad for the Cadillac Allanté. Appearing

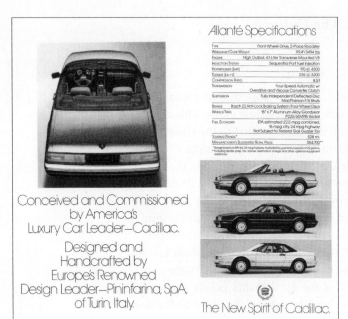

Allanté Specifications

Type	Front-Wheel-Drive, 2-Place Roadster
Wheelbase/Curb Weight	99.4"/3494 lbs
Engine	High Output, 4.1-Liter Transverse-Mounted V8
Induction System	Sequential Port Fuel Injection
Horsepower (bhp)	170 @ 4300
Torque (lb.-ft.)	235 @ 3200
Compression Ratio	8.5:1
Transmission	Four-Speed Automatic w/ Overdrive and Viscous Converter Clutch
Suspension	Fully Independent/Deflected-Disc MacPherson F/R Struts
Brakes	Bosch III Anti-Lock Braking System/Four-Wheel Discs
Wheels/Tires	15" x 7" Aluminum Alloy/Goodyear P225/60VR15 Radial
Fuel Economy	EPA-estimated 22.8 mpg combined, 16 mpg city, 24 mpg highway Not Subject to Federal Gas Guzzler Tax
Touring Range*	528 mi.
Manufacturer's Suggested Retail Price	$54,700**

*Range based on EPA-est. 24 mpg highway multiplied by gas tank capacity of 22 gallons.
**Including dealer prep. Tax, license, destination charge and other optional equipment additional.

Conceived and Commissioned
by America's
Luxury Car Leader—Cadillac.

Designed and
Handcrafted by
Europe's Renowned
Design Leader—Pininfarina, SpA,
of Turin, Italy.

The New Spirit of Cadillac.

as a full-color, four-page insert in *Time*, the ad seems to say "I'm special—and so is this car" even before we've begun to read it. Rather than being printed on the ordinary, flimsy pages of the magazine, the Allanté spread appears on glossy coated stock. The unwritten message here is that an extraordinary car deserves an extraordinary advertisement, and that both car and ad are aimed at an extraordinary consumer, or at least one who wishes to appear extraordinary compared to his more ordinary fellow citizens.

Ads of this kind work by creating symbolic associations between their product and what is most coveted by the consumers to whom they are addressed. It is significant, then, that this ad insists that the Allanté is virtually an Italian rather than an American car—an automobile, as its copy runs, "Conceived and Commissioned by America's Luxury Car Leader—Cadillac" but "Designed and Handcrafted by Europe's Renowned Design Leader—Pininfarina, SpA, of Turin, Italy." This is not simply a piece of product information; it's a sign of the prestige that European luxury cars enjoy in today's automotive marketplace. Once the luxury car of choice for America's status drivers, Cadillac has fallen far behind its European competitors in the race for the prestige market. So the Allanté essentially represents Cadillac's decision, after years of resisting the trend toward European cars, to introduce its own European import—whose high cost is clearly printed on the last page of the ad. Although $54,700 is a lot of money to pay for a Cadillac, it's about what you'd expect to pay for a top-of-the-line Mercedes-Benz. That's precisely the point the ad is trying to make: the Allanté is no mere car. It's a potent status symbol you can associate with the other major status symbols of the 1980s.

American companies manufacture status symbols because American consumers want them. As Alexis de Tocqueville recognized a century and a half ago, the competitive nature of democratic societies breeds a desire for social distinction, a yearning to rise above the crowd. But given the fact that those who do make it to the top in socially mobile societies have often risen from the lower ranks, they still look like everyone else. In the socially immobile societies of aristocratic Europe, generations of fixed social conditions produced subtle class signals. The accent of one's voice, the shape of one's nose, or even the set of one's chin immediately communicated social status. Aside from the nasal bray and uptilted head of the Boston Brahmin, Americans do not have any native sets of personal status signals. If it weren't for his Mercedes-Benz and Manhattan townhouse, the parvenu Wall Street millionaire often couldn't be distinguished from the man who tailors his suits. Hence, the demand for status symbols, for the objects that mark one off as a social success, is particularly strong in democratic nations — stronger even than in aristocratic societies, where the aristocrat so often looks and sounds different from everyone else.

Status symbols, then, are signs that identify their possessors' place in a social hierarchy, markers of rank and prestige. We can all think of any number of status symbols — Rolls-Royces, Beverly Hills mansions, even Shar Pei puppies (whose rareness has rocketed them beyond Russian wolfhounds as status pets and has inspired whole lines of wrinkle-faced stuffed toys) — but how do we know that something is a status symbol? The explanation is quite simple: when an object (or puppy!) either costs a lot of money or requires influential connections to possess, anyone who possesses it must also possess the necessary means and influence to acquire it. The object itself really doesn't matter, since it ultimately disappears behind the presumed social potency of its owner. Semiotically, what matters is the signal it sends, its value as a sign of power. One traditional sign of social distinction is owning a country estate and enjoying the peace and privacy that attend it. Advertisements for Mercedes-Benz, Jaguar, and Audi automobiles thus frequently feature drivers motoring quietly along a country road, presumably on their way to or from their country houses.

Advertisers have been quick to exploit the status signals that belong to body language as well. As Hegel observed in the early nineteenth century, it is an ancient aristocratic prerogative to be seen by the lower orders without having to look at them in return. Tilting his chin high in the air and gazing down at the world under hooded eyelids, the aristocrat invites observation while refusing to look back. We can find such a pose exploited in an advertisement for Cadillac Seville in which an elegantly dressed woman goes out for a drive with her husband in their new Cadillac. If we look closely at the woman's body language, we see her glance inwardly with a satisfied smile on her face but not outward toward the camera that represents our gaze. She is glad to be seen by us in her Seville, but she isn't interested in looking at us!

Ads that are aimed at a broader market take the opposite approach. If the American dream encourages the desire to arrive, to vault above the mass, it also fosters a desire to be popular, to "belong." Populist commercials accordingly transform products into signs of belonging, utilizing such common icons as country music, small-town life, family picnics, and farmyards. All of these icons are incorporated in GM's "Heartbeat of America" campaign for its Chevrolet line. Unlike the Seville commercial, the faces in the Chevy ads look straight at us and smile. Dress is casual, the mood upbeat. Quick camera cuts take us from rustic to suburban to urban scenes, creating an American montage filmed from sea to shining sea. We all "belong" in a Chevy.

Discussion Questions

1. Jack Solomon sets up an interesting contrast between "manipulate" and "persuade" at the beginning of this excerpt. How does his description of these ads mirror our understanding of arguments? In your own words, how would you describe the differences he establishes between manipulating and persuading?

2. In Solomon's analysis of the Cadillac and Chevrolet ads, where does he address the claims and reasons given by the advertisers to buy their products? Do the ads address assumptions?

3. How does Solomon characterize the appeals made by both advertisements? Where does he describe appeals to ethos? Logos? Pathos?

Insider Example
Student Analysis of an Advertisement

Timothy Holtzhauser, a student in a first-year writing class, wrote the following analysis of an advertisement as a course assignment. He used elements of rhetorical analysis and argument analysis to understand the persuasive effects of the advertisement he chose. Notice, also, that he followed Modern Language Association (MLA) style conventions, especially when citing sources within his paper and documenting them at the end of the paper. (See Chapter 4 and the Appendix for additional information on documentation styles.)

Timothy Holtzhauser

ENG 101-79

February 13, 201-

Rhetoric of a 1943 War Bonds Ad

From the front covers of magazines at the store, to the ads by Google on sidebars of websites, to the incessant commercials on television, advertisements are visible everywhere. Whether the advertisement announces or insinuates its purpose, all advertisements attempt to change the audience's manner of thinking or acting. In "Masters of Desire: The Culture of American Advertising," Jack Solomon describes the motive behind advertising as pure and simple manipulation: "'Manipulate' is the word here, not 'persuade'; for advertising campaigns are not sources of product information, they are exercises in behavior modification" (60). Even the most innocent advertisement performs this maneuver, and the

"Death Warrant . . . US War Bonds" advertisement drawn by S. J. Woolf is no different. This 1943 ad, printed in the *New York Daily News* for Bloomingdale's department store, not only encourages the purchase of U.S. war bonds by exaggerating Hitler's negative aspects, but also depicts the growing influence and activism of the United States during this era.

The main claim, or thesis

When this advertisement appeared, the United States was rapidly becoming more involved in the hostilities of World War II. While not yet engaged in the war in Europe, the United States was providing supplies and manpower for the war in the Pacific, and the government was in serious need of funds to keep the war machine rolling. The main method that the government used to obtain these funds was selling war bonds and advertising, to push the sale of these bonds. War bonds were used as a tool to raise money for the government by selling certificates that promised a return on the investment after a period of time in exchange for the investment. In New York City, publishing city of the *New York Daily News* and home of Bloomingdale's main store, there was tremendous outrage at the atrocities being committed as a result of the war. Due to this, the general public showed interest in ending the war, especially the war in the Pacific. For the most part, the city trended toward the progressive democratic mind-set and agreed with the mostly democratic-controlled government of the era (Duranti 666). While factors such as these propelled the citizens to purchase bonds as the advertisement suggests, there were other factors resisting this push as well. Particularly important was the ever-present aftermath of the Great Depression. The combination of these factors created a mixed feeling about the purchase of war bonds, but the fear of Hitler's reign continuing tended to bias the populace toward purchasing the bonds.

The next two paragraphs provide the reader with historical context for the ad and its publication. This information clarifies the rhetorical situation for readers and sets the stage for the analyses of the ad's elements that follow.

Drawing courtesy of S. J. Woolf

TO BRING CLOSER THE HAPPY DAY SHOWN
ABOVE—BUY MORE AND MORE WAR BONDS

BLOOMINGDALE'S
Lexington Avenue and 59th Street

At the time of the release of this ad, the *New York Daily News* was a fairly new newspaper in New York City, as it had been initially released about twenty years beforehand. Even as a new publication, it had an extremely wide readership due to its tabloid format, which focused on images, unlike other New York papers. At the time of the printing of this ad, the *Daily News* was known to be slightly biased toward the democratic mind-set common among the citizens of the city ("New York Daily News"). The publishing of this advertisement at this time could be viewed as an appeal to ethos in order to push the patriotic sense of the paper. The advertisement can also be seen as an appeal to ethos by Bloomingdale's, as the company was seeking to portray itself as a patriotic firm. With that context in mind, several components of the advertisement make more sense and can be more effectively analyzed.

The analysis now focuses on specific elements of the ad. In this paragraph, the student analyzes features of Hitler's face: the bug eyes, the dropped jaw, the tufts of hair. These, he suggests, express Hitler's fear of American strength, which stems at least partially from the selling and purchasing of war bonds.

The most prominent feature in the advertisement is Hitler's face, and in particular, his facial expression. Woolf's image here uses two primary components to make the facial expression stand out: the humorously exaggerated bug-eyed stare and the dropped jaw. The effect created by these two factors is compounded by the addition of the buck teeth and the protruding ears. The bug eyes commonly serve in American imagery to express shock, and they perform that role excellently here in this advertisement. The dropped jaw is used very frequently as well, especially in cartoons, and here it strengthens the shocked expression. The buck teeth and protruding ears are two images that are used in American culture to convey the idea of a buffoon. In addition to these features, Woolf comically adds in two tufts of hair in imitation of devil horns to further enhance Hitler's evil image. When these two are added to the previous facets, it creates an image of a completely dumbfounded and baffled Hitler. The image was designed in this manner to enhance the feeling that purchasing U.S. war bonds would benefit society by eliminating the severe hindrance known as Hitler.

The next feature that stands out is the death warrant and war bond itself and Hitler's hands clutching it. Woolf draws Hitler's hands in a manner that makes them appear to be tightly gripping the paper as in anger. The paper itself shows only the words "death warrant" and "U.S. War Bonds," but one can infer from the context that the warrant is for Hitler. The fact that the warrant is printed on a war bond suggests that the U.S. government completely backs the killing of Hitler and will take action to see it through. The document appeals to the viewer's logos through the suggestion that war bonds will end the war sooner and save countless lives in the process. There is also an inherent appeal to ethos in the suggestion of the character of Bloomingdale's as a firm that strongly opposes the horrors committed by Hitler and his followers. In addition, there is an appeal to pathos, with the ad attempting to home in on the audience's moral code. This apparent encouragement of killing Hitler, coupled with the text at the bottom of the advertisement, creates a mood of vengeance directed toward Hitler.

The next major feature of the advertisement is the caption at the bottom of the image, which reads, "To bring closer the happy day shown above — buy more and more war bonds." The image shown above the text in most scenarios would not be considered a happy day for most people. The thought of death is normally enough to ruin anyone's day, but this image banks on the public having a burning vengeance that justifies the end of Hitler. The idea of vengeance is generally viewed as having serious negative repercussions, but this article portrays the idea in a positive manner by making an appeal to the audience's logos. The appeal here could best be described as sacrificing one to save millions. The caption also makes an appeal to pathos in the manner that it tries to connect with the viewer's sense of morals that Hitler has almost definitely broken in numerous ways.

The next aspect of the advertisement that stands out is the use of shading. Woolf's decision here may have been influenced by requirements of the *Daily News* at the time, but even viewed in that light it has a rhetorical effect on the advertisement. The usage of shading here creates the appearance of an unfinished image, further enhancing the idea that Hitler has just been served his death warrant hot off the press by the United States and its war bonds. It also creates a worried cast to Hitler's face through the heavy shading in the creases along his jawline. The overall image of Hitler created through the use of shading comes off as dark and sinister, representative of the common American's view on Hitler's character. In contrast, the war bond is virtually untouched by shading, leaving it nearly white. This creates the image of a beacon of hope shining through the darkness that provides a means to eliminate this terror. Additionally, the presence of a heavily shaded advertisement among the more crisp images, popular among tabloids, accents this advertisement and its message.

The final aspect of the advertisement that draws major attention is the overall construction of the image. The layout emphasizes the two key components of the advertisement: Hitler's face and the war bond. Not only does this accentuate the relationship between buying war bonds and bringing the hammer down on Hitler, but it also provides further depth to the image's rhetorical context. Hitler is posed hunched over as if to imply a deformity in his body and represent a deformity of his mind. The statement here runs on the classic American stereotype that a malformed person is either inferior or evil, a stereotype popularly used in comical representations such as this one. In addition, the hunched posture can be interpreted as the weight of the American war machine, fueled by the war bond purchases, dragging Hitler down to end his reign of terror.

The writer shifts focus to analyze the ad's caption.

With each of these analyzed aspects in mind, the advertisement can serve as an effective description of the period similar to what Jack Solomon suggests is possible in "Masters of Desire." He uses the following statement to show how advertisements are indicative of the culture of their audiences: "But by semiotically reading the signs that advertising agencies manufacture to stimulate consumption, we can plot the precise state of desire in the audiences to which they are addressed" (61). Based upon the patriotic push shown through this advertisement's attack on Hitler and visualization of handing him a death warrant, the advertisement shows the general patriotic mood of America at the time. Given the war footing of the country during this era, this patriotic pride fits well into the time frame. It also shows the growing influence of the United States across the world. Up until this point in time, America was not taken very seriously, and U.S. foreign policy was mostly designed to ignore the rest of the world and preserve America. With the serving of the death warrant to Hitler shown in this advertisement, the change in ideology is starkly apparent. Instead of the wait-and-see mentality common in America before World War II, the highly proactive and aggressive nature of America today begins to show. For a small snippet in a tabloid newspaper, this advertisement packs quite a rhetorical punch.

Notice how the ending addresses elements of the paper's thesis statement, or how the ad "depicts the growing influence and activism of the United States during this era."

Taking into account all the elements of this advertisement, rhetorical and otherwise, the advertisement creates an astounding patriotic push for the purchase of war bonds through exaggeration and establishes the United States as a globally significant force through the implications of the death warrant for a foreign citizen. All aspects used in this advertisement work well to cleverly goad readers of the paper to purchase war bonds from Bloomingdale's, holding true to Jack Solomon's statement about advertisements not seeking to provide information, but to manipulate the audience. In the end, however, this advertisement does not convey the negative connotation often associated with manipulative advertising; rather, it uses manipulative elements to try to create a better future for the readers.

Works Cited

Bloomingdale's. Advertisement. *New York Daily News*. 1943. Print.

Duranti, Marco. "Utopia, Nostalgia, and World War at the 1939–40 New York World's Fair." *Journal of Contemporary History* 41.4 (2006): 663–83. Web. 29 Jan. 2012.

"New York Daily News." *Encyclopaedia Britannica Online*. Encyclopaedia Britannica, 2012. Web. 5 Feb. 2012.

Solomon, Jack. "Masters of Desire: The Culture of American Advertising."
*The Signs of Our Time: Semiotics: The Hidden Messages of Environments,
Objects, and Cultural Images*. Los Angeles: Jeremy P. Tarcher, 1988.
59–76. Print.

Discussion Questions

1. Where does Timothy Holtzhauser state his thesis? Why do you think he phrases his thesis in the way that he does?

2. How does Timothy use logos in his own argument? Why do you think he relies on logos to support his claim?

3. Who is the intended audience for this argument?

4. What scholarly or popular conversation(s) is Timothy joining in?

5. Which claim(s) do you find most convincing and least convincing for Timothy's rhetorical situation? Why?

WRITING PROJECT **Composing a Rhetorical Analysis of an Advertisement**

For this project, we ask you to consider the ways in which rhetorical context and appeals work together in an advertisement to create an argument.

- To begin, choose a print or online advertisement that you can analyze based on its rhetorical context and the appeals it uses to persuade the intended audience.

- Then, drawing on the principles of rhetorical analysis from Chapter 2 and the discussion of developing arguments in this chapter, compose an analysis examining the ad's use of appeals in light of the rhetorical situation the ad constructs.

RHETORICAL CONTEXT (SEE CHAPTER 2)

Central Question: How do the elements of the rhetorical context affect the way the advertisement is structured?

Author _____

Audience _____

Topic _____

Purpose _____

RHETORICAL APPEALS (SEE CHAPTER 3)

Central Question: What appeals does the advertisement use, and why?

Ethos _____

Logos _____

Pathos _____

Keep in mind that a rhetorical analysis makes an argument, so your analysis should have a central claim that you develop based on what you observed, through the frameworks of rhetorical context and rhetorical appeals, in the advertisement. Make your claim clear, and then support it with reasons and evidence from the advertisement.

tip sheet

Developing Arguments

- **Presenting an argument is different from merely stating an opinion.** Presenting and supporting an argument mean establishing a claim that is backed by reasons and evidence.

- **The unifying element of any academic argument is its primary or central claim.** A unifying claim may take the form of a thesis, a hypothesis, or a more general statement of purpose. There are numerous kinds of claims, including claims of value, definition, and policy.

- **Reasons are generated from and supported by evidence.** Evidence may take the form of inartistic proofs (including statistics and raw data) or artistic proofs, including the rhetorical appeals of ethos (appeal to credibility), logos (appeal to reason and logic), and pathos (appeal to emotion).

- **Claims presented as part of a chain of reasoning are linked by (often) unstated assumptions.** Assumptions should be analyzed carefully for their appropriateness (acceptability, believability) in a particular rhetorical context.

- **Considering and/or incorporating counterarguments is an excellent way to strengthen your own arguments.** You may rebut counterarguments, or you may concede (or partially concede) to them and modify your own argument in response.

- **Analyzing others' arguments is a good way to develop your skills at arguing,** particularly in an academic context.

Academic Research

Conducting Research

R esearch projects have all kinds of starting points. Sometimes we start them because a course instructor or an employer asks us to. At other times, we embark on research projects because we want to learn about something on our own. In all these cases, though, our research responds to a question or set of questions that we need to answer. These are called **research questions**, and identifying them and narrowing them down is usually the first step of starting a research project, especially in an academic context.

DEVELOPING A RESEARCH QUESTION

For many students, choosing a subject to research is incredibly difficult. The best way to start is by thinking about issues that matter to you. Writers tend to do their best work when writing about things in which they have a personal investment. Even if you're conducting research in a course with a topic that has been assigned, think about how you might approach the topic from an angle that matters to you or brings in your own unique point of view.

Another challenge that many students face is narrowing down a solid research question once they've selected an issue of interest. If a research question is too broad, then it may not be feasible to respond to it adequately in the scope of your research assignment. If it's too narrow, though, it might not be researchable; in other words, you might not be able to find enough sources to support a solid position on the issue.

As you work on drafting a research question, keep these five criteria in mind:

ANDREA TSURUMI

1. **Personal Investment** Is this an issue you care about?
2. **Debatable Subject** Might reasonable people looking at evidence about this issue come to different conclusions?
3. **Researchable Issue** Is there adequate published evidence to support a position on this issue?
4. **Feasibility** Is the scope of the research question manageable?
5. **Contribution** Will your response to the question contribute to the ongoing conversation about the issue?

INSIDE WORK **Writing a Research Question**

As you begin your research project, you should identify a research question that will guide your research and keep you on track. Start by brainstorming a list of possible research questions for ten minutes, and then use the five criteria below to narrow down your list to a research question that might work for you. If your answer to any of the questions is a definitive "No," then the research question might not be a good choice, or you might need to revise it to make it work for a research project.

1. **Personal Investment** Is this an issue you care about? If the issue is too broad, is there a way you can narrow down the topic to an aspect of the issue that is of the most importance to you?
2. **Debatable Subject** Could two reasonable people looking at evidence about this issue come to different conclusions?
3. **Researchable Issue** Can you find adequate published evidence to support a position on this issue?
4. **Feasibility** Is the scope of the research question manageable, given the amount of time you have to research the issue and the amount of space in which you will make your argument?
5. **Contribution** Will your response to your question contribute to the on-going conversation about the issue? ▶

LaunchPadSolo

A political scientist emphasizes the importance of supporting evidence.

CHOOSING PRIMARY AND SECONDARY SOURCES

To respond to any research question, a writer must collect evidence to prove or disprove a hypothesis or to support a claim. Once you have identified a solid research question, you must decide whether you need to collect *primary* and/or *secondary sources* to support your research aims.

Writers can choose from among several types of sources to support their research. When considering sources to support an argument, writers must study them for information that can serve as specific *evidence* to address aspects of their claims, all the while keeping their target audience in mind.

What kind of evidence will likely be convincing to the target audience? If researchers are reviewing the existing literature on a topic or are trying to understand what has already been written about an issue before conducting a study of their own, they must search for sources that provide information about the ongoing conversation concerning that topic or issue. Then the researchers might collect data to answer a clearly defined research question that has grown out of reading those sources.

Primary sources include the results of data that researchers might collect on their own. If you're making a claim about how to interpret a work of art and you've studied the piece carefully for images and symbols that you discuss in your argument, then the work of art is your primary source. Or perhaps you've designed and conducted a survey of people's experiences with a particular phenomenon. In this case, the results you've gathered from your survey are a primary source from which you can provide evidence to answer a research question or support an argument. Other forms of primary sources include original historical documents and results from interviews you may have conducted.

Insider's View
Primary research in writing studies
MORIAH McCRACKEN, WRITING STUDIES

"I like to try to introduce my students to qualitative research in their first year, when our students have to interview a professor. Sometimes I'll help them develop survey questions and questionnaires so they can have that kind of experience, and I'll teach them about double-entry notebooks so they can do some observations in the classroom. I like to bring in qualitative methods so that students realize there are different kinds of questions to ask, and depending on my question, I'm going to have to try something a little bit different and learn how to do this kind of research in my discipline."

Find additional advice on doing primary research.

INSIDE WORK   **Collecting Primary Evidence**

Freewrite for five to ten minutes about a time in the past when you had to collect data on your own to answer a research question.

- Why were you collecting the data? What question were you trying to answer?

- What data did you collect, and how did you collect it? Did you observe something? Conduct a survey? Interview someone?

- If you were to try to answer that research question now, what data would you collect? Would you do anything differently? Why or why not? ▶

Based on the scope of your argument and the expectations of your audience, you may also need to engage **secondary sources**, or research collected by and/or commented on by others. Let's say that your literature professor wants you to offer an interpretation of a poem. You study the poem carefully as your primary source and arrive at a conclusion or claim about the work.

But imagine that the assignment also requires you to use scholarly opinions to support your own position or interpretation. As a result, you spend time in the library or searching online databases to locate articles or books by scholars who provide their own interpretations or perspectives on the poem. The articles or books you rely on to support your interpretation are secondary sources because the interpretations were developed by others, commenting on the poem. Likewise, if you cite as part of your own argument the results of a survey published in an academic article, then that article serves as a secondary source of information to you. Other secondary sources include newspapers and magazines, textbooks, and encyclopedias. Many of the researched arguments you'll produce in college will require you to use both primary and secondary sources as support.

INSIDE WORK) **Using Primary and Secondary Sources**

Read Timothy Holtzhauser's ad analysis on pages 52–57 of Chapter 3. After reviewing his analysis, look at the list of works cited at the end of his essay. Then answer the following questions.

- What primary source(s) does Timothy use to support his argument? Why do you think he chooses the primary source(s) he does?

- What would the impact be if Timothy didn't use primary sources in his argument? Would his argument be more or less persuasive to his audience?

- What secondary sources does Timothy use to support his argument?

- Why do you think he chooses these particular secondary sources? What impact do they have on the development of his argument?

- If Timothy had only used primary sources and no secondary sources, what would the impact have been on the persuasiveness of his argument? ▶

SEARCHING FOR SOURCES

In Part Two, we discuss collecting primary sources to support claims in specific disciplinary areas or genres in more detail. In the rest of this chapter, though, we provide support for collecting secondary sources, which provide a foundation for research and writing in academic contexts. Even if the main evidence used to support an academic research project comes from primary sources, secondary sources can provide an overview of what other scholars have already argued with regard to a particular issue or topic. Keep in mind that academic writing and research essentially comprise a series of extended conversations about different issues, and secondary sources help you understand what part of the conversation has already happened before you start researching a topic on your own, or before you consider entering an established conversation on a topic or issue.

Identifying Search Terms

The school, college, or university you attend likely offers many avenues to help navigate the processes for conducting library research at your institution. Most of these processes include searching for source materials online. When you search for secondary sources online to support the development of a research study or to support a claim in an argument, it's important to consider your **search terms**, the key words and phrases you'll use while you're searching. Let's say that you're interested in understanding the effects of using cell phones while driving, a topic we explored in Chapter 2. You might begin your research with a question that reads something like this:

What are the effects of using cell phones while driving?

The first step in your research process would likely be to find out what others have already written about this issue. To start, you might rephrase your research question to ask:

What have scholars written about the effects of using cell phones while driving?

To respond, you'll need to identify the key terms of your question that will focus your search for secondary sources about the subject. You might highlight some of the key terms in the question:

What have scholars written about the effects of using cell phones while driving?

If you started your search by typing "cell phones and driving" into Google, your search would return millions of results:

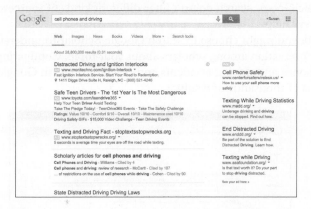

These results include links to images of people on cell phones in their cars, to news articles, and to statistics from insurance companies, to name a few. After careful evaluation, you may decide that some of these sources of data would be useful for your research, but you can also see that the results produce far too many hits to manage. There's simply no way you can comb through the millions of hits to find information that is appropriate for your purposes. As a result, you may choose to narrow your search to something that emerges as a specific issue, like "reaction time." If you narrowed your search to "cell phones and reaction time," you would see results like this:

Focusing your research terms further narrows the scope of your search somewhat, but you still have far too many results to review. One concern to keep in mind, then, is that basic Google searches are not very useful in helping to locate the kinds of sources you might rely on for your research, especially in an academic context. If you want to understand what scholars have written about your topic, then you need to find scholarly or academic sources as support. A basic Google search doesn't filter different kinds of sources, so it's not generally very helpful.

Instead, you might choose to search Google Scholar to understand the ongoing conversation among scholars about your topic. Conducting a search for "cell phones and driving accidents and reaction time" in Google Scholar returns tens of thousands of results:

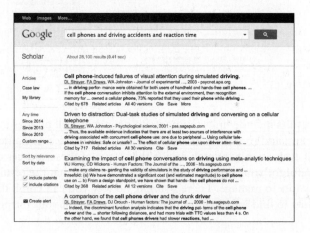

If you take a close look at the left-hand side of the screen, however, you'll notice that you can limit your search in several ways. By limiting the search to sources published since 2014, you can reduce your results significantly:

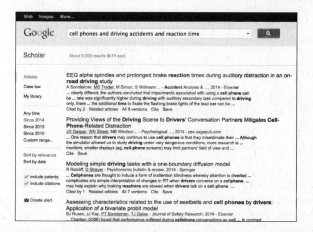

You can continue refining your search until you end up with a more manageable number of hits to comb through. Although the number is still large, thousands of results are more manageable than millions. Of course, you would likely need to continue narrowing your results. As part of this narrowing process, you are simultaneously focusing in on the conversation you originally wanted to understand: what scholars have written about your topic. Consider the criteria that would be most meaningful for your project as you refine your search by revising your search terms.

INSIDE WORK **Generating Search Terms**

Think of a controversial social issue that interests you. We chose driving while using a cell phone, but you should choose something you would potentially be interested in learning more about. Then follow these instructions, preferably working with classmates.

- Brainstorm the search terms you would use for that topic. What terms would you enter into a search engine?

- List your search terms in the box for Round 1 below, and then try doing a search using your preferred web search engine.

- How many hits did you get? Write the number in the box for Round 1.

- Switch seats with a classmate so that you can look at someone else's search terms. Should the search be narrowed? If so, revise your classmate's search terms to narrow them slightly. Write those in the box for Round 2. Try the search, and record the number of hits.

- Follow the instructions again for Rounds 3 and 4.

	Search Terms	Number of Hits
Round 1		
Round 2		
Round 3		
Round 4		

After you have finished the exercise, reflect on the following questions.

- How did your classmates narrow your search terms? What changes worked well, and what changes didn't work as well?

- If you were going to write advice for students using search engines for research, what advice would you give about search terms? ❿

Keep in mind that general search engines such as Google are not always the best places to conduct academic research, although they can often be useful starting points. Experienced researchers generally rely on more specialized databases to find the kinds of sources that will support their research most effectively.

Using Journal Databases

If you are conducting academic research, then one of the first types of sources you should look for is peer-reviewed journal articles. You may wonder why we don't recommend beginning your search by scouring your library's catalog for books. The answer is that academic books, which are often an excellent source of information, generally take much longer to make their way through the publishing process before they appear in libraries. Publishing the results of research in academic journal articles, however, is a faster method for academics to share their work with their scholarly communities. Academic journals, therefore, are a valuable resource precisely because they offer insight into the most current research being conducted in a field.

Additionally, like other scholarly work, most academic journals publish research only after it has undergone rigorous scrutiny through a peer-review process by other scholars in the relevant academic field. Work that has gone through the academic peer-review process has been sent out, with the authors' identifying information removed, and reviewed by other scholars who determine whether it makes a sufficiently significant contribution to the field to be published. Work published in a peer-reviewed academic journal has been approved not only by the journal's editor but also by other scholars in the field.

If you've ever browsed through your school's library, you've probably noticed that there are thousands of academic journals, and many are available online and easy to locate via the Internet. If you're associated with a college or university, you likely have access to a wide array of online academic journals that can be explored through databases via the library's website. You can search general library databases by refining search terms, as we discussed in the examples of using Google, but you can also find relevant resources by searching in specific disciplinary databases.

Searching for Journal Articles by Discipline

One way of searching for journal articles through your school's library is to explore the academic databases by subject or discipline. These databases usually break down the major fields of study into the many subfields that make up smaller disciplinary communities. Individual schools, colleges, and universities choose which databases they subscribe to. In the following image from the North Carolina State University's library website, you can see that agriculture is divided into various subfields: agricultural economics, animal science, crop science, and so on.

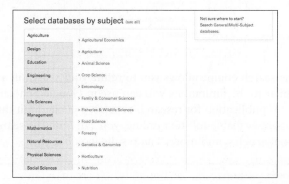

Let's say you need to find information on post-traumatic stress disorder (PTSD) among veterans of the Iraq War that began in March 2003. Consider the subfields of the social sciences where you're most likely to find research on PTSD. You might search databases in history, sociology, political science, and psychology, for instance. If you choose "Psychology," then you see a screen that lists major research databases in psychology, along with some related databases. Choosing the database at the top of the page, "PsycINFO," gains you access to one of the most comprehensive databases in that field of study.

Psychology

Databases

PsycINFO

PsycINFO, from the American Psychological Association (APA), contains more than 2 million citations and summaries of scholarly journal articles, book chapters, books, and dissertations, all in psychology and related disciplines, dating as far back as the 1800s. The database also includes information about the psychological aspects of related fields such as medicine, psychiatry, nursing, sociology, education, pharmacology, physiology, linguistics, anthropology, business, law and others. Journal coverage, which spans 1887 to present, includes international material selected from nearly 2,000 periodicals in more than 25 languages.

Selecting "PsycINFO" grants access to the PsycINFO database via a search engine—in this case, EbscoHOST. You can now input search terms such as "PTSD and Iraq war veterans" to see your results.

Notice that the search engine allows you to refine your search in a number of ways, very similar to the limitations you can use in Google Scholar: you can limit the years of publication for research articles, you can limit the search to sources that are available full-text online, you can limit the search to peer-reviewed journal articles, and more. The results look like this:

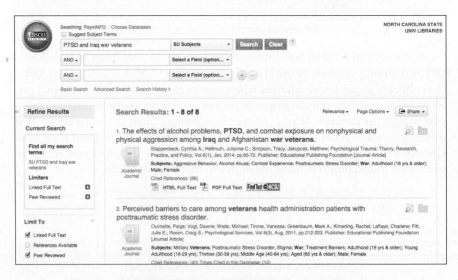

You can now access the texts of journal articles that you find interesting or that might be most relevant to your research purposes. Depending on the number and content of the results, you may choose to revise your search terms and run the search again.

EVALUATING SOURCES

Distinguishing between Scholarly and Popular Sources

As we have said, using search engines makes finding sources easy. The difficult part is deciding which sources are worth your time. If you are working on an academic paper, it is particularly useful to be able to distinguish between popular and scholarly sources.

Depending on your research and writing context, you might be able to use both scholarly and popular sources to support your research. However, in some writing situations it is most appropriate to rely on scholarly sources. For this reason, you should understand the difference between scholarly and popular sources, which comes down to a matter of audience and the publication process. **Scholarly sources** are produced for an audience of other scholars, and **popular sources** are produced for a general audience. Scholarly sources have undergone the peer-review process prior to publication, while popular sources typically have been vetted only by an editor. Generally speaking, popular sources are not very useful for supporting academic research. Let's examine a number of publication types in terms of the kind of information, scholarly or popular, they most often provide:

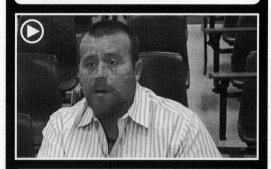

Insider's View
On distinguishing scholarly sources
JONATHAN MORRIS, POLITICAL SCIENCE

"We have to teach our students what's scholarly literature and what isn't. Peer-review journal articles, books—that's scholarly literature. When you pull things off of Wikipedia, when you go even to newspaper articles from the *New York Times*—that's not scholarly research. They need to know that differentiation."

LaunchPadSolo
Get expert advice on finding scholarly sources.

Examples of Scholarly Sources

- **Academic Journals**   Most journal articles are produced for an audience of other scholars, and the vast majority are peer-reviewed before they are published in academic journals.

- **Books Published by Academic Presses**   Academic presses publish books that also go through the peer-review process. You can sometimes identify academic presses by their names (e.g., a university press), but sometimes you need to dig deeper to find out whether a press generally publishes scholarly or popular sources. Looking at the press's website can often help answer that question.

Examples of Popular Sources

- **Newspapers**   Most newspaper articles are reviewed by editors for accuracy and reliability. However, they typically provide only information that would be of interest to a general audience. They are not specifically intended for an academic audience. A newspaper might report the results of a study published in an academic journal, but it will generally not publish original academic research.

- **Magazines** Like newspaper articles, magazine articles are typically reviewed by editors and are intended for a general reading audience, not an academic one.

Although it may seem easy to classify sources into one of these two categories, in fact it is often difficult to determine if a source is scholarly or not. Understanding the nature of scholarly and popular sources and recognizing their differences as you do your research will help you develop more effective arguments.

Scholarly works, for instance, are typically built on other sources, so they generally include references to other works that are documented in the text and listed in a complete bibliography at the end. Imagine for a moment, though, that you locate a study published on the Internet that you think would be a really good source for your research. It looks just like an article that might appear in a journal, and it has a bibliography that includes other academic sources. However, as part of your analysis of the source, you discover that the article, published only on a website, has never been published by a journal. Is this a scholarly work? It might be. Could this still be a useful scholarly work for your purposes? Perhaps. Still, as a writer and researcher, you would need to know that the article you're using as part of your own research has never been peer-reviewed or published by a journal or an academic press. This means that the validity of the work has never been assessed by other experts in the field. If you use the source in your own work, you would probably want to indicate that it has never been peer-reviewed or published in an academic journal as part of your discussion of that source.

Answering the following questions about your sources can help you evaluate their credibility and reliability:

1. Who are the authors?
2. Who is the intended audience?
3. Where is the work published?
4. Does the work rely on other reputable sources for information?
5. Does the work seem biased?

As a writer, you must ultimately make the decisions about what is or is not an appropriate source, based on your goals and an analysis of your audience. Answering the questions above can help you assess the appropriateness of sources.

INSIDE WORK   **Evaluating Sources**

For this exercise, either look at the sample essay from Timothy Holtzhauser on pages 52–57 of Chapter 3 or look at an essay that you wrote for a class in the past. Choose one of the references listed in the essay's bibliography, and write answers to the following questions.

1. Who are the authors? Do they possess any particular credentials that make them experts on the topic? With what institutions or organizations are the authors associated?

2. Who is the intended audience—the general public or a group of scholars? How do you know?

3. Where is the work published? Do works published there undergo a peer-review process?

4. Does the work rely on other reputable sources for information? What are those sources, and how do you know they are reputable?

5. Does the work seem biased? How do you know this? Is the work funded or supported by individuals or parties who might have a vested interest in the results? If so, is there a potential conflict of interest? ◗

SUMMARIZING, PARAPHRASING, AND QUOTING FROM SOURCES

Once you've located and studied the sources you want to use in a research paper, then you're ready to begin considering ways to integrate that material into your own work. There are a number of ways to integrate the words and ideas of others into your research, and you've likely already had experience summarizing, paraphrasing, and quoting from sources as part of an academic writing assignment. For many students, though, the specifics of how to summarize, paraphrase, and quote accurately are often unclear, so we'll walk through these processes in some detail.

Summarizing

Summarizing a text is a way of condensing the work to its main ideas. A summary therefore requires you to choose the most important elements of a text and to answer these questions: *What* is this work really trying to say, and *how* does it say it? Composing a summary of a source can be valuable for a number of reasons. Writing a summary can help you carefully analyze the content of a text and understand it better, but a summary can also help you identify and keep track of the sources you want to use in the various parts of your research. You may sometimes be able to summarize a source in only a sentence or two. We suggest a simple method for analyzing a source and composing a summary:

1. Read the source carefully, noting the **rhetorical context**. Who composed the source? For whom is the source intended? Where was it published? Identify the source and provide answers to these questions at the beginning of your summary, as appropriate.

2. Identify the **main points**. Pay close attention to topic sentences at the beginning of paragraphs, as they often highlight central ideas in the overall structure of an argument. Organize your summary around the main ideas you identify.

3. Identify **examples**. You will want to be able to summarize the ways the writer illustrates, exemplifies, or argues the main points. Though you will likely not discuss all of the examples or forms of evidence you identify in detail as part of your summary, you will want to comment on one or two, or offer some indication of how the writer supports his or her main points.

The following excerpt is taken from the fuller text of Jack Solomon's "Masters of Desire: The Culture of American Advertising," which appears on pages 49–52 in Chapter 3:

> Status symbols, then, are signs that identify their possessors' place in a social hierarchy, markers of rank and prestige. We can all think of any number of status symbols — Rolls-Royces, Beverly Hills mansions, even Shar Pei puppies (whose rareness and expense has rocketed them beyond Russian wolfhounds as status pets and has even inspired whole lines of wrinkle-faced stuffed toys) — but how do we know that something is a status symbol? The explanation is quite simple: when an object (or puppy!) either costs a lot of money or requires influential connections to possess, anyone who possesses it must also possess the necessary means and influence to acquire it. The object itself really doesn't matter, since it ultimately disappears behind the presumed social potency of its owner. Semiotically, what matters is the signal it sends, its value as a sign of power. One traditional sign of social distinction is owning a country estate and enjoying the peace and privacy that attend it. Advertisements for Mercedes-Benz, Jaguar, and Audi automobiles thus frequently feature drivers motoring quietly along a country road, presumably on their way to or from their country houses.

A summary of this part of Solomon's text might read something like this:

> In "Masters of Desire: The Culture of American Advertising," Jack Solomon acknowledges that certain material possessions may be understood as representations of an individual's rank or status. He illustrates this point by identifying a number of luxury automobiles that, when observed, cause us to consider the elevated economic status of the vehicles' owners (63).

You'll notice that this summary eliminates discussion of the specific examples Solomon provides. Further, it removes any discussion of the concept of semiotics. Though Solomon's ideas are clearly condensed and the writer of this summary has carefully selected the ideas to be summarized in order to further his or her own aims, the core of Solomon's idea is accurately represented.

Paraphrasing

Sometimes a writer doesn't want to summarize a source because condensing its ideas risks losing part of its importance. In such a case, the writer has to choose whether to paraphrase or quote directly from the source. **Paraphrasing** means translating the author's words and sentence structure into your own for the purpose of making the ideas clear for your audience. A paraphrase may be the same length or even longer than the part of a text being paraphrased, so the purpose of paraphrase is not really to condense a passage, as is the case for summary.

Often, writers prefer to paraphrase sources rather than to quote from them, especially if the exact language from the source isn't important, but the ideas are. Depending on your audience, you might want to rephrase highly technical language from a scientific source, for example, and put it in your own words. Or you might want to emphasize a point the author makes in a way that isn't as clear in the original language. Many social scientists and most scientists routinely paraphrase sources as part of the presentation of their own research because the results they're reporting from secondary sources are more important than the exact language used to explain the results. Quotations should be reserved for instances when the exact language of the original source is important to the point being made. Remember that paraphrasing requires you to restate the passage in your own words and in your own sentence structure. Even if you are putting the source's ideas in your own words, you must acknowledge where the information came from by providing an appropriate citation.

The following paragraph was taken from William Thierfelder's article "Twain's *Huckleberry Finn*," published in *The Explicator*, a journal of literary criticism.

> An often-noted biblical allusion in *Huckleberry Finn* is that comparing Huck to the prophet Moses. Like Moses, whom Huck learns about from the Widow Douglas, Huck sets out, an orphan on his raft, down the river. In the biblical story, it is Moses' mother who puts him in his little "raft," hoping he will be found. In the novel, Huck/Moses takes charge of his own travels. . . .

Inappropriate Paraphrase

> William Thierfelder suggests that Huckleberry is often compared to the prophet Moses. Huck, an orphan like Moses, travels down a river on a raft (194).

Although some of the language has been changed and the paraphrase includes documentation, this paraphrase of the first two sentences of Thierfelder's passage is inappropriate because it relies on the language of the original text and employs the author's sentence structure. An appropriate paraphrase that uses new language and sentence structure might look like this:

> William Thierfelder notes that numerous readers have linked the character of Huckleberry Finn and the biblical figure of Moses. They are both orphans who take a water journey, Thierfelder argues. However, Moses's journey begins because of the actions of his mother, while Huck's journey is undertaken by himself (194).

Quoting

Depending on your rhetorical context, you may find that **quoting** the exact words of a source as part of your argument is the most effective strategy. The use of quotations is much more common in some academic fields than in others. Writers in the humanities, for example, often quote texts directly because the precise language of the original is important to the argument. You'll find, for instance, that literary scholars often quote a short story or poem (a primary source) for evidence. You may also find that a secondary source contains powerful or interesting language that would lose its impact if you paraphrased it. In such circumstances, it is entirely appropriate to quote the text. Keep in mind that your reader should always be able to understand why the quotation is important to your argument. We recommend three methods for integrating quotations into your writing. (The examples below follow American Psychological Association style conventions; see "Understanding Documentation Systems" on pages 76–77 and the Appendix for more information about documentation styles.)

1. **Attributive Tags**   Introduce the quotation with a tag (with words like *notes*, *argues*, *suggests*, *posits*, *maintains*, etc.) that attributes the language and ideas to its author. Notice that different tags suggest different relationships between the author and the idea being cited. For example:

   De Niet, Tiemens, Lendemeijer, Lendemei, and Hutschemaekers (2009) argued, "Music-assisted relaxation is an effective aid for improving sleep quality in patients with various conditions" (p. 1362).

2. **Further Grammatical Integration**   You may also fully integrate a quotation into the grammar of your own sentences. For example:

   Their review of the research revealed "scientific support for the effectiveness of the systematic use of music-assisted relaxation to promote sleep quality" in patients (De Niet et al., 2009, p. 1362).

3. **Introduce with Full Sentence + Punctuation**   You can also introduce a quotation with a full sentence and create a transitional link to the quotation with punctuation, like the colon. For example:

   The study reached a final conclusion about music-assisted relaxation: "It is a safe and cheap intervention which may be used to treat sleep problems in various populations" (De Niet et al., 2009, p. 1362).

INSIDE WORK   **Summarizing, Paraphrasing, and Quoting from Sources**

Choose a source that you have found on a topic of interest to you, and find a short passage (only one or two sentences) that provides information that might be useful in your own research. Then complete the following steps and write down your responses.

1. Summarize the passage. It might help to look at the larger context in which the passage appears.

2. Paraphrase the passage, using your own words and sentence structure.

3. Quote the passage, using the following three ways to integrate the passage into your own text:
   a. attributive tags
   b. grammatical integration
   c. full sentence + punctuation

For your own research, which approach (summarizing, paraphrasing, quoting) do you think would be most useful? Consider your writing context and how you would use the source. ▶

AVOIDING PLAGIARISM

Any language and ideas used in your own writing that belong to others must be fully acknowledged and carefully documented, including in-text citations and full bibliographic documentation. Failure to include either of these when source materials are employed could lead to a charge of **plagiarism**, perhaps the most serious of academic integrity offenses. The procedures for documenting cited sources vary from one rhetorical and disciplinary context to another, so always clarify the expectations for documentation with your instructor when responding to an assigned writing task. Regardless, you should always acknowledge your sources when you summarize, paraphrase, or quote, and be sure to include the full information for your sources in the bibliography of your project.

Insider's View
On accidental plagiarism
KAREN KEATON JACKSON, WRITING STUDIES

"Many students come in who are already familiar with using direct quotations. But when it comes to paraphrasing and summarizing, that's when I see a lot of accidental plagiarism. So it's really important for students to understand that if you don't do the research yourself, or if you weren't there in the field or doing the survey, then it's not your own idea and you have to give credit."

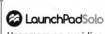

LaunchPadSolo
Hear more on avoiding plagiarism.

INSIDE WORK **Understanding Plagiarism**

Most schools, colleges, and universities have established definitions of plagiarism and penalties or sanctions that may be imposed on students found guilty of plagiarism. You should become familiar with the definitions of plagiarism used by your institution as well as by your individual instructors.

• Locate a resource on campus (e.g., a student handbook or the website of your institution's Office of Student Conduct) that provides a definition of plagiarism from the perspective of your institution. You may discover that in addition to defining plagiarism, your institution provides avenues of support to foster academic integrity and/or presents explanations of the consequences or penalties for violating rules of academic integrity.

- Locate a resource from one of your classes (e.g., a course website, a course syllabus) that provides a definition of plagiarism from the perspective of one of your instructors.

- Consider what is similar about the two definitions. Consider the differences between them. What do these similarities and differences reveal about your instructor's expectations and those of the larger academic community in which you participate? ❱

UNDERSTANDING DOCUMENTATION SYSTEMS

Documentation systems are often discipline-specific, and their conventions reflect the needs and values of researchers and readers in those particular disciplines. For these reasons, you should carefully analyze any writing situation to determine which documentation style to follow. You'll find examples of specific documentation systems in the disciplinary chapters in Part Two. Here are some of the most common ones:

1. **Modern Language Association (MLA)**   MLA documentation procedures are generally followed by researchers in the humanities. One of the most important elements of the in-text citation requirements for the MLA documentation system is the inclusion of page numbers in a parenthetical reference. Though page numbers are used in other documentation systems for some in-text citations (as in the APA system when quoting a passage directly), page numbers in MLA are especially important because they serve as a means for readers to assess your use of sources, both primary and secondary, and are used whether you are quoting, paraphrasing, or summarizing a passage. Page numbers enable readers to quickly identify cited passages and evaluate the evidence: readers may verify that you've accurately represented a source's intent when citing the author's words, or that you've fully examined all the elements at play in your analysis of a photograph or poem. Of course, this kind of examination is important in all disciplines, but it is especially the case in the fields of the humanities, where evidence typically takes the form of words and images. Unlike some other documentation systems, the MLA system does not require dates for in-text citations, because scholars in this field often find that past discoveries or arguments are just as useful today as when they were first observed or published. Interpretations don't really expire; their usefulness remains valid across exceptionally long periods of time. Learn more about the style guides published by the Modern Language Association, including the *MLA Handbook for Writers of Research Papers* and the *MLA Style Manual and Guide to Scholarly Publishing*, along with more information about the MLA itself, at www.mla.org.

2. American Psychological Association (APA)   APA documentation procedures are generally followed by researchers in many areas of the social sciences and related fields. Although you will encounter page numbers in the in-text citations for direct quotations in APA documents, you're much less likely to find direct quotations overall. Generally, researchers in the social sciences are less interested in the specific language or words used to report research findings than they are in the results or conclusions. Therefore, social science researchers are more likely to paraphrase information than to quote information. Additionally, in-text documentation in the APA system requires the date of publication for research (see the examples on p. 74, and consult the Appendix for more information). This is a striking distinction from the MLA system. Social science research that was conducted fifty years ago may not be as useful as research conducted two years ago, so it's important to cite the date of the source in the text of the argument. Imagine how different the results would be for a study of the effects of violence in video games on youth twenty years ago versus a study conducted last year. Findings from twenty years ago probably have very little bearing on the contemporary social context and would not reflect the same video game content as today's games. As a result, the APA system requires including the date of research publication as part of the in-text citation. The date enables readers to quickly evaluate the currency, and therefore the appropriateness, of the research being referenced. Learn more about the *Publication Manual of the American Psychological Association* and the APA itself at its website: www.apa.org.

3. The Council of Science Editors (CSE)   As the name suggests, the CSE documentation system is most prevalent among disciplines of the natural sciences, although many of the applied fields of the sciences, like engineering and medicine, rely on their own documentation systems. As in the other systems described here, CSE requires writers to document all materials derived from sources. Unlike MLA or APA, however, CSE allows multiple methods for in-text citations, corresponding to alternative forms of the reference page that appears at the end of research reports. For more detailed information on CSE documentation, consult the latest edition of *Scientific Style and Format: The CSE Manual for Authors, Editors, and Publishers.* You can learn more about the Council of Science Editors at its website: www.councilscienceeditors.org.

WRITING PROJECT   **Writing an Annotated Bibliography**

The annotated bibliography is a common genre in several academic disciplines because it provides a way to compile and take notes on—that is, annotate— resources that are potentially useful in a research project. *Annotated bibliographies* are essentially lists of citations, formatted in a consistent documentation style, that include concise summaries of source material. Some annotated bibliographies include additional commentary about the sources—perhaps evaluations of their usefulness for the research project or comments about how the sources complement one another within the bibliography (perhaps by providing multiple perspectives). Annotated bibliographies are usually organized alphabetically, but longer bibliographies can be organized topically or in sections with subheadings. Each source entry gives the citation first and then a paragraph or two of summary, as in this example using MLA style:

> Carter, Michael. "Ways of Knowing, Doing, and Writing in the
> Disciplines." *College Composition and Communication* 58.3 (2007):
> 385–418. Print.
>
> In this article, Carter outlines a process for helping faculty across
> different academic disciplines to understand the conventions of writing
> in their disciplines by encouraging them to think of disciplines as "ways
> of doing." He provides examples from his own interactions with faculty
> members in several disciplines, and he draws on data collected from
> these interactions to describe four "metagenres" that reflect ways
> of doing that are shared across multiple disciplines: problem-solving,
> empirical inquiry, research from sources, and performance. Finally, he
> concludes that the metagenres revealed by examining shared ways of
> doing can help to identify "metadisciplines."

For this assignment, you should write an annotated bibliography that seeks to find sources that will help you respond to a specific research question. Your purpose in writing the annotated bibliography is threefold: (1) to organize and keep track of the sources you've found on your own topic, (2) to better understand the relationships among different sources that address your topic, and (3) to demonstrate knowledge of the existing research about it.

To meet this purpose, choose sources that will help answer your research question, and think about a specific audience who might be interested in the research you're presenting. Your annotated bibliography should include the following elements.

- An introduction that clearly states your research question and describes the scope of your annotated bibliography.

- As many as eight to twelve sources (depending on the scope of the sources and the number of perspectives you want to represent), organized alphabetically. If you choose a different organization (e.g., topical), explain how you have organized your annotated bibliography in the introduction.

- An annotation for each source that includes:
  - A summary of the source that gives a concise description of the main findings, focused on what is most important for responding to your research question
  - Relevant information about the authors or sponsors of the source to indicate credibility, bias, perspective, and the like

- An indication of what this source brings to your annotated bibliography that is unique and/or how it connects to the other sources
- A citation (see the Appendix) in a consistent documentation style

WRITING PROJECT ## Developing a Supported Argument on a Controversial Issue

For this writing assignment, you will apply your knowledge from Chapter 3 about developing an argument and from this chapter on finding and documenting appropriate sources. The sources you find will be evidence for the argument you develop. We ask you to make a claim about a controversial issue that is of importance to you and support that claim with evidence to persuade a particular audience of your position. As you write, you might follow the steps below to develop your argument.

- Begin by identifying an issue that you care about and likely have some experience with. We all write best about things that matter to us. For many students, choosing an issue that is very specific to their experience or local context makes a narrower, more manageable topic to write about. For example, examining recycling options for students on your college campus would be more manageable than tackling the issue of global waste and recycling.

- Once you have identified an issue, start reading about it to discover what people are saying and what positions they are taking. Use the suggestions in this chapter to find scholarly sources about your issue so that you can "listen in on" the conversations already taking place about your issue. You might find that you want to narrow your topic further based on what you find.

- As you read, begin tracking the sources you find. These sources can serve as evidence later for multiple perspectives on the issue; they will be useful both in supporting your claim and in understanding counterarguments.

- Identify a clear claim you would like to support, an audience you would like to persuade, and a purpose for writing to that audience. Whom should you talk to about your issue, and what can they do about it?

As you work to develop your argument, consider the various elements of an argument you read about in Chapter 3.

- Identify a clear central claim, and determine if it should be a simple or complex thesis statement.

- Develop clear reasons for that claim, drawn from your knowledge of the issue and the sources you have found.

- Choose evidence from your sources to support each reason that will be persuasive to your audience, and consider the potential appeals of ethos, logos, and pathos.

- Identify any assumptions that need to be explained to or supported for your audience.

- Develop responses to any counterarguments you should include in your argument.

Insider Example
Student Argument on a Controversial Issue

The following sample student argument, produced in a first-year writing class, illustrates many of the principles discussed in Chapters 3 and 4. As you read, identify the thesis, reasons, and sources used as support for the argument. Notice also that the student, Ashlyn Sims, followed MLA style conventions throughout her paper.

Ashlyn Sims

ENG 100

November 15, 201-

Project II

Condom Distribution in High School

A day rarely goes by when a teenager does not think about sex. It races back and forth in the teenage mind, sneaking its way into conversations all the time. We live in a society where sex is quickly becoming more and more common at younger ages; however, it is still considered a rather taboo topic, generating more discomfort from one generation to the next when you consider the values and beliefs of varying generations. Many teens learn things about sex through their peers because discussions of sex can be less awkward among friends, and thus a chain of risky, uninformed sex patterns can been created. Most teens will avoid talking to their parents about sex at all costs. Typically, this is because parents do not establish an open line of communication, or they make it clear that consequences will be enacted if their kids are having sex. This only keeps the cycle going, spreading sexually transmitted diseases around campuses and causing hundreds of thousands of unwanted pregnancies. So who is left to pick up the slack when parents become unapproachable to teens? Schools need to step in for the vast number of parents who do not know how to effectively educate their teens. Accessible contraceptives and sex education are necessary in schools because they can prevent sexually transmitted diseases and unwanted pregnancies while recognizing the reality that teens will inevitably have sex and steps need to be taken to ensure it is safe sex.

Sexually transmitted diseases are spreading quickly throughout high schools because teenagers do not know how to engage in safe sex practices by using condoms. Studies show that approximately one in four sexually active teens will contract an STD ("U.S. Teen Sexual Activity"). Schools need to provide condoms to students in order to slow the spread of STDs and keep their schools safer for sexually active teens. The purpose of schools is

Can you begin to identify a specific audience to whom the author is writing?

Compare the author's claim with the principles for writing a claim discussed on pages 39–41 of Chapter 3.

Why do you think the author uses this statistical data to support this reason? Where did this statistic come from? Think about whom she is writing to and what that audience might find persuasive.

to educate students and give them every tool necessary in order to succeed in the world. Sex education should be no exception. By giving students information about using some form of birth control, they can prevent the negative effects of having an STD, such as low self-esteem and self-worth, and send the strongest possible students out into the world to prosper. In more extreme cases, students can contract HIV, and it becomes a matter of life and death. Approximately half of the new cases of HIV every year occur in people under the age of twenty-five ("U.S. Teen Sexual Activity"). Although contracting HIV is not an end result for all sexually active teens, it is still a major risk factor, and the spread can be slowed with the help of condoms.

As you see places where the student has cited information from sources, think about whether she has paraphrased, summarized, or quoted. Why do you think she makes the choices she does?

Compared to older adults, adolescents are at a higher risk for acquiring STDs for a number of reasons, including limited access to contraceptives and regular health care ("U.S. Teen Sexual Activity"). When parents won't help their children practice safe sex, it becomes the schools' job to protect students and educate them accordingly. Adolescents face many obstacles to obtaining and using condoms given outside of school. Some of these obstacles include confidentiality, cost, access, transportation, embarrassment, objection by a partner, and the perception that the risks of pregnancy and infection are low (Dodd). School should be a place where students go to obtain condoms, which gives students the means to have safe sex. Because STDs are spreading at an alarming rate, schools should do their best to prevent them by distributing condoms.

Here the student reiterates the central point of the paragraph.

Pregnancies in teenagers are almost always unplanned, and they are usually the consequences of having sex without birth control. Schools need to supply students with contraceptives because a teenage pregnancy is the number one reason girls drop out of high school, and it sets them up for a life of hardships. Girls who get pregnant at an early age drop out 70% of the time (Mangal). The teenagers may not have known the importance of using contraceptives and practicing safe sex because no one ever talked to them about it. It should be the responsibility of our academic institutions to safeguard these students from pregnancies by educating them when nobody else has done so. Schools have the ability to provide contraceptives and sex education in order to prevent pregnancies and ensure that more girls will graduate and have better odds of getting a higher-paying job. The cost of a condom by the government is nothing compared to the cost it takes to raise the child of a mother who did not graduate from high school and needs welfare in order to survive. It would be absurd to spend thousands of dollars on a child when a condom costs only a few dollars.

The student offers a reason to support the distribution of condoms in schools.

The student is embedding reasons together here and developing a logical chain of reasons to support her argument.

The student's chain of reasons continues here.

Additionally, children of teen mothers are 22% more likely to have children of their own before the age of twenty (Maynard). The early childbearing could then become a cycle.

The teen years should be focused on learning everything necessary in order to succeed in life. Students need to complete their education and focus solely on making good grades and learning the skills necessary to get into college, and schools should provide anything students need in order to fulfill their greatest potential. Providing condoms is the more effective way to ensure that students can make smart decisions and focus on school, rather than raising a child.

The author makes a controversial claim here. How does she support it with her sources?

While many schools try to fight the growing numbers of STDs and pregnancies with abstinence-only classes, they are failing to face the reality that the classes do not prevent students from engaging in sex. By providing condoms for students, schools can acknowledge that students will have sex. Many schools ignore the problem and assume that if students need condoms, they can get them themselves. The reality is that many high school students cannot drive because they are under the age of sixteen or do not have a car. Others cannot afford condoms or choose to take the risk in order to avoid spending money. The difficulty in getting a condom behind parents' backs, combined with the preconceived notion that it is unlikely that one will get pregnant or an STD, creates a risky pattern of unsafe behaviors. In 1997, a study followed two thousand middle-school and elementary-aged students into high school. The study concluded that abstinence-only sex education does not keep teenagers from having sex. Neither does it increase or decrease the likelihood that if they do have sex, they will use a condom (Stepp). Changes need to be made to the programs taught in schools to best persuade students to practice safe sex. To be most effective, schools need to meet students halfway: schools will acknowledge the reality of sex among teens but will also teach them safe sex. A school that acknowledges that teens will have sex and provides condoms shows that it cares about the success and safety of its students.

The author acknowledges a potential counterargument here. How does she use her sources to refute that counterargument?

Many parents would argue that by providing access to condoms, a school is promoting the sexual behaviors of teens. Then this leads to the fear that by having more sexually active teens, the STD and pregnancy rate will increase and only produce more affected teens who would otherwise not be affected. However, at least one study has shown that a teen who is not sexually active is no more inclined to get a condom and become sexually active just because of the easy access (Kirby and Brown). Students who need condoms will be able to get them, and those who do not will know that they are available but will not have any reason to use them.

The author identifies another possible counterargument. What evidence is provided to refute the counterargument?

People might also argue that it is not a school's place to make decisions for the parents about whether students should have access to condoms. However, the reality is that teens will have sex, and although it is not the school's place to make these decisions, teens who have no other way to gain access will be able to protect themselves. If no more students are influenced to have sex, then the distribution of condoms is not creating any risk; it is only offering protection to the one in four teens who will contract an STD and the thousands of girls who will get pregnant. It is only giving students access to protect themselves. By providing condoms, a school does not encourage sexual activity among young adults, but rather encourages safe sex and provides options for teens who would otherwise have no options and would engage in high-risk activities anyway.

Overall, providing condoms does not encourage risky behavior; it gives high-risk students options when they cannot afford or obtain condoms. The access to condoms helps prevent sexually transmitted diseases and pregnancies. A school that does not acknowledge the high risk of teens having sex is only hurting its students. Schools need to provide condoms so that students have greater chances of fulfilling their full potential in life and do not have to work against the odds when faced with pregnancy. In order to lower the rates of STDs and pregnancies, all schools should provide condoms in the interest of the safety of sexually active students.

Works Cited

Dodd, Kerri J. "School Condom Availability." *Advocates for Youth*. 1998. Web. 20 Sept. 2015. <http://www.advocatesforyouth.org/publications /449?task=view>.

Kirby, Douglas B., and Nancy L. Brown. "Condom Availability Programs in U.S. Schools." *Family Planning Perspectives* 28.5 (1996): 196–202. JSTOR. Web. 21 Sept. 2015. <http://www.jstor.org/stable/2135838>.

Mangal, Linda. "Teen Pregnancy, Discrimination, and the Dropout Rate." *American Civil Liberties Union of Washington*. ACLU, 25 Oct. 2010. Web. 21 Sept. 2015. <http://www.aclu-wa.org/blog/teen-pregnancy -discrimination-and-dropout-rate>.

Notice what kinds of sources the author has cited. If she were to conduct additional research to support her argument, what do you think might strengthen it?

Maynard, Rebecca A. "Kids Having Kids." *The Urban Institute | Research of Record*. Web. 21 Sept. 2015. <http://www.urban.org/pubs/khk/summary.html>.

Stepp, Laura Sessions. "Study Casts Doubt on Abstinence-Only Programs." *Washington Post*. 14 Apr. 2007. Web. 26 Sept. 2015. <http://www.washingtonpost.com/wp-dyn/content/article/2007/04/13/AR2007041301003.html>.

"U.S. Teen Sexual Activity." *Kaiser Family Foundation*. Jan. 2005. Web. 21 Sept. 2015. <http://www.kff.org/youthhivstds/upload/U-S-Teen-Sexual-Activity-Fact-Sheet.pdf>.

Discussion Questions

1. Whom do you think Ashlyn Sims is targeting as her audience in this assignment? Why do you think that is her audience?

2. What is Ashlyn's thesis, and what does she provide as the reasons and evidence for her claim?

3. What assumptions connect her thesis to her reasons? Additionally, what assumptions would her audience have to accept in order to find her evidence persuasive? Really dig into this question, because this area is often where arguments fall apart.

4. What counterarguments does Ashlyn address in her essay? Why do you think she addresses these particular counterarguments? Can you think of others that she might have addressed?

5. What kinds of sources does she use in her essay? How does she integrate them into her argument, and why do you think she has made those choices?

6. What would make this essay more persuasive and effective?

Academic Research

- **Research typically begins with a research question, which establishes the purpose and scope of a project.** As you develop research questions, keep in mind the following evaluative criteria: personal investment, debatable subject, researchable issue, feasibility, and contribution.

- **A researcher who has established a clear focus for her research, or who has generated a claim, must decide on the kinds of sources needed to support the research focus:** primary, secondary, or both.

- While both scholarly and popular sources may be appropriate sources of evidence in differing contexts, be sure to understand what distinguishes these types of sources so that you can choose evidence types purposefully.

- **Primary sources are the results of data that researchers might collect on their own.** These results could include data from surveys, interviews, or questionnaires. **Secondary sources include research collected by and/or commented on by others.** These might include information taken from newspaper articles, magazines, scholarly journal articles, and scholarly books, to name a few.

- **Keep in mind that as you do research, you will likely have cause to refine your search terms.** This process involves carefully selecting or narrowing the terms you use to locate information via search engines or databases.

- **Be aware of the challenges of conducting basic searches for sources via Internet search engines** like Google. While Google Scholar may be a better means of searching for sources in the academic context, researchers often rely on more specialized research databases.

- **Peer-reviewed academic journals are an excellent source of information for academic arguments.** The publication process for journal articles is typically much shorter than for books, so using journal articles allows you access to the most current research.

- **Be aware of the strategies you can use to integrate the ideas of others into your own writing:** summarizing, paraphrasing, and/or quoting.

- **When you integrate the words or ideas of others, take care to ensure that you are documenting their words and ideas carefully to avoid instances of plagiarism,** and make sure you understand what constitutes plagiarism at your institution and/or in your individual classes. Follow appropriate rules for documenting your sources and constructing a bibliography. In academic contexts, this often means using MLA, APA, or CSE documentation systems.

Inside Academic Writing

PART TWO

Inside Academic Writing

Reading and Writing in Academic Disciplines

The four chapters that follow this one introduce four broad disciplinary areas in higher education: humanities, social sciences, natural sciences, and applied fields. While some differences distinguish each of these areas, certain similarities show shared values that provide ways to analyze and understand the conventions of writing and research in those areas.

To help you navigate these chapters, we have organized Chapters 6 through 8 around the same key concerns:

- **Research in the Discipline**   Every academic discipline has established conventions of research. One thing that unites them is the importance of **observation**. Whether you're a humanities scholar observing texts, or a social scientist observing human behavior, or a scientist observing the natural world, careful methods of observation are central to developing research questions and writing projects in each disciplinary area. Similarly, all disciplines rely on the concepts of **primary research** and **secondary research**. (If you gather data of your own, you're doing primary research. If you gather data by studying the research of others, you're doing secondary research.) Academic writers in a variety of disciplines engage in both primary and secondary research and find that they inform each other. For example, a social scientist studying human behavior might conduct secondary research first to learn what others have done and to develop her research questions. Then she might conduct primary research to test a hypothesis and report results.

ANDREA TSURUMI

Similarly, a humanities scholar studying historical documents might conduct secondary research to build a preliminary research question and to develop a review of literature before conducting primary research by analyzing a historical document to develop a thesis about his interpretation of that document.

- **Conventions of Writing in the Discipline**   Each academic discipline has expectations about academic writing in its field. The chapters that follow this one all include sections that describe and help you analyze the *conventions* of writing in the disciplines, using the principles of rhetoric (the strategies of communication and persuasion) introduced in this chapter.

- **Genres in the Discipline**   Each chapter also provides examples of *genres*, or common types of academic writing, that often cross disciplines. These *Insider Examples* of writing, not only by professionals in the disciplines but also by students entering the discipline and composing in particular genres, are annotated to reveal key features that prompt your own analysis of them.

Insider's View
Writing should be different in various situations
KAREN KEATON JACKSON, WRITING STUDIES

"I think students should consider that writing has to be and should be different in various situations. Students need to go through a kind of meta-process of thinking about their own writing, one that allows them to see that the skills they learn in first-year writing can transfer. When students go into their history class or psychology class, for instance, the expectations may be different, but they'll see how they can transfer what they've learned in first-year writing to that situation."

LaunchPadSolo

Learn more about rhetorical situations.

Chapter 9 then explores the kinds of work and genres produced in a number of applied fields, including nursing, education, business, and law.

Additionally, the chapters share other common features to help you broaden your understanding of each disciplinary area: *Insider's View* excerpts of scholars discussing disciplinary writing; *Inside Work* activities that prompt you to reflect on what you've learned; *Writing Projects* that help you develop your own academic compositions; and *Tip Sheets* that summarize key information.

Throughout these chapters, we ask you to analyze and practice writing in various academic disciplines. Keep in mind, though, that we *do not* expect you to master the writing of these communities by taking just one class or by reading one book. Instead, we introduce you to the concepts associated with **disciplinary discourse**, or the writing and speaking that is specific to different disciplines. Using these concepts, you can analyze future writing situations and make choices appropriate to the rhetorical contexts. It's worth noting that such rhetorical awareness may help you enter other **discourse communities**, or groups that share common values and similar communication practices, outside of your college classes as well, socially and professionally.

Disciplinary conventions and styles are not just patterns to follow; rather, they represent shared values. In other words, there's a reason why academic texts are communicated in the way that they are: scholars in the same discipline might have similar ways of thinking about an issue, and they follow common ways of researching and investigating that represent their shared values and perspectives. The information we offer you on different academic disciplines in this book is not necessarily something to memorize, but rather something to analyze through the frame of *rhetorical context*. Ultimately, we want you to be able to look at an academic text and determine what the rhetorical context is and what conventions influence that text. As you write for different courses throughout your college career, this ability will help you determine and follow the expectations of writing for the different academic contexts you encounter. It will also help you read the assignments in your other classes because you'll understand some of the reasons that texts are written in the way that they are.

Analyzing Genres and Conventions of Academic Writing

As you know, different writing situations call for different types of writing. Different types of writing—from short items such as tweets, bumper stickers, and recipes to longer and more complex compositions such as Ph.D. dissertations, annual reports, and novels—are called *genres*. Scholars write in many different genres depending on their disciplinary areas, the kinds of work they do, and the situation in which they're writing. You have probably written in several different academic genres in your education already. You might have written a literary analysis in an English class, a lab report in a science class, a bibliography for a research paper, and maybe a personal narrative. Each of these genres has a common set of expectations that you must be familiar with in order to communicate effectively with your intended audience. In this text, you'll find information about writing in many of these genres—such as literary/artistic interpretations, rhetorical analyses, annotated bibliographies, reviews of literature, lab reports, and memos—with the ultimate goal of learning to analyze the rhetorical context so that you can determine the expected conventions of a genre in any writing situation.

Genres are not always bound by discipline, however. You'll find that the conventions of some genres are similar from one disciplinary area to another. As you read Chapters 6 through 9 on humanities, the social sciences, the natural sciences, and applied fields, pay attention to which genres are repeated and how the conventions of those genres shift or remain constant from one disciplinary context to another.

You'll notice that similar writing situations within, and even sometimes across, disciplines call for a similar genre. In other words, academics might approach a piece of writing in the same (or a similar) way even though they come from different academic disciplines.

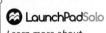
For example, you'll notice that scholars in all disciplines write reviews of literature for their research. Likewise, when reporting on the results of a research study, many academics follow the **IMRAD (Introduction, Methods, Results, and Discussion) format** or a variation of it to record and publish the results of their research, regardless of their discipline. There might be some subtle differences from one discipline or one situation to another, but common elements are evident. Literature reviews and IMRAD reports are two examples of common genres of academic writing.

As we begin to talk about specific disciplinary contexts, keep in mind these strategies to analyze the conventions of academic writing. When you read and write academic texts, you'll want to:

- understand the overall rhetorical context of the piece of writing: the author, the audience, the topic, and the purpose for writing;

- identify and understand the disciplinary area—humanities, the social sciences, the natural sciences, applied fields—and make connections to what you know about that discipline;

- consider which elements of structure, language, and reference (explained below) govern the writing situation;

- identify the genre, or category, that the writing fits into, and discover the common conventions and expectations for that genre within the rhetorical context;

- analyze the persuasive strategies used, if the author is developing an argument. (What claims are presented? How are they supported by reasons and evidence? What assumptions are in play?)

These analytical strategies will help you to approach any academic writing situation confidently and effectively.

Adapting to Different Rhetorical Contexts: An Academic Writer at Work

Even though some genres are more common in specific disciplines than others, many scholars write in more than one genre on a regular basis. Scholars write

Insider's View
Scientists must write all sorts of things
MIKE BROTHERTON, ASTRONOMY

"Aspiring scientists often don't appreciate the importance of communication skills. Science doesn't count until it's communicated to the rest of the scientific community, and eventually the public. Moreover, scientists must write all sorts of things to have a successful career, from journal articles to grant applications to press releases.

"Probably the most important thing to do well when writing as a scientist is simply to get everything right. Science is a methodology for developing reliable information about the world we live in, and getting things wrong is the surest way for scientists to lose their reputation; and for a scientist, reputation is the coin of the realm. While nearly everyone scientifically inclined finds getting things right to be an obvious and principal goal, it is also critically important to identify the audience of any particular piece of writing and address that audience in an effective way. The writing examples included in this text are all targeted for a different readership, and that represents a primary difference between them.

"Scientists write and are asked to write for all sorts of audiences. This isn't an easy task, but success in that adaptation can be the difference between a great career and failure, so it's important to treat it seriously. There isn't magic to this, and while brilliance can be challenging to achieve, competence can certainly be learned. It just takes some practice and thought."

for different rhetorical contexts all the time, and they adapt their writing to the audience, topic, and purpose of the occasion. We'd like to take an in-depth look at one scholar's writing to show you an example of how he shifts the conventions of his writing for different contexts—often academic, but sometimes more general. We've chosen to look at a scholar in a scientific field that is rarely discussed in English classes: astronomy. Mike Brotherton is an astronomer at the University of Wyoming, and we'll look at two types of writing that he does on a regular basis. Brotherton writes scholarly articles in his field to report on his research to an audience of other academics—his peers. He also sometimes writes press releases about his research, and these are intended to help journalists report news to the general public. Each piece of writing represents a different genre intended for a different audience, but together they show us the varying ways that Brotherton shares his work in the field of astronomy. Both of these rhetorical contexts call for an awareness of different conventions.

INSIDE WORK **Reflecting on a Discipline**

In his Insider's View, "Scientists must write all sorts of things," Mike Brotherton makes several generalizations about science, scientists, and scientific writing. Which of these comments, if any, surprised you, and which ones didn't? Explain why. ▶

Using Rhetorical Context to Analyze Writing for a Non-Academic Audience

First we'll take a look at a piece of writing that Mike Brotherton composed for a non-academic audience of journalists who might be interested in research he conducted. Brotherton wrote a press release to communicate the results of his research in a genre familiar to journalists. As you read the press release, which we've annotated, keep in mind the elements of rhetorical context that are useful in analyzing all kinds of writing:

- *author* (who is the writer, and what does he or she bring to the text?)
- *audience* (for whom is the text intended?)
- *topic* (what issue is the text addressing?)
- *purpose* (why did the author write the text?)

Specifically, consider the following questions:

- How might Brotherton's position as the *author* of the press release influence the way he wrote it? What might have been different if someone else had written the press release after talking to him about his research?
- Who is the *audience* for this piece? What choices do you think Brotherton made that were specific to his audience for the press release?
- How does the *topic* of the press release affect the choices the author made? Would you have made different choices to approach the topic for a general audience? What would they be?
- What is the *purpose* for writing the press release? How might that influence Brotherton's choices as a writer? Do you think he has met that purpose? Why or why not?

Excerpt from **Hubble Space Telescope Spies Galaxy/Black Hole Evolution in Action**

MIKE BROTHERTON

Identifies the **topic** of the research study and its relevant findings

Identifies members of the research team, who are all **authors** of the study upon which the press release is based

JUNE 2ND, 2008—A set of 29 Hubble Space Telescope (HST) images of an exotic type of active galaxy known as a "post-starburst quasar" show that interactions and mergers drive both galaxy evolution and the growth of super-massive black holes at their centers. Mike Brotherton, Associate Professor at the University of Wyoming, is presenting his team's findings today at the American Astronomical Society meeting in St. Louis, Missouri. Other team members include Sabrina Cales, Rajib Ganguly, and Zhaohui Shang of the University of Wyoming, Gabriella Canalizo of the University of California at Riverside, Aleks Diamond-Stanic of the University of Arizona, and Dan Vanden Berk of the Penn State University. The result is of special interest because the images provide support for a leading theory of the evolution of massive galaxies, but also show that the situation is more complicated than previously thought.

Over the last decade, astronomers have discovered that essentially every galaxy harbors a super-massive black hole at its center, ranging from 10,000 times the mass of the sun to upwards of 1,000,000,000 times solar, and that there exists a close relationship between the mass of the black hole and properties of its host. When the black holes are fueled and grow, the galaxy becomes active, with the most luminous manifestation being a quasar, which can outshine the galaxy and make it difficult to observe.

In order to explain the relationships between galaxies and their central black holes, theorists have proposed detailed models in which both grow together as the result of galaxy mergers. This hierarchical picture suggests that large galaxies are built up over time through the assembly of smaller galaxies with corresponding bursts of star formation, and that this process also fuels the growth of the black holes, which eventually ignite to shine as quasars. Supernova explosions and their dusty debris shroud the infant starburst until the activated quasar blows out the obscuration.

Brotherton and his team turned the sharp-eyed Hubble Space Telescope and its Advanced Camera for Surveys to observe a subset of these post-starburst quasars that had the strongest and most luminous stellar content. Looking at these systems 3.5 billion light-years away, Hubble, operating without the distortions of an atmosphere, can resolve sub-kiloparsec scales necessary to see nuclear structure and host galaxy morphology.

"The images started coming in, and we were blown away," said Brotherton. "We see not only merger remnants as in the prototype of the class, but also post-starburst quasars with interacting companion galaxies, double nuclei, starbursting rings, and all sorts of messy structures."

Astronomers have determined that our own Milky Way galaxy and the great spiral galaxy of Andromeda will collide three billion years from now. This event will create massive bursts of star formation and most likely fuel nuclear activity a few hundred million years later. Hubble has imaged post-starburst quasars three and a half billion light-years away, corresponding to three and a half billion years ago, and three and a half billion years from now our own galaxy is probably going to be one of these systems.

This work is supported by grants from NASA, through the Space Telescope Science Institute and the Long-Term Space Astrophysics program, and the National Science Foundation.

Fulfills the **purpose** of a press release by stating the importance of the research project. Appears in the first paragraph to make it prominent for the audience

Provides relevant background information about the topic for the **audience**

Provides a brief overview of the study's methods

Acknowledges funding support for the research project, giving credit to funding agencies that might also be **audiences** for the journalists' news articles

"It isn't always the case that scientists write their own press releases. Often, there are writers on staff at various institutions who specialize in writing press releases and who work with scientists. I've written press releases solo (e.g., the contribution included here) and in collaboration with staff journalists at the University of Texas, Lawrence Livermore National Laboratory, and the University of Wyoming. Press releases should be able to be run as news stories themselves and contain enough content to be adapted or cut to length. The audience for a press release is very general, and you can't assume that they have any background in your field. You have to tell them why your result is important, clearly and briefly, and little else.

"While I don't think my effort here is bad, it is far from perfect and suffers one flaw. Reporters picking up press releases want to know what single result they should focus upon. They want to keep things simple. I tried to include several points in the release, rather than focusing on a single result. Some reporters became distracted about the notion that the Milky Way and Andromeda would someday merge and might become a post-starburst galaxy, which was not a result of my research project. Even though it gave the work some relevance, in hindsight I should have omitted it to keep the focus on the results of my research."

INSIDE WORK Reflecting on Rhetorical Context

In his Insider's View, "The audience for a press release is very general," Mike Brotherton explains some of the specifics of writing a press release and what he sees as the strengths and weaknesses of his own press release. Review the press release with Brotherton's comments in mind, and explain whether you agree with his assessment of it. What advice might you give him for revising the press release? ❯

Using Structure, Language, and Reference to Analyze Academic Writing

While rhetorical context provides a useful framework for analyzing a variety of types of writing, the categories of **structure**, **language**, and **reference** **(SLR)*** offer more specific help in analyzing the conventions of academic writing at a deeper level. Although discourse conventions vary from discipline to discipline, once you understand how to analyze academic writing through these

*The SLR concept originated in the following essay: Patricia Linton, Robert Madigan, and Susan Johnson, "Introducing Students to Disciplinary Genres: The Role of the General Composition Course," *Language and Learning Across the Disciplines* 1, no. 2 (1994): 63–78.

categories, you can determine what conventions and choices are appropriate for nearly any academic writing situation.

- **Structure, or Format and Organization** Written texts are often organized according to specific disciplinary conventions. For example, scholars in the social sciences and natural sciences usually organize experimental study reports with an introduction first, followed by a description of their research methods, then their data/results, then the analysis of that data, and finally a discussion and conclusion (IMRAD format, discussed in more detail in Chapters 7 and 8 on the social sciences and natural sciences). By contrast, scholars in the humanities tend to write and value essays that are driven by a clear thesis (or main claim: what you are trying to prove) near the beginning of the essay that indicates the direction the argument will take. Scholars in the humanities also don't tend, as much, to use headings to divide a text.

- **Language, or Style and Word Choice** The language used in academic writing follows disciplinary conventions. Consider the use of the active and passive voices. You may recall that in the active voice the subject performs the action, while in the passive voice the subject is acted upon. (Active voice: *Inez performed the experiment*; passive voice: *The experiment was performed by Inez*.) Often, the passive voice is acceptable in specific situations in the natural sciences, but it is usually not favored in the humanities. A scholar in the sciences might write, *It was determined that the two variables have a negative correlation*, a sentence that obscures the subject doing the determining (generally, the researcher or research team). Such uses of the passive voice rarely occur in the humanities, where scholars prefer the active voice. Likewise, qualifiers (words such as *might, could, likely*) are often used in the natural and social sciences to indicate the interpretive power of the data collected and to help persuade an audience to accept the results because they are not generalizing inappropriately (*The positive correlation between the variables likely indicates a strong relationship between the motivation of a student and his or her achievement of learning objectives*). When qualifiers are used in the humanities, however, they often demonstrate uncertainty and weaken an argument (*Hamlet's soliloquies in acts 2 and 4 might provide an interesting comparison because they frame the turning point of the play in act 3*).

- **Reference, or Citation and Documentation** The conventions of how scholars refer to one another's work can also shift by discipline. You might already know, for example, that many scholars in the humanities use the documentation style of the Modern Language Association (MLA), while those in the social sciences generally use the style guide published by the American Psychological Association (APA). Conventions of how often scholars quote, paraphrase, and summarize one another's work can also vary.

LaunchPadSolo
Get astronomer Mike Brotherton's take on qualifying and hedging.

In the next example of Mike Brotherton's work, we'll look at the abstract and introduction to a scholarly journal article that he wrote with several co-authors. If we consider the *structure*, *language*, and *reference conventions* used in the piece, we can gain some insight into the way such writing is structured within the sciences—and specifically in the field of astronomy.

As you read the excerpt from Brotherton's co-authored article, notice the structure, language, and reference conventions. The article contains a lot of specific scientific language, and for the purpose of your analysis right now it's not important to understand the concepts as much as it is to recognize some of the elements that make this writing unique from other writing you may have encountered in English classes in the past. Consider the following questions:

- Even though the entire article is not included, what conclusions can you draw about its **structure**? What comes first in the article, and how is it organized in the beginning?

- How would you describe the **language** that Brotherton and his co-authors choose to use in the article? What does it tell you about the audience for the article?

- What **reference conventions** does the article follow? Does the documentation style used for the parenthetical references look familiar? How often are other scholars cited, and what is the context for citing their work? What purpose do those references serve in the article?

Excerpt from **A Spectacular Poststarburst Quasar**

M. S. BROTHERTON, WIL VAN BREUGEL, S. A. STANFORD, R. J. SMITH, B. J. BOYLE, LANCE MILLER, T. SHANKS, S. M. CROOM, AND ALEXEI V. FILIPPENKO

ABSTRACT

The **language** is highly specific and technical.

We report the discovery of a spectacular "poststarburst quasar" UN J10252–0040 ($B = 19$; $z = 0.634$). The optical spectrum is a chimera, displaying the broad Mg II $\lambda2800$ emission line and strong blue continuum characteristic of quasars, but is dominated in the red by a large Balmer jump and prominent high-order Balmer absorption lines indicative of a substantial young stellar population at similar redshift. Stellar synthesis population models show that the stellar component is consistent with a 400 Myr old instantaneous starburst with a mass of $\leq 10^{11}$ $M_\odot$. A deep, K_s-band image taken in $\sim 0''.5$ seeing shows a point source surrounded by asymmetric extended fuzz. Approximately 70% of the light is unresolved, the majority of which is expected to be emitted by the starburst. While starbursts and galaxy interactions have been previously associated with quasars, no quasar ever before has been seen with such an extremely luminous young stellar population.

1. INTRODUCTION

Headings indicate a particular kind of **structure**.

Is there a connection between starbursts and quasar activity? There is circumstantial evidence to suggest so. The quasar 3C 48 is surrounded by nebulosity that shows the high-order Balmer absorption lines characteristic of A-type stars (Boroson & Oke 1984; Stockton & Ridgeway 1991). PG 1700+518 shows a nearby starburst ring (Hines et al. 1999) with the spectrum of a 10^8 yr old starburst (Stockton, Canalizo, & Close 1998). Near-IR and CO mapping reveals a massive ($\sim 10^{10}\ M_\odot$) circumnuclear starburst ring in I Zw 1 (Schinnerer, Eckart, & Tacconi 1998). The binary quasar member FIRST J164311.3+315618B shows a starburst host galaxy spectrum (Brotherton et al. 1999).

In addition to these individual objects, *samples* of active galactic nuclei (AGNs) show evidence of starbursts. Images of quasars taken with the *Hubble Space Telescope* show "chains of emission nebulae" and "near-nuclear emission knots" (e.g., Bahcall et al. 1997). Seyfert 2 and radio galaxies have significant populations of $\sim$100 Myr old stars (e.g., Schmitt, Storchi-Bergmann, & Cid Fernandes 1999). Half of the ultraluminous infrared galaxies (ULIRGs) contain simultaneously an AGN and recent (10–100 Myr) starburst activity in a 1–2 kpc circumnuclear ring (Genzel et al. 1998).

The advent of *IRAS* provided evidence for an evolutionary link between starbursts and AGNs. The ULIRGs ($L_{IR} > 10^{12}\ L_\odot$) are strongly interacting merger systems with copious molecular gas [$(0.5-2) \times 10^{10}\ M_\odot$] and dust heated by both starburst and AGN power sources. The ULIRG space density is sufficient to form the quasar parent population. These facts led Sanders et al. (1988) to hypothesize that ULIRGs represent the initial dust-enshrouded stage of a quasar. Supporting this hypothesis is the similarity in the evolution of the quasar luminosity density and the star formation rate (e.g., Boyle & Terlevich 1998; Percival & Miller 1999). Another clue is that supermassive black holes appear ubiquitously in local massive galaxies, which may be out-of-fuel quasars (e.g., Magorrian et al. 1998). AGN activity may therefore reflect a fundamental stage of galaxy evolution.

Introduction **references** multiple prior studies by other scholars.

We report here the discovery of a poststarburst quasar. The extreme properties of this system may help shed light on the elusive AGN-starburst connection. We adopt $H_0 = 75$ km s^{-1} Mpc^{-1} and $q_0 = 0$.

INSIDE WORK **Reflecting on Disciplinary Writing**

In his Insider's View "Accuracy trumps strong writing" on page 100, Mike Brotherton provides some guidelines for analyzing his scientific article through the lenses of structure, language, and reference. Write down a few points he makes about each lens that will be helpful when you approach reading a scientific article on your own.

Accuracy trumps strong writing

MIKE BROTHERTON, ASTRONOMY

"The audience for a scientific journal should be experts in your field but also beginning graduate students. Articles should be specific, succinct, and correct. For better or worse, in scientific articles it is necessary to use a lot of qualifications, adverbs, and modifying phrases, to say exactly what you mean even though the result is not as strong or effective.

Accuracy trumps strong writing here, although there is plenty of room for good writing. Every piece of writing, fiction or non-fiction, should tell an interesting story. The format for a scientific article is rather standard.

"There is also an abstract that gives a summary of all the parts of the paper. In many instances, the entire paper is not read but skimmed, so being able to find things quickly and easily makes the paper more useful. Audiences for scientific papers are often measured only in the dozens, if that. While popular papers can be read and used by thousands, most papers have a small audience and contribute to advancement in some niche or other, which may or may not turn out to be important.

"Some people cite heavily, and some people don't cite as heavily. And, again, you need to keep in mind your audience and what's appropriate. In writing a telescope proposal, for instance, which is not quite the same as a scientific article but has the same conventions, some reviewers want you to cite a lot of things just to prove that you know the field. This is especially true for beginning students writing proposals."

- Reread the excerpt from "A Spectacular Poststarburst Quasar" (see pp. 98–99) and reflect on any new things you notice.

- Read the excerpt again, this time with an eye to rhetorical context (author, audience, topic, and purpose for writing). Try to generalize about the usefulness of the two approaches to your reading.

- Annotate a paper you've written for another class, noting the rhetorical and SLR elements as we have in our annotations on the press release and the scholarly article. What practices about your own writing do these approaches suggest? ❯

WRITING PROJECT **Writing a Rhetorical Analysis of an Academic Article**

For this project, you will analyze a full-length study in a discipline of your choice, published as an article in an academic journal. Your instructor may assign an article or may ask you to seek his or her approval for the article you choose to use for this project.

Using the convention categories of *structure*, *language*, and *reference*, describe the basic rhetorical features of the article you've chosen to study. In addition, try to explain why those conventions are the most appropriate for the writer in light of the goals of his or her article and for his or her intended academic audience.

The introduction to your paper should name the article you will analyze, describe the primary methods you will use to analyze it, and explain the goal of your analysis—to demonstrate and analyze features of discourse in an academic article. The body of your paper might be organized around the three convention categories—structure, language, and reference—or you might focus on one or two of the features that are of specific interest in your article. Of course, you can subdivide these categories to address specific elements of the larger categories. Under the conventions of the language category, for instance, you could address the use of qualifiers, the use of passive and active voice, and so on, providing examples from the article and commenting on their usefulness for the writer. In your conclusion, reflect on what you've found. Are there other issues still to be addressed? What other rhetorical strategies could be explored to analyze the work further? How effective are the strategies the author used, given the intended audience?

WRITING PROJECT **Writing a Comparative Rhetorical Analysis**

The goal of this writing project is to allow you to consider further the shifts in conventional expectations for writing across two disciplinary areas.

Use what you've learned about structure, language, and reference to compare and contrast the conventional expectations for writing in two different disciplines. To begin, you'll need two comparable studies: locate two articles about the same topic in academic journals representing different disciplines. For example, you might find two articles discussing the issue of increasing taxes on the wealthy to deal with the U.S. national debt. You might find one article written by an economist that addresses the impact of the national debt and projects the feasibility of different solutions, and another article written by a humanist discussing how the media has portrayed the issue.

Once you have your articles, begin by thinking about what kinds of questions the authors ask. Then examine both articles in terms of the structure, language, and reference conventions discussed in this chapter. Formulate a thesis that assesses the degree to which the rhetorical features in each category compare or contrast. Throughout your paper (which should be organized around the three areas of convention—structure, language, and reference), execute your comparisons and contrasts by illustrating your findings with examples from the texts. For example, if you find that one article (perhaps from the humanities) uses the active voice almost exclusively, then provide some examples. If the other article relies heavily on the passive voice, then provide examples of this use. End each section with a consideration of the implications of your findings: What does it say about the humanities that the writing is so characterized by active voice? Do not avoid discussing findings that might contradict your assumptions about writing in these two academic domains. Instead, study them closely and try to rationalize the authors' rhetorical decision-making.

Comparing Scholarly and Popular Articles

Choose a scholarly article and an article written for a more general audience on a common topic. You might reread the discussion of the differences between scholarly and popular articles in Chapter 4 as you're looking for articles to choose. Then use the framework for rhetorical context from Chapter 2 to conduct a rhetorical analysis of each article. In your comparison of the rhetorical contexts and decisions the authors have made, consider the questions below.

- How do the rhetorical contexts for writing compare?
- Which writing conventions are similar, and which ones are different?
- Why do you think the authors made the choices that they did in writing?

Finally, use the framework of structure, language, and reference to analyze the scholarly article. What conclusions can you draw about the conventions of the type of academic writing you're looking at by analyzing these three elements?

Translating Scholarly Writing for Different Rhetorical Contexts

At times, writing for an academic context, like Mike Brotherton's work, must be repurposed for presentation in another, more general context. Sometimes the writer does the translating, and sometimes other writers may help communicate the importance of a piece of scholarly writing to another audience.

Insider Example
Student Translation of a Scholarly Article

Jonathan Nastasi, a first-year writing student, translated a scholarly article about the possible habitability of another planet from the journal *Astronomy & Astrophysics* into a press release for a less specialized audience. He condensed the information into a two-page press release for a potential audience interested in publishing these research results in news venues. Also, he followed his writing instructor's advice to apply MLA style even though the article he summarized is scientific.

Release Date: 18 September 2014

Contact: W. von Bloh
bloh@pik-potsdam.de
Potsdam Institute for Climate Impact Research

Life May Be Possible on Other Planets

New data shows that a new planet found outside of our solar system may be habitable for life.

RALEIGH (SEPTEMBER 18, 2014)—A study from the Potsdam Institute for Climate Impact Research shows that a planet in another solar system is in the perfect position to harbor life. Additionally, the quantity of possibly habitable planets in our galaxy is much greater than expected.

An artist's rendition of Gliese 581g orbiting its star.

Gliese 581g is one of up to six planets found to be orbiting the low-mass star Gliese 581, hence its name. Gliese 581g and its other planetary siblings are so-called "Super Earths," rocky planets from one to ten times the size of our Earth. This entire system is about twenty light-years away from our Sun. W. Von Bloh, M. Cuntz, S. Franck, and C. Bounama from the Potsdam Institute for Climate Impact Research chose to research Gliese 581g because of its size and distance from its star, which make it a perfect candidate to support life.

A planet must be a precise distance away from a star in order to sustain life. This distance is referred to as the habitable zone. According to von Bloh et al., the habitable zones "are defined as regions around the central star where the physical conditions are favourable for liquid water to exist at the planet's surface for a period of time sufficient for biological evolution to occur." This "Goldilocks" zone can be affected by a number of variables, including the temperature of the star and the composition of the planet.

The actual distance of Gliese 581g from its star is known; the goal of this study was to find out if the planet is capable of supporting life at that distance. The researchers began by finding the habitable zone of the star Gliese 581—specifically, the zone that allowed for photosynthesis. Photosynthesis is the production of oxygen from organic life forms and is indicative of life. In order for the planet to harbor this kind of life, a habitable zone that allows for a specific concentration of CO_2 in the atmosphere as well as liquid water would have to be found.

The scientists used mathematical models based on Earth's known attributes and adjusted different variables to find out which scenarios yielded the best results. Some of these variables include surface temperature, mass of the planet, and geological activity. The scientists also considered settings where the surface of the planet was all-land, all-water, or a mix of both.

Considering all of these scenarios, von Bloh et al. determined that the habitable zone for Gliese 581g is between 0.125 and 0.155 astronomical units, where an astronomical unit is the distance between the Earth and the Sun. Other studies conclude that the *actual* orbital distance of Gliese 581g is 0.146 astronomical units. Because Gliese 581g is right in the middle of its determined habitable zone, the error and uncertainty in the variables that remain to be determined are negligible.

However, the ratio of land to ocean on the planet's surface is key in determining the "life span" of the habitable zone. The habitable zone can shift over time due to geological phenomena caused by a planet having more land than ocean. According to von Bloh et al., a planet with a land-to-ocean ratio similar to ours would remain in the habitable zone for about seven billion years, shorter than Gliese 581g's estimated age. In other words, if Gliese 581g has an Earth-like composition, it cannot sustain life. But if the ratio is low (more ocean than land), the planet will remain in its habitable zone for a greater period of time, thus allowing for a greater chance of life to develop.

The researchers conclude that Gliese 581g is a strong candidate for life so long as it is a "water world." According to the authors, water worlds are defined as "planets of non-vanishing continental area mostly covered by oceans."

The discovery of Gliese 581g being a strong candidate for sustaining life is especially important considering the vast quantity of planets just like it. According to NASA's *Kepler Discoveries* Web page, the Kepler telescope alone has found over 4,234 planet candidates in just five years. With the collaboration of other research, 120 planets have been deemed "habitable," according to *The Habitable Exoplanets Catalog*.

"Our results are another step toward identifying the possibility of life beyond the Solar System, especially concerning Super-Earth planets, which appear to be more abundant than previously surmised," say the authors. More and more scientists are agreeing with the idea that extraterrestrial life is probable, given the abundance of Earth-like planets found in our galaxy already. If this is true, humanity will be one step closer to finding its place in the universe.

"[W]e have to await future missions to identify the pertinent geodynamical features of Gl[iese] 581g . . . to gain insight into whether or not Gl[iese] 581g harbors life," write the researchers. The science community agrees: continued focus in researching the cosmos is necessary to confirm if we have neighbors.

The full journal article can be found at <http://www.aanda.org.prox.lib.ncsu .edu/articles/aa/full_html/2011/04/aa16534-11/aa16534-11.html>.

Astronomy & Astrophysics, published by EDP Sciences since 1963, covers important developments in the research of theoretical, observational, and instrumental astronomy and astrophysics. For more information, visit <http://www.aanda.org/>.

Works Cited

Annual Review of Astronomy and Astrophysics. Annual Reviews, 2014. Web. 17 Sept. 2014.

"Astronomy & Astrophysics (About)." *Astronomy & Astrophysics*, n.d. Web. 17 Sept. 2014.

Cook, Lynette. "Planets of the Gliese 581 System." 29 Sept. 2010. NASA. *NASA Features*. Web. 17 Sept. 2014.

The Habitable Exoplanets Catalog. Planetary Habitability Laboratory, 2 Sept. 2014. Web. 16 Sept. 2014.

Kepler Discoveries. NASA, 24 July 2014. Web. 16 Sept. 2014.

Kepler Launch. NASA, 2 Apr. 2014. Web. 16 Sept. 2014.

Von Bloh, W., M. Cuntz, S. Franck, and C. Bounama. "Habitability of the Goldilocks Planet Gliese 581g: Results from Geodynamic Models." *Astronomy & Astrophysics* 528.A133 (2011): n. pag. *Summon*. Web. 15 Sept. 2014.

Discussion Questions

1. Who was Jonathan Nastasi's audience as he wrote his press release? What cues in the writing tell you whom Jonathan views as his audience?

2. How well did he tailor his description of the research to that audience?

3. What is the purpose behind Jonathan's communication of the research findings?

4. What other genre might work for translating this research to a public audience? What would Jonathan need to do differently in that rhetorical situation?

Translating a Scholarly Article for a Public Audience

The goal of this project is to translate a scholarly article for a public audience. To do so, you will first analyze the scholarly article rhetorically and then shift the genre through which the information in your article is reported. You will produce two documents in response to this assignment:

- the translation of your scholarly article
- a written analysis of the choices you made as you wrote your translation

STEP ONE: IDENTIFYING YOUR NEW AUDIENCE AND GENRE
To get started, you'll need to identify a new audience and rhetorical situation for the information in your selected article. The goal here is to shift the audience from an academic one to a public one. You may, for instance, choose to report the findings of the article in a magazine targeted toward a general audience of people who are interested in science, or you may choose to write a newspaper article that announces the research findings. You might also choose to write a script for a news show that reports research findings to a general television audience. Notice that once you change audiences, then the form in which you report will need to shift as well. The genre you produce will be contingent on the audience you're targeting and the rhetorical situation: magazine article, newspaper article, news show script. There is an array of other possibilities for shifting your audience and genre as well.

STEP TWO: ANALYZING YOUR TARGET AUDIENCE AND GENRE EXPECTATIONS
Closely analyze an example or two of the kind of genre you're attempting to create, and consider how those genre examples fulfill the expectations of the target audience. Your project will be assessed according to its ability to reproduce those genre expectations, so you will need to explain, in detail, the rhetorical changes and other choices you had to make in the construction of your piece. Be sure that you're able to explain the rhetorical choices you make in writing your translation. Consider all four elements of rhetorical context: author, audience, topic, purpose.

STEP THREE: CONSTRUCTING THE GENRE
At this point, you're ready to begin constructing or translating the article into the new genre. The genre you're producing could take any number of forms. As such, the form, structure, and development of your ideas are contingent on the genre of public reporting you're attempting to construct. If you're constructing a magazine article, for example, then the article you produce should really look like one that would appear in a magazine. Try to mirror how the genre would appear in a real situation.

STEP FOUR: WRITING THE ANALYSIS
Once your translation is complete, compose a reflective analysis. As part of your analysis, consider the rhetorical choices you made as you constructed your translation. Offer a rationale for each of your decisions that connects the features of your translation to your larger rhetorical context. For example, if you had to translate the title of the scholarly article for a public audience, explain why your new title is the most appropriate one for your public audience.

- **You should not expect to master the writing of every academic discipline by reading one book,** even this one.

- **It's important to become familiar with key concepts of disciplinary writing in academic discourse communities:** *research* expectations; *conventions* (expectations) of writing; *genres* (types) of writing.

- **Genres are not always bound by discipline, although their conventions may vary somewhat from discipline to discipline.** For example, you can expect to write literature reviews in many different courses across the curriculum.

- **Analyzing academic writing is a multistep process.** (1) Understand the rhetorical context (author, audience, topic, purpose for writing); (2) identify the disciplinary area and what you know about it; (3) consider how expectations for features of *structure*, *language*, and *reference* govern the writing situation; (4) identify the genre of writing and the conventions that apply; (5) analyze the persuasive strategies if the writer is developing an argument.

- **Remember SLR.** The acronym for *structure*, *language*, and *reference* offers categories that can help you determine conventions and choices appropriate for most academic writing situations.

  – *Structure* concerns how texts are organized. *Example:* IMRAD—signifying Introduction, Methods, Results, and Discussion—is a common format in both the social and natural sciences.

  – *Language* encompasses conventions of style or word choice. *Example:* Active voice is typically favored in the humanities, and passive voice is more characteristic of writing in the social and natural sciences.

  – *Reference* concerns the ways writers engage source material, including their use of conventions of citation and documentation. *Example:* Many humanities scholars use MLA style; many social science scholars use APA style.

- **Academic research is important beyond the academy.** Therefore, academic writing that conveys such research often must be repurposed—translated—for different venues and audiences.

CHAPTER 6

Reading and Writing in the Humanities

Introduction to the Humanities

An interest in exploring the meaning, or interpretation, of something and how it reflects on the human experience is one of the defining characteristics of the **humanities** that sets it apart from the social sciences, the natural sciences, and applied fields. Look at the tree at the bottom of this page, and see if you recognize any fields within the humanities with which you're already familiar.

Scholars in the humanities are interested in, and closely observe, human thought, creativity, and experience. The American Council of Learned Societies explains that humanistic scholars "help us appreciate and understand what distinguishes us as human beings as well as what unites us." Scholars in the humanities ask questions such as these:

- What can we learn about human experience from examining the ways we think and express ourselves?

- How do we make sense of the world through various forms of expression?
- How do we interpret what we experience, or make meaning for ourselves and for others?

Professor John McCurdy teaches history at Eastern Michigan University. Dr. McCurdy's research focuses on the history of early America, and he teaches courses on the colonial era and the American Revolution. In his Insider's View comments, he offers thoughts on

ANDREA TSURUMI

what humanists do and value, as well as the kind of research questions they ask. These comments come from an interview with him about his writing and about research in the humanities in general.

TEXTS AND MEANING

To understand the human condition and respond to these questions, humanists often turn to artifacts of human culture that they observe and interpret. These might be films, historical documents, comic strips, paintings, poems, religious artifacts, video games, essays, photographs, and songs. They might even include graffiti on the side of a building, a Facebook status update, or a YouTube video.

In addition to tangible artifacts, humanist writers might turn their attention to events, experiences, rituals, or other elements of human culture to develop meaning. When Ernest Hemingway wrote *Death in the Afternoon* about the traditions of bullfighting in Spain, he carefully observed and interpreted the meaning of a cultural ritual. And when historians interpret Hemingway's text through the lens of historical context, or when literary scholars compare the book to Hemingway's fiction of a later period, they are extending that understanding of human culture. Through such examination and interpretation of specific objects of study, scholars in the humanities can create artistic texts and develop theories that explain human expression and experience.

In this chapter, we'll often refer to artifacts and events that humanistic scholars study as **texts**. The ability to construct meaning from a text is an essential skill within the scholarship of the humanities. In high school English classes, students are often asked to interpret novels, poetry, or plays. You've likely written such analyses in the past, so you've developed a set of observational and interpretive skills that we'd like to build upon in this chapter. The same skills, such as the observational skills that lead you to find evidence in a literary text to develop and support an interpretation, can help you analyze other kinds of texts.

INSIDE WORK **Thinking about Texts**

Write your responses to the following questions.

- What experiences do you already have with interpretation of texts in the humanities? Have you had to write a formal interpretation of a text before? If so, what questions did you ask?

- Imagine a text with which you are familiar. It might be a novel, a song, a painting, a sculpture, a play, a building, or a historical document. Brainstorm a list of *why* questions that you could ask about that text. ❯

OBSERVATION AND INTERPRETATION

You probably engage every day in observation of the kinds of things studied in the humanities, but you might not be doing it in the systematic way that humanistic scholars do. When you listen to music, how do you make meaning? Perhaps you listen to the words, the chord progressions, or repeated phrases. Or maybe you look to specific matters of context such as who wrote the song, what other music the artist has performed, and when it was recorded. You might consider how it is similar to or different from other songs. In order to understand the song's meaning, you might even think about social and cultural events surrounding the period when the song was recorded. These kinds of observational and interpretive acts are the very things humanists do when they research and write; they just use careful methods of observing, documenting, and interpreting that are generally more systematic than what most of us do when listening to music for enjoyment. Humanists also develop and apply theories of interpretation or build on the theories of others that help still other scholars determine how to observe and interpret texts and find meaningful connections among them. In this chapter, you will learn about some of those methods of observation and interpretation, and you will also have the opportunity to practice some of the kinds of writing and research typically seen in the humanities.

INSIDE WORK **Observing and Asking Questions**

For this activity, pick a place to sit and observe, and bring something to write with. You might choose to do the activity in your dorm room or apartment, your workplace, a classroom, outside, in a restaurant or coffee shop, or at a gym, to name a few possibilities. For ten minutes, freewrite about all the things you see around you that could be "texts" that a humanist might interpret. Then think about the kinds of questions that a humanist might ask about those texts. Try to avoid writing about the actual activities people are engaging in; human behavior is more within the realm of the social sciences, not the humanities. Instead, think creatively about the kinds of artifacts that a humanist might analyze to understand and interpret human experience.

For example, if you observe and write in a coffee shop, you might consider the following artifacts, or texts.

- **The Sign or Logo Used for the Store**   Is there a logo? What does it include? How is it designed, and why? Is there a slogan? Whom might it relate to? What does it say about the store?

- **The Clothing of the People Working behind the Counter**   Do they have a dress code? Are they wearing uniforms? If so, what do the colors, materials, and/or style of the uniforms represent? What do they potentially tell you about the values of the business?

- **The Furniture**   Is it comfortable? New? Old? How is it arranged? What might the coffee shop be communicating to customers through that arrangement?

- **The Music Playing in the Background**   Is there music? What is playing? How loud is the music? What mood does it convey? Does it match the arrangement of the rest of the space? What emotions might the music evoke from customers?

- **The Materials Used to Serve Coffee**   Are the cups and napkins recycled? Does the store use glass or ceramic cups that can be washed and reused? Are there slogans or logos on the materials? If so, what do they say? What does the store communicate to customers through the materials used?

- **The Menu**   What kinds of items does the coffee shop serve? What language is used to describe menu items? How are the items written on the menu? Where is it displayed? Is food served? If so, what types of food are available, and what does that communicate to customers?

See how many different texts you can identify and how many questions you can generate. You might do this activity separately in the same place with a partner and then compare notes. What texts did you or your partner find in common? Which ones did you each identify that were unique? Why do you think you noticed the things you did? What was the most interesting text you identified? ◗

Hear more about the different kinds of texts scholars draw on in their research.

Research in the Humanities

The collection of information, or data, is an integral part of the research process for scholars in all academic disciplines. The data that researchers collect form the foundation of evidence they use to answer a question. In the humanities, data are generally gathered from texts. Whether you're reading a novel, analyzing a sculpture, or speculating on the significance of a cultural ritual, your object of analysis is a text and the primary source of data you collect to use as evidence typically originates from that text.

Academic fields within the humanities have at their heart the creation and interpretation of texts. A history scholar may pore through photographs of Civil

War soldiers for evidence to support a claim. An actor in a theater class might scour a script in order to develop an interpretation of a character he will perform onstage. And those who are primarily the creators of texts—visual artists, novelists, poets, playwrights, screenwriters, musicians—read widely in the field in order to master elements of style and contribute to their art in original and innovative ways. In the humanities, it's all about the text. Humanists are either creators or interpreters of texts, and often they are both.

To understand the research and writing in a specific disciplinary area, it is important to know not only what the objects of study are but also what methods scholars in that area use to analyze and study the objects of their attention. In the humanities, just as in other disciplines, scholars begin with observation. They closely observe the texts that interest them, looking for patterns, meaning, and connections that will help generate and support an interpretation. Humanists use their observations to pose questions about the human condition, to gather evidence to help answer those questions, and to generate theories about the human experience that can extend beyond one text or set of texts.

INSIDE WORK) **Observing and Interpreting Images**

Consider each of the following images—a movie poster (A), graffiti (B), and a painting (C)—as texts that have something to say about human experience. Write your ideas in response to the following questions.

- What does the image mean?

- How do you make meaning from the image? What do you analyze to make meaning?

- What does the image make you think about?

- What emotion does the artist want you to feel? What aspect of the text do you base this on?

- Why do you think someone created this image? ❱

A. Movie Poster as Text

B. Graffiti as Text

C. Painting as Text

THE ROLE OF THEORY IN THE HUMANITIES

When scholars in the humanities analyze and interpret a text, they often draw on a specific theory of interpretation to help them make meaning. Theories in the humanities offer a particular perspective through which to understand human experience. Sometimes those perspectives are based on ideas about *how* we make meaning from a text; such theories include Formalism (sometimes called New Criticism, though it is far from new), Reader Response, and Deconstruction. Other theories, such as Feminist Theory and Queer Theory, are based more on ideas about how identity informs meaning-making. Still other theories, such as New Historicism, Postcolonialism, and Marxism, are centrally concerned with how historical, social, cultural, and other contexts inform meaning.

These are only a few of the many prominent theories of humanistic interpretation, barely scratching the surface of the theory-building work that has taken place in the humanities. Our goal is not for you to learn specific names of theories at this point, though. Rather, we want you to understand that when scholars in the humanities draw on a theory in the interpretation of a text, the theory gives them a *lens* through which to view the text and a set of questions they might ask about it. Different theories lead to different sets of questions and varying interpretations of the same text.

CLOSE READING IN THE HUMANITIES

To develop clear claims about the texts they're interpreting, scholars in the humanities must closely observe their texts and learn about them. Close observation might involve the kinds of reading strategies we discussed in Chapter 2, especially if the text is alphabetic (i.e., letter based), such as a book, a story, or a poem. One method that humanities scholars use is close reading, or careful observation of a text. It's possible to do a close reading of a story, of course, but one can also do a close reading of non-alphabetic texts such as films, buildings, paintings, events, or songs.

Most college students are highly skilled at reading for content knowledge, or for information, because that's what they're most often asked to do as students. This is what a professor generally expects when assigning a reading from a textbook. As you read such texts, you're primarily trying to figure out what the text is saying rather than thinking about how it functions, why the author makes certain stylistic choices, or how others might interpret the text. As we mentioned in Chapter 2, you might also read to be entertained, to learn, or to communicate.

Close observation or *reading* in the humanities, however, requires our focus to shift from reading for information to reading to understand how a text functions and how we can make meaning of it. Because texts are the primary sources of data used in humanistic research, it's important for those who work in the humanities to examine how a text conveys meaning to its audience. This kind of work—observing a text critically to analyze what it means and how it conveys meaning—is what we call **close reading**.

Insider Example
Professional Close Reading

In the following example of a close reading of a text, Dr. Dale Jacobs discusses how he constructs meaning from comics. He argues that comics are more complicated to interpret than texts composed only of words (e.g., a novel or short story) because graphic novel readers must also interpret visual, gestural, and spatial language at work in the panels. In doing so, Dr. Jacobs offers his own observation. Furthermore, he concludes his interpretation by calling on instructors to challenge students to think critically about how they construct meaning from texts. As you read his article, you might reflect on this question: When reading a text, how do you make meaning?

More Than Words: Comics as a Means of Teaching Multiple Literacies

DALE JACOBS

Over the last several years, comics have been an ever more visible and well-regarded part of mainstream culture. Comics are now reviewed in major news-papers and featured on the shelves of independent and chain bookstores. Major publishing houses such as Pantheon publish work in the comics medium, including books such as Marjane Satrapi's *Persepolis* and David B.'s *Epileptic*. Educational publishers such as Scholastic are also getting in on the act; in January 2005, Scholastic launched its own graphic novels imprint, Graphix, with the publication of Jeff Smith's highly acclaimed Bone series. At the NCTE Annual Convention, graphic novels and comics are displayed in ever greater numbers. School and public libraries are building graphic novels collections to try to get adolescents into the library. Comics have, indeed, emerged from the margins into the mainstream.

   With all this activity and discussion surrounding comics, it is timely to con-sider how we as literacy teachers might think about the practice of using comics in our classrooms and how this practice fits into ongoing debates about comics and literacy. In examining these links between theory and practice, I wish to move beyond seeing the reading of comics as a debased or simplified word-based literacy. Instead, I want to advance two ideas: (1) reading comics involves a complex, multimodal literacy; and (2) by using comics in our classrooms, we can help students develop as critical and engaged readers of multimodal texts.

THE HISTORY OF ATTITUDES TOWARD COMICS AND LITERACY

Prior to their current renaissance, comics were often viewed, at best, as popular entertainment and, at worst, as a dangerous influence on youth. Such attitudes were certainly prevalent in the early 1950s when comics were at their most popular, with critics such as Fredric Wertham voicing the most strenuous arguments against comics in his 1954 book *Seduction of the Innocent* (for an extended discussion of this debate, see Dorrell, Curtis, and Rampal). Wertham baldly asserts that "[c]omic books are death on reading" (121). He goes on, "Reading troubles in children are on the increase. An important cause of this increase is the comic book. A very large proportion of children who cannot read well habitually read comic books. They are not really readers, but gaze mostly at the pictures, picking up a word here and there. Among the worst readers is a very high percentage of comic-book addicts who spend very much time 'reading' comic books. They are book-worms without books" (122). According to this thinking, children who read comic books are not really reading; they are simply looking at the pictures as a way to avoid engaging in the complex processes of learning to read. The problem, according to Wertham, is that in reading comics children focus far too much on the image to make meaning and avoid engaging with the written word, a semiotic system that Wertham clearly sees as both more complex and more important. Though he sees the visuality of comics as dangerous, Wertham shares the notion with current proponents of comics that the visual is more easily ingested and interpreted than the written. Whether the visual acts as a hindrance or a help to the acquisition of word-based literacy, the key idea remains that the visual is subservient to the written.

When I was growing up in the 1970s, I never saw comics in school or in the public library unless they were being read surreptitiously behind the cover of a novel or other officially sanctioned book. Over the last decade, however, there has been a movement to claim a value for comics in the literacy education of children. Comics have made their way into schools mainly as a scaffold for later learning that is perceived to be more difficult, in terms of both the literate practices and content involved. For example, *Comics in Education*, the online version of Gene Yang's final project for his master's degree at California State University, Hayward, embodies thinking that is typical of many educators who advocate the use of comics in the classroom. Yang, a teacher and cartoonist, claims that the educational strength of comics is that they are motivating, visual, permanent, intermediary, and popular. In emphasizing the motivational, visual permanency (in the way it slows down the flow of information), intermediacy, and the popular, such approaches inadvertently and ironically align themselves with Wertham's ideas about the relationship between word and image, even while bringing comics into the mainstream of education. Comics in this formulation are seen simply as a stepping stone to the acquisition of other, higher skills. As a teaching tool, then, comics are seen primarily as a way to motivate through their popularity and to help slow-learning students, especially in the acquisition of reading skills (see Haugaard; Koenke). While I agree with these attempts to argue for the value of comics in education, such an approach has limited value.

Libraries have also been important in the reconsideration of the place of comics as appropriate texts for children in their literacy learning and acquisition. Recently, many librarians have been arguing for the introduction of comics into library collections, usually in the form of graphic novels, as a way to get children into the library and interested in reading. The main thrust of this argument is that the presence of graphic novels will make the library seem cool and interesting, especially among the so-called reluctant readers, mainly adolescent boys, who seem to show little interest in reading or in libraries (see Crawford; Simmons). Graphic novels can compete with video games, television, and movies, giving the library the advantage it needs to get this specifically targeted demographic through the door. Many public libraries and librarians have seen the power of comics and graphic novels as a tool for drawing young people into the library, getting them first to read those comics and then building on that scaffold to turn them into lifelong readers. Again, while I agree with the inclusion of comics and graphic novels in library collections, such an approach places severe limitations on the possibilities of our uses of the medium as literacy educators.

To think through these ideas, let's assume that this strategy has some of its desired effects in drawing reluctant readers into the library and coaxing them to read. What can we then say about the effects of this approach and its conception of comics and their relation to developing literate practices? On the one hand, the use of graphic novels is seen as one strategy in teaching and encouraging literacy and literate practices; on the other hand, graphic novels are still regarded as a way station on the road to "higher" forms of literacy and to more challenging and, by implication, worthwhile texts. I'm not trying to suggest that reading comics or graphic novels exists apart from the world of word-based texts as a whole or the complex matrix of literacy acquisition. Rather, I'm simply pointing out that in the development of children's and adolescents' literacies, reading comics has almost always been seen as a debased form of word-based literacy, albeit an important intermediate step to more advanced forms of textual literacy, rather than as a complex form of multimodal literacy.

COMICS AS MULTIMODAL LITERACY: THE THEORY

If we think about comics as multimodal texts that involve multiple kinds of meaning making, we do not give up the benefits of word-based literacy instruction but strengthen it through the inclusion of visual and other literacies. This complex view of literacy is touched on but never fully fleshed out in two excellent recent articles on comics and education: Rocco Versaci's "How Comic Books Can Change the Way Our Students See Literature: One Teacher's Perspective" and Bonny Norton's "The Motivating Power of Comic Books: Insights from Archie Comic Readers." By situating our thinking about comics, literacy, and education within a framework that views literacy as occurring in multiple modes, we can use comics to greater effectiveness in our teaching at all levels by helping us to arm students with the critical-literacy skills they need to negotiate diverse systems of meaning making.

I'm going to offer an example of how comics engage multiple literacies by looking at Ted Naifeh's *Polly and the Pirates*, but first let me give a brief outline of these multiple systems of meaning making. As texts, comics provide a complex environment for the negotiation of meaning, beginning with the layout of the page itself. The comics page is separated into multiple panels, divided from each other by gutters, physical or conceptual spaces through which connections are made and meanings are negotiated; readers must fill in the blanks within these gutters and make connections between panels. Images of people, objects, animals, and settings, word balloons, lettering, sound effects, and gutters all come together to form page layouts that work to create meaning in distinctive ways and in multiple realms of meaning making. In these multiple realms of meaning making, comics engage in what the New London Group of literacy scholars calls *multimodality*, a way of thinking that seeks to push literacy educators, broadly defined and at all levels of teaching, to think about literacy in ways that move beyond a focus on strictly word-based literacy. In the introduction to the New London Group's collection, *Multiliteracies: Literacy Learning and the Design of Social Futures*, Bill Cope and Mary Kalantzis write that their approach "relates to the increasing multiplicity and integration of significant modes of meaning-making, where the textual is also related to the visual, the audio, the spatial, the behavioural, and so on.... Meaning is made in ways that are increasingly multimodal—in which written-linguistic modes of meaning are part and parcel of visual, audio, and spatial patterns of meaning" (5). By embracing the idea of multimodal literacy in relation to comics, then, we can help students engage critically with ways of making meaning that exist all around them, since multimodal texts include much of the content on the Internet, interactive multimedia, newspapers, television, film, instructional textbooks, and many other texts in our contemporary society.

Such a multimodal approach to reading and writing asserts that in engaging with texts, we interact with up to six design elements, including linguistic, audio, visual, gestural, and spatial modes, as well as multimodal design, "of a different order to the others as it represents the patterns of interconnections among the other modes" (New London Group 25). In the first two pages from

Polly and the Pirates, all of these design elements are present, including a textual and visual representation of the audio element. Despite the existence of these multiple modes of meaning making, however, the focus in thinking about the relationship between comics and education is almost always on the linguistic element, represented here by the words in the words balloons (or, in the conventions of comics, the dialogue from each of the characters) and the narrative text boxes in the first three panels (which we later find out are also spoken dialogue by a narrator present in the story).

As discussed earlier, comics are seen as a simplified version of word-based texts, with the words supplemented and made easier to understand by the pictures. If we take a multimodal approach to texts such as comics, however, the picture of meaning making becomes much more complex. In word-based texts, our interaction with words forms an environment for meaning making that is extremely complex. In comics and other multimodal texts, there are five other elements added to the mix. Thought about in this way, comics are not just simpler versions of word-based texts but can be viewed as the complex textual environments that they are.

COMICS AS MULTIMODAL LITERACY:
POLLY AND THE PIRATES IN THE CLASSROOM

In comics, there are elements present besides words, but these elements are just as important in making meaning from the text. In fact, it is impossible to make full sense of the words on the page in isolation from the audio, visual, gestural, and spatial. For example, the first page of *Polly and the Pirates* (the first issue of a six-issue miniseries) opens with three panels of words from what the reader takes to be the story's narrative voice. Why? Partially it is because of *what* the words say—how they introduce a character and begin to set up the story—but also it is because of the text boxes that enclose the words. That is, most people understand from their experiences of reading comics at some point in their history that words in text boxes almost always contain the story's narrative voice and denote a different kind of voice than do words in dialogue balloons. What's more, these text boxes deviate in shape and design from the even rectangles usually seen in comics; instead, they are depicted more like scrolls, a visual element that calls to mind both the time period and genre associated with pirates. Not only does this visual element help to place the reader temporally and generically, but it, along with lettering and punctuation, also aids in indicating tone, voice inflection, cadence, and emotional tenor by giving visual representation to the text's audio element. We are better able to "hear" the narrator's voice because we can see what words are emphasized by the bold lettering, and we associate particular kinds of voices with the narrative voice of a pirate's tale, especially emphasized here by the shape of the text boxes. Both the visual and the audio thus influence the way we read the words in a comic, as can be seen in these three opening panels.

It seems to me, however, that the key lies in going beyond the way we make meaning from the words alone and considering the other visual elements, as well as the gestural and spatial. If I were teaching this text, I would engage students in a discussion about how they understand what is going on in the story and how they make meaning from it. Depending on the level of the class, I would stress different elements at varying levels of complexity. Here I will offer an example of how I make meaning from these pages and of some of the elements I might discuss with students.

In talking about the visual, I would consider such things as the use of line and white space, shading, perspective, distance, depth of field, and composition. The gestural refers to facial expression and body posture, while the spatial refers to the meanings of environmental and architectural space, which, in the case of comics, can be conceived as the layout of panels on the page and the relation between these panels through use of gutter space. The

opening panel depicts a ship, mainly in silhouette, sailing on the ocean; we are not given details, but instead see the looming presence of a ship that we are led to believe is a pirate ship by the words in the text boxes. The ship is in the center of an unbordered panel and is the only element in focus, though its details are obscured. The unbordered panel indicates openness, literally and metaphorically, and this opening shot thus acts much in the same way as an establishing shot in a film, orienting us both in terms of place and in terms of genre. The second panel pulls in closer to reveal a silhouetted figure standing on the deck of the ship. She is framed between the sails, and the panel's composition draws our eyes toward her as the central figure in the frame. She is clearly at home, one arm thrust forward while the other points back with sword in hand, her legs anchoring herself securely as she gazes across the ocean. The third panel pulls in even farther to a close-up of her face, the top half in shadow and the bottom half showing a slight smile. She is framed by her sword on the left and the riggings of the ship on the right, perfectly in her element, yet obscured from our view. Here

and in the previous panel, gestural and visual design indicate who is the center of the story and the way in which she confidently belongs in this setting. At the same time, the spatial layout of the page and the progression of the panels from establishing shot to close-up and from unbordered panels to bordered and internally framed panels help us to establish the relationship of the woman to the ship and to the story; as we move from one panel to the next, we must make connections between the panels that are implied by the gutter. Linguistic, visual, audio, gestural, and spatial elements combine in these first three panels to set up expectations in the reader for the type of story and its narrative approach. Taken together, these elements form a multimodal system of meaning making.

What happens in the fourth panel serves to undercut these expectations as we find out that the narrative voice actually belongs to one of the characters in the story, as evidenced by the shift from text box to dialogue balloon even though the voice is clearly the same as in the first three panels of the page. Spatially, we are presented with a larger panel that is visually dominated by the presence of a book called *A History of the Pirate Queen*. This book presumably details the story to which we had been introduced in the first three panels. The character holding the book is presenting it to someone and, because of the panel's composition, is also effectively presenting it to us, the readers. The gesture becomes one of offering this story up to us, a story that simultaneously becomes a romance as well as a pirate story as evidenced by the words the character says and the way she says them (with the bold emphasis on *dream* and *marry*). At this point, we do not know who this character is or to whom she is speaking, and the answers to these questions will be deferred until we turn to the second page.

On the first panel of page 2, we see three girls, each taking up about a third of the panel, with them and the background in focused detail. Both the words and facial expression of the first girl indicate her stance toward the story, while the words and facial expression of the second girl indicate her indignation at the attitude of the first girl (whom we learn is named Sarah). The third girl is look-ing to the right, away from the other two, and has a blank expression on her face. The next panel depicts the second and third girls, pulling in to a tighter close-up that balances one girl and either side of the panel and obscures the background so that we will focus on their faces and dialogue. The unbordered panel again indicates openness and momentary detachment from their surroundings. Polly is at a loss for words and is not paying attention to the other girl, as indicated by the ellipses and truncated dialogue balloons, as well as her eyes that are point-ing to the right, away from the other girl. Spatially, the transition to panel 3 once more encloses them in the world that we now see is a classroom in an over-head shot that places the students in relation to the teacher. The teacher's words restore order to the class and, on a narrative level, name the third of the three girls and the narrative voice of the opening page. The story of the pirates that began on page 1 is now contained within the world of school, and we are left to wonder how the tensions between these two stories/worlds will play out in the remaining pages. As you can see, much more than words alone is used to make meaning in these first two pages of *Polly and the Pirates*.

CONCLUSION

My process of making meaning from these pages of *Polly and the Pirates* is one of many meanings within the matrix of possibilities inherent in the text. As a reader, I am actively engaging with the "grammars," including discourse and genre conventions, within this multimodal text as I seek to create/negotiate meaning; such a theory of meaning making with multimodal texts acknowledges the social and semiotic structures that surround us and within which we exist, while at the same time it recognizes individual agency and experience in the creation of meaning. Knowledge of linguistic, audio, visual, gestural, and spatial conventions within comics affects the ways in which we read and the meanings we assign to texts, just as knowledge of conventions within word-based literacy affects the ways in which those texts are read. For example, the conventions discussed above in terms of the grammar of comics would have been available to Naifeh as he created *Polly and the Pirates*, just as they are also available to me and to all other readers of his text. These conventions form the underlying struc-ture of the process of making meaning, while familiarity with these conventions, practice in reading comics, interest, prior experience, and attention given to that reading all come into play in the exercise of agency on the part of the reader (and writer). Structure and agency interact so that we are influenced by design conventions and grammars as we read but are not determined by them; though we are subject to the same set of grammars, my reading of the text is not neces-sarily the same as that of someone else.

Reading and writing multimodal texts, then, is an active process, both for creators and for readers who by necessity engage in the active production of meaning and who use all resources available to them based on their familiarity with the comics medium and its inherent grammars, their histories, life experiences, and interests. In turn, every act of creating meaning from a multimodal text, happening as it does at the intersection of structure and agency, contributes to the ongoing process of becoming a multimodally literate person. By teaching students to become conscious and critical of the ways in which they make meaning from multimodal texts such as comics, we can also teach students to become more literate with a wide range of multimodal texts. By complicating our view of comics so that we do not see them as simply an intermediary step to more complex word-based literacy, we can more effectively help students become active creators, rather than passive consumers, of meaning in their interactions with a wide variety of multimodal texts. In doing so, we harness the real power of comics in the classroom and prepare students for better negotiating their worlds of meaning.

WORKS CITED

B., David. *Epileptic*. New York: Pantheon, 2005.

Cope, Bill, and Mary Kalantzis. "Introduction: Multiliteracies: The Beginnings of an Idea." *Multiliteracies: Literacy Learning and the Design of Social Futures*. Ed. Bill Cope and Mary Kalantzis. New York: Routledge, 2000. 3–8.

Crawford, Philip. "A Novel Approach: Using Graphic Novels to Attract Reluctant Readers." *Library Media Connection* 22.5 (Feb. 2004): 26–28.

Dorrell, Larry D., Dan B. Curtis, and Kuldip R. Rampal. "Book-Worms without Books? Students Reading Comic Books in the School House." *Journal of Popular Culture* 29 (Fall 1995): 223–34.

Haugaard, Kay. "Comic Books: Conduits to Culture?" *The Reading Teacher* 27.1 (Oct. 1973): 54–55.

Koenke, Karl. "The Careful Use of Comic Books." *The Reading Teacher* 34.5 (Feb. 1981): 592–95.

McCloud, Scott. *Understanding Comics: The Invisible Art*. New York: Harper, 1993.

Naifeh, Ted. *Polly and the Pirates* 1 (Sept. 2005): 1–2.

New London Group, The. "A Pedagogy of Multiliteracies: Designing Social Futures." *Multiliteracies: Literacy Learning and the Design of Social Futures*. Ed. Bill Cope and Mary Kalantzis. New York: Routledge, 2000. 9–37.

Norton, Bonny. "The Motivating Power of Comic Books: Insights from Archie Comic Readers." *The Reading Teacher* 57.2 (Oct. 2003): 140–47.

Satrapi, Marjane. *Persepolis*. New York: Pantheon, 2003.

Simmons, Tabitha. "Comic Books in My Library?" *PNLA Quarterly* 67.3 (Spring 2003): 12, 20.

Versaci, Rocco. "How Comic Books Can Change the Way Our Students See Literature: One Teacher's Perspective." *English Journal* 91.2 (Mar. 2001): 61–67.

Wertham, Fredric. *Seduction of the Innocent*. New York: Rinehart, 1954.

Yang, Gene. *Comics in Education*. 2003. 29 Aug. 2006 <http://www.humblecomics.com/comicsedu/index.html>.

Discussion Questions

1. In your own words, describe how Dr. Jacobs constructs meaning from the comics panels analyzed in this article.

2. What do you think he means by the phrase *multimodal text*?

3. Study one of the comics panels for a minute, and consider how you make meaning from it. Freewrite for five minutes about your own process for making sense of what the comic means.

4. Freewrite for five minutes discussing something you were asked to interpret in the past: perhaps a painting, a novel, a poem, or something else. How did you make meaning of what you were observing and interpreting?

STRATEGIES FOR CLOSE READING AND OBSERVATION

For most of us, when we observe a printed text closely, we highlight, underline, and take notes in the margins. If we're analyzing a visual or aural text, we might take notes on our thoughts, observations, and questions. We might keep a separate notebook or computer file in which we expand on our notes or clarify meaning. As with any skill, the more you practice these steps, the better you'll become at interpretation. We encourage you to take detailed notes, underline passages if applicable, and actively engage with a text when conducting your observation.

We recommend two specific data-collection steps for humanistic inquiry. First, we suggest that you take notes in the margins for a printed text or on a separate sheet of paper as you read, view, or listen to a text to be interpreted. These notes will draw your attention to passages that may serve as direct evidence to support points you'll make later. Additionally, you can elaborate in more detail when something meaningful in the text draws your attention. Jotting down page numbers, audio/video file time markers, and paragraph numbers is often a helpful step for cataloging your notes. The key is to commit fully to engaging with a text by systematically recording your observations.

Second, we recommend developing a **content/form-response grid** to organize the essential stages of your interpretation. The "content" is what happens in the text, and the "form" is how the text's creator structures the piece. In the case of a painting, you might comment on the materials used, the artist's technique, the color palette and imagery choice, or the historical context of the piece. In the case of a religious or political text, you might examine style, language, and literary devices used. The "response" is your interpretation of what the elements you've identified might mean.

Now read the opening paragraphs from "The Story of an Hour," a very brief short story by Kate Chopin published in 1894 that is now recognized as a classic work of American literature. The excerpt includes a student's notes in the margins followed by a content/form-response grid. Notice the frequency of notes the student takes in the margins and the kinds of questions she asks at this early stage. She offers a fairly equal balance of questions and claims. Pay attention to how she follows the two steps of humanistic inquiry mentioned above:

1. Examine the text and take careful notes. Try keeping marginal notes (if appropriate) and/or separate notebook or sheets of paper to expand on your notes.
2. Complete a content/form-response grid based on the notes you collect.

Excerpt from **The Story of an Hour**

KATE CHOPIN

Heart trouble? I wonder what kind of trouble.

The news of her husband's death is delivered by her sister.

Knowing that Mrs. Mallard was afflicted with a heart trouble, great care was taken to break to her as gently as possible the news of her husband's death. It was her sister Josephine who told her, in broken sentences; veiled hints that revealed in half concealing. Her husband's friend Richards was there, too, near her. It was he who had been in the newspaper office when intelligence of the railroad disaster was received, with Brently Mallard's name leading the list of "killed." He had only taken the time to assure himself of its truth by a second telegram, and had hastened to forestall any less careful, less tender friend in bearing the sad message.

Why would she act differently from other women hearing the same kind of news?

Interesting comparison. The storm-like quality of her grief.

Why is she "exhausted"? Interesting word choice.

She did not hear the story as many women have heard the same, with a paralyzed inability to accept its significance. She wept at once, with sudden, wild abandonment, in her sister's arms. When the storm of grief had spent itself she went away to her room alone. She would have no one follow her.

There stood, facing the open window, a comfortable, roomy armchair. Into this she sank, pressed down by a physical exhaustion that haunted her body and seemed to reach into her soul.

There are lots of images of life here. This really contrasts with the dark news of the story's opening.

She could see in the open square before her house the tops of trees that were all aquiver with the new spring life. The delicious breath of rain was in the air. In the street below a peddler was crying his wares. The notes of a distant song which some one was singing reached her faintly, and countless sparrows were twittering in the eaves.

This student's annotations can be placed into a content/form-response grid that helps her keep track of the ideas she had as she read and observed closely, both for information (*what*) and for ways the text shaped her experience of it (*how*). Notice that the student uses the Content/Form section to summarize the comments from her annotations, and then she reflects on her annotations in the Response section:

Content/Form Notes (*what* and *how*)	Response (What effect does it have on me?)
Heart trouble? I wonder what kind of trouble.	*There's a mystery here. What's wrong with Mrs. Mallard's heart?*
The news of her husband's death is delivered by her sister.	*Interesting that a female relative is chosen to deliver the news. A man would be too rough?*
Why would she act differently from other women hearing the same kind of news?	*I wonder what is special about Mrs. Mallard that causes her reaction to be different. Is she putting on a show? Story says her reaction was "sudden" and "wild."*
Why is she "exhausted"? Interesting word choice.	*Maybe this has to do with her heart condition or with how physically draining her mourning is.*
There are lots of images of life here. This really contrasts with the dark news of the story's opening.	*This is a sudden change in feeling. Everything is so calm and pleasant now. What happened?*

The purpose of this activity is to construct meaning from the text based on the student's close observation of it. This is an interpretation. We can already see that major complexities in the story are beginning to emerge in the student's response notes—such as the importance of the story's setting and the change that occurs in Mrs. Mallard.

Because content/form-response grids like the one above allow you to visualize both your ideas and how you arrived at those ideas, we recommend using this activity anytime you have to observe a text closely in order to interpret its meaning. For a non-alphabetic text, start with the content/form-response grid and use it to log your initial notes as you observe; then reflect later. In the end, such an activity provides a log of details that can help explain how you arrived at a particular conclusion or argument about the text.

INSIDE WORK **Annotating a Text**

Use this activity as an opportunity to practice close reading. Read the whole text of Kate Chopin's "The Story of an Hour" on pages 126–28, and then annotate the text as you read, paying particular attention to the following elements.

- **Content:** what is being said (the facts, the events, and who the characters are)

- **Form:** how it is being said (the style, language, literary techniques, and narrative perspective)

A follow-up activity at the conclusion of the story asks you to draw a content/ form-response grid like the example above. It's important to take extensive marginal notes (perhaps one or two comments per paragraph) and highlight and underline passages as you read the story. These notes will help shape your content/form-response grid and will strengthen your interpretation. We encourage you to expand on your notes on a separate sheet of paper while you read the story. ◗

The Story of an Hour

KATE CHOPIN

Knowing that Mrs. Mallard was afflicted with a heart trouble, great care was taken to break to her as gently as possible the news of her husband's death.

It was her sister Josephine who told her, in broken sentences; veiled hints that revealed in half concealing. Her husband's friend Richards was there, too, near her. It was he who had been in the newspaper office when intelligence of the railroad disaster was received, with Brently Mallard's name leading the list of "killed." He had only taken the time to assure himself of its truth by a second telegram, and had hastened to forestall any less careful, less tender friend in bearing the sad message.

She did not hear the story as many women have heard the same, with a paralyzed inability to accept its significance. She wept at once, with sudden, wild abandonment, in her sister's arms. When the storm of grief had spent itself she went away to her room alone. She would have no one follow her.

There stood, facing the open window, a comfortable, roomy armchair. Into this she sank, pressed down by a physical exhaustion that haunted her body and seemed to reach into her soul.

She could see in the open square before her house the tops of trees that were all aquiver with the new spring life. The delicious breath of rain was in the air. In the street below a peddler was crying his wares. The notes of a distant song which some one was singing reached her faintly, and countless sparrows were twittering in the eaves.

There were patches of blue sky showing here and there through the clouds that had met and piled one above the other in the west facing her window.

She sat with her head thrown back upon the cushion of the chair, quite motionless, except when a sob came up into her throat and shook her, as a child who has cried itself to sleep continues to sob in its dreams.

She was young, with a fair, calm face, whose lines bespoke repression and even a certain strength. But now there was a dull stare in her eyes, whose gaze was fixed away off yonder on one of those patches of blue sky. It was not a glance of reflection, but rather indicated a suspension of intelligent thought.

There was something coming to her and she was waiting for it, fearfully. What was it? She did not know; it was too subtle and elusive to name. But she felt it, creeping out of the sky, reaching toward her through the sounds, the scents, the color that filled the air.

Now her bosom rose and fell tumultuously. She was beginning to recognize this thing that was approaching to possess her, and she was striving to beat it back with her will—as powerless as her two white slender hands would have been.

When she abandoned herself a little whispered word escaped her slightly parted lips. She said it over and over under her breath: "free, free, free!" The vacant stare and the look of terror that had followed it went from her eyes. They stayed keen and bright. Her pulses beat fast, and the coursing blood warmed and relaxed every inch of her body.

She did not stop to ask if it were or were not a monstrous joy that held her. A clear and exalted perception enabled her to dismiss the suggestion as trivial.

She knew that she would weep again when she saw the kind, tender hands folded in death; the face that had never looked save with love upon her, fixed and gray and dead. But she saw beyond that bitter moment a long procession of years to come that would belong to her absolutely. And she opened and spread her arms out to them in welcome.

There would be no one to live for during those coming years; she would live for herself. There would be no powerful will bending hers in that blind persistence with which men and women believe they have a right to impose a private will upon a fellow-creature. A kind intention or a cruel intention made the act seem no less a crime as she looked upon it in that brief moment of illumination.

And yet she had loved him—sometimes. Often she had not. What did it matter! What could love, the unsolved mystery, count for in face of this possession of self-assertion which she suddenly recognized as the strongest impulse of her being!

"Free! Body and soul free!" she kept whispering.

Josephine was kneeling before the closed door with her lips to the keyhole, imploring for admission. "Louise, open the door! I beg, open the door—you will make yourself ill. What are you doing, Louise? For heaven's sake open the door."

"Go away. I am not making myself ill." No; she was drinking in a very elixir of life through that open window.

Her fancy was running riot along those days ahead of her. Spring days, and summer days, and all sorts of days that would be her own. She breathed a quick prayer that life might be long. It was only yesterday she had thought with a shudder that life might be long.

She arose at length and opened the door to her sister's importunities. There was a feverish triumph in her eyes, and she carried herself unwittingly like a goddess of Victory. She clasped her sister's waist, and together they descended the stairs. Richards stood waiting for them at the bottom.

Some one was opening the front door with a latchkey. It was Brently Mallard who entered, a little travel-stained, composedly carrying his grip-sack and umbrella. He had been far from the scene of accident, and did not even know there had been one. He stood amazed at Josephine's piercing cry; at Richards' quick motion to screen him from the view of his wife.

But Richards was too late.

When the doctors came they said she had died of heart disease—of joy that kills.

INSIDE WORK **Preparing a Content/Form-Response Grid**

Based on your annotations and notes, construct a content/form-response grid modeled after the example on page 125. Be sure to include your responses to the items you identify in the Content/Form column. Remember that in this case "content" relates to what happens in the story, and "form," in the context of a literary text, relates to how the writer makes the story function through style, narrative perspective, and literary techniques.

Once you've completed your close reading, you might pair up with a classmate or two and share your content/form-response grids. When doing so, consider the following questions as part of your discussion.

1. What facts or events did you note about the story?

2. What did you notice about the ways Chopin shapes your experience of the story? What style or literary techniques did you note?

3. What patterns do you see in the notes you've taken in the Form column? What repeated comments did you make, or what elements strike you in a similar way? How would you explain the meaning of those patterns? ▶

RESPONDING TO THE INTERPRETATIONS OF OTHERS

Before, during, and after observing a text, humanistic scholars also draw on the work of other scholars to build and support their interpretations. If you were interpreting Chopin's story, for example, you might review the notes you made in your content/form-response grid, search for interesting patterns, and then see if other scholars have noticed the same things. You might look for an element of the story that doesn't make sense to you and see if another scholar has already offered an interpretation. If you agree with the interpretation, you might cite it as support for your own argument. If you disagree, you might look for evidence in the story to show why you disagree and then offer your own interpretation.

As in other disciplines, scholars in the humanities draw on the work of others to make sure they're contributing something new to the ongoing

LaunchPadSolo

Learn more about incorporating sources into your writing.

conversation about the artifact, event, or phenomenon they're studying. They also read the
work of others to determine if they agree or
disagree with an interpretation. Because of the
importance of specific language and detail in the
humanities, scholars in the humanities quote one
another's exact words often, and they also quote
directly from their primary sources. We'll discuss
some of the reasons for these conventions, and
others, in the next section.

Conventions of Writing in the Humanities

Some writing conventions are shared across
different fields in the humanities. Because the
kinds of texts humanistic scholars examine can
vary so much, though, there are also sometimes
distinctions in writing conventions among its
various fields. One of the challenges of learning the conventions of a disciplinary discourse
community is figuring out the specific expectations for communicating with a specific academic
audience. In this section, we turn our attention
from *research in the humanities* to examine and
interpret artifacts themselves, to *strategies of rhetorical analysis* that help us examine how scholars
in the humanities write about those artifacts.

Many scholars learn about disciplinary
writing conventions through imitation and
examination of articles in their fields. Recall that
in Chapter 5 we introduced a three-part method
for analyzing an academic text by examining the
conventions of structure, language, and reference.
Applying this analytical framework to professional writing in the various humanities fields can
help you further understand conventions appropriate for any given subfield. An awareness of the
conventions for writing in any academic context
may facilitate your success in writing in those contexts.

Dr. Shelley Garrigan teaches Spanish language and literature at North
Carolina State University. As Dr. Garrigan describes in her Insider's View,
scholars learn conventions of writing in their field through a variety of means,
including learning from peers.

STRUCTURAL CONVENTIONS

From your experience in high school, you might already be familiar with common structural features of writing in the humanities. Arguments in the humanities are generally "thesis-driven"; that is, they make an interpretive claim about a text and then support that claim with specific evidence from the text and sometimes with material from other sources that support their interpretation. By contrast, arguments in the social sciences and the natural sciences are usually driven by a hypothesis that must be tested to come to a conclusion, which encourages a different structure (see Chapters 7 and 8). First we'll talk about how humanistic scholars develop research questions and thesis statements. Then we'll turn our attention to a common structure that many students learn in secondary school to support their thesis statements with evidence, which is loosely based on the structure of the thesis-driven argument, and we'll compare it with published scholarship in the humanities.

Insider's View
The research is going to support your own ideas
KAREN KEATON JACKSON, WRITING STUDIES

"When we talk about what the paper should look like, I let them know that the research part of your paper is not the longest part. I always say the longest part of your paper is this brainchild, your program that you're coming up with. And I say that purposely because I don't want the research running your paper. This is your paper, your voice. The research is going to support your own ideas.

"I think this sends the message that there's more to it than this; you can be more creative and not just rely on the research."

Get expert advice on incorporating research.

DEVELOPING RESEARCH QUESTIONS AND THESIS STATEMENTS

An important part of the interpretation process is using observations to pose questions about a text. From these close observations, humanists develop *research questions* that they answer through their research. A research question in the humanities is the primary question a scholar asks about a text or set of texts. It is the first step in interpretation because questions grow out of our observations and the patterns or threads that we notice. A *thesis statement* is an answer to a research question and is most persuasive when supported by logical evidence. Thesis statements are discussed in more detail in Chapter 3 as the central claim of an argument. It's important to note that developing a research question works best when it is generated prior to writing a thesis statement. Novice writers can sometimes overlook this crucial step in the writing process and attempt to make a thesis statement without formulating a well-realized research question first.

As John McCurdy mentions earlier in this chapter, some of the most important questions for humanists begin by asking, "Why?" Why does George befriend Lenny in *Of Mice and Men*? Why did Pablo Picasso begin experimenting with cubism in his paintings in the early 1900s? Why did President Lincoln frequently use religious imagery and language in public discourse? To answer such questions, humanistic scholars must collect evidence to support their claims, and in the humanities, evidence often originates from texts.

Many students confess to struggling with the process of writing a good thesis statement. A key to overcoming this hurdle is to realize that a good thesis statement comes first from asking thoughtful questions about a text and searching for answers to those questions through observation.

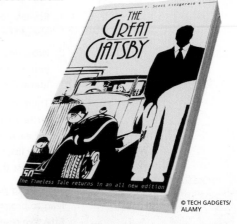

© TECH GADGETS/
ALAMY

Examples of Research Questions and Corresponding Thesis Statements

Research Question: Why does F. Scott Fitzgerald use the adjective *great* to describe Gatsby in *The Great Gatsby*?

Thesis Statement: The adjective *great* is used both ironically and derisively throughout F. Scott's Fitzgerald's novel *The Great Gatsby*, as evidenced by the use of Nick Carraway as the narrator and the carnival-like depictions of Gatsby's home and parties.

Research Question: Why did Georges-Pierre Seurat experiment with pointillism in the mid-1800s?

Thesis Statement: Georges-Pierre Seurat drew upon the scientific research of Ogden Rood and other color theorists to create paintings with minute brushstrokes in a style now called pointillism, which Seurat believed unified optically to make colors more vivid than in traditional painting styles of the time.

SUNDAY AFTERNOON ON THE ISLAND OF LA GRANDE JATTE, 1884–86 (OIL ON CANVAS), SEURAT, GEORGES-PIERRE (1859–91)/THE ART INSTITUTE OF CHICAGO, IL, USA/BRIDGEMAN IMAGES

Once you have carefully observed a text, gathered thorough notes, and developed a content/form-response grid as discussed earlier in the chapter, you're in a great position to begin brainstorming and drafting research questions. Recall that we encourage open-ended questions (*who, what, when, where, why*, and *how*) as opposed to closed, *yes/no* questions (questions that can be answered with a *yes* or *no*) as a pivotal step before drafting a thesis statement. Scholars in the humanities often start by asking questions that begin with *why*, but you might also consider questions of *what* and *how*.

INSIDE **WORK** **Developing *Why*, *What*, and *How* Questions**

The process of asking questions after conducting a close reading of a text is part of interpretation, and it can help you generate effective research questions to guide the development of a thesis. In this activity, we walk you through developing potential research questions from your notes on "The Story of an Hour." You could easily follow these steps after observing another kind of text as well.

1. Review your notes on "The Story of an Hour," and develop three questions about the story's content and form using *Why* as a starter word.

2. Next, develop three questions using *What* as your starter word. Try to focus your questions on different aspects of the story's characters, language, style, literary techniques, or narrative perspective.

3. Then use *How* as a starter word to develop three more questions. Again, write your questions with a different aspect of the story as the central focus for each. That is, don't just repeat the same questions from your *What* or *Why* list, inserting *How* instead. Think of different questions that can help address the story's meaning.

Try sharing your questions with a fellow student, and discuss which ones might lead to promising thesis statements to ground an extended interpretation. Effective research questions have the following characteristics.

- They can be answered with specific evidence from the text and from your notes: an effective research question can be answered with evidence and not just feelings or opinions.

- They can be answered in more than one way (i.e., they might require you to make a claim as opposed to being questions of fact): an effective research question is debatable. ❯

DEVELOPING EFFECTIVE THESIS STATEMENTS

The thesis statement, or the central claim, asserts *what* the author intends to prove, and it may also provide insight into *how* it will be proven. Providing both of these elements in a thesis allows writers to establish a blueprint for the structure of their entire argument—what we describe as a complex thesis statement in Chapter 3. Based on the thesis alone, a reader can determine the central claim and see how the writer intends to go about supporting it.

In the following example, Sarah Ray provides a thesis for her interpretation of Chopin's "The Story of an Hour." Notice that she includes clues as to how she will prove her claim in the thesis statement itself:

Blueprint for how Sarah will prove her claim

Sarah's interpretation of the story, provided as a clear claim

> Through Mrs. Mallard's emotional development and the concomitant juxta-position of the vitality of nature to the repressive indoors, Chopin exposes the role of marriage in the oppression of one's true self and desires.

Although it's not uncommon for thesis statements in humanistic scholarship to remain implied, as opposed to being stated explicitly, most interpretations explicitly assert a claim close to the beginning of the argument, often in the introductory paragraph (or, in a longer piece, paragraphs). Thesis statements may appear as single-sentence statements or may span multiple sentences.

Notice, for example, how Zenia Kish, a professor of American studies, states her claim at the end of the introductory section to her article "'My FEMA People': Hip-Hop as Disaster Recovery in the Katrina Diaspora." In the full text of the article, Kish builds up to this statement through several paragraphs of explanation, which all contribute to her thesis statement, shown here:

> I will examine how both national and local New Orleans artists identify with and rebel against the forces of marginalization that produced different senses of being a refugee, and also how they exploit marginality and the hustle as strategies to return home, however different or new that home may be. Providing listeners with an affective mapping of the social, economic, and discursive contradictions that produced the Katrina diaspora as refugees, post-Katrina hip-hop is a critical site for interrogating the ongoing tragedy of African American bodies that don't matter. (p. 673)

[Margin annotations:] Blueprint for how Kish will prove her claim — Reasons provided for Kish's claim — Clear statement of Kish's claim

INSIDE WORK **Drafting Thesis Statements**

Review the questions and responses you drafted in the "Developing *Why*, *What*, and *How* Questions" Inside Work activity. Some scholars use "I" in thesis statements, like the example from Zenia Kish, while others avoid using "I." Make sure you pay attention to requirements for the particular type of writing you're doing in your discipline. (Don't hesitate to ask your professor if "I" statements are acceptable.) You can always edit the thesis statement later to take out "I" if needed, but sometimes it helps when figuring out what you want to say to include yourself in the statement. So, for now, consider structuring your responses to your two selected questions as separate thesis statements, using an "I" statement in the following form.

By examining _____ (a, b, c, etc.—the evidence you have found), I argue that _____ (your claim).

Example Thesis Statement: **By examining Mrs. Mallard's emotional development and the juxtaposition of the vitality of nature to the repressive indoors in the story, I argue that Chopin exposes the role of marriage in the story to show the oppression of a person's true self and desires.**

Now test the appropriateness of your claim by asking the following questions about it.

- **Is the thesis debatable?** Claims in the humanities are propositions, not statements of fact. For example, the assertion that "The Story of an Hour" deals with a wife's response to the news of her husband's death is a fact. It is not, therefore, debatable and will not be a very useful thesis. If, however, we assert that the wife's response to her husband's death demonstrates some characteristic of her relationship with her husband and with the institution of marriage, then we're proposing a debatable claim. This is a proposition we can try to prove, instead of a fact that is already obviously true.

- **Is the thesis significant?** Claims about texts should offer substantial insight into the meaning of the artifacts. They should account for as much of the artifacts as possible and avoid reducing their complexity. Have you paid attention to all of the evidence you collected, and have you looked at it in context? Are you considering all of the possible elements of the text that might contribute to your interpretation?

- **Does the thesis contribute to an ongoing scholarly conversation?** Effective thesis statements contribute to an ongoing conversation without repeating what others have already said about the text. How does the claim extend, contradict, or affirm other interpretations of the text?

Once you've analyzed Chopin's story and constructed two separate thesis statements, consider sharing them with a classmate, identifying strengths and weaknesses in both. How is your claim both argumentative and significant? How many direct quotes from the story would help support your points? Which of the two thesis statements offers a more significant insight into the story's meaning? ▶

FIVE-PARAGRAPH ESSAYS AND OTHER THESIS-DRIVEN TEMPLATES

Many students learn to write academic arguments following a template taught in primary and secondary school as the **five-paragraph essay**. This template places a thesis, or claim, at the front of the argument (often at the end of an introductory paragraph), devotes the body of the essay to supporting the thesis, and then offers a final paragraph of conclusion that connects all the parts of the argument by summarizing the main points and reminding readers of the argument's overall significance.

LaunchPadSolo

See more on the transition into college writing.

While the premise behind this structure is based on some conventions of the humanities, following the template too closely could get you into trouble. Not every thesis has three points to prove, for example, giving you three body paragraphs in which to present evidence. And sometimes an introduction needs to be longer than one paragraph—as in the case of Zenia Kish's article "'My FEMA People': Hip-Hop as Disaster Recovery in the Katrina Diaspora," which originally appeared in the academic journal *American Quarterly*. The elements of the template that tend to be consistent in scholarship in the humanities, though, are these:

- Thesis statements generally appear toward the beginning of the argument in an introduction that explains the scope and importance of the topic.

- The body of the argument presents evidence gathered from the text to support the thesis.

- The conclusion connects the parts of the argument together to reinforce the thesis, summarizing the argument's important elements and reminding readers of its overall significance.

A template such as this one can provide a useful place to start as you organize your argument, but be careful not to allow a template to restrict your argument by oversimplifying your understanding of how humanistic scholars structure their writing.

OTHER STRUCTURAL CONVENTIONS IN THE HUMANITIES

There are other structural features conventional of writing in the humanities that you should consider when you begin a project in the discipline.

Title

Scholars in the humanities value the artistic and creative use of language, and titles of their work often reflect that value. In contrast to articles in the social sciences and the natural sciences, which often have descriptive titles that directly state the topic of study, articles in the humanities tend to have titles that play with language in creative ways, sometimes using quotations from the text in interesting ways. Humanistic scholars are also notorious for their love of subtitles. Here are a few examples:

- *Burlesque West: Showgirls, Sex, and Sin in Postwar Vancouver*
- "'The Fault of Being Purely French': The Practice and Theory of Landscape Painting in Post-Revolutionary France"
- "Reforming Bodies: Self-Governance, Anxiety, and Cape Colonial Architecture in South Africa, 1665–1860"
- "Resident Franchise: Theorizing the Science Fiction Genre, Conglomerations, and the Future of Synergy"

Paragraphs and Transitions

In arguments in the humanities, paragraphs tend to link back to the thesis by developing a reason and providing evidence. The paragraphs are often connected through **transitional words or phrases** (e.g., *similarly, in addition, in contrast, for example*) that guide readers by signaling shifts between and among the parts of an argument. These words and phrases help the reader understand the order in which the reasons are presented and how one paragraph connects to the preceding one.

LANGUAGE CONVENTIONS IN THE HUMANITIES

Writing in the humanities generally follows several conventions of language use that might sound familiar because they're often taught in English classes. Keep in mind, though, that even though these conventions are common in the humanities, they aren't necessarily conventional in other disciplinary areas.

Descriptive and Rhetorical Language

Writers in the humanities often use language that is creative or playful, not only when producing artistic texts but sometimes also when writing interpretations of texts. For example, you might notice that writing in the humanities uses figurative language and rhetorical devices (similes, metaphors, and alliteration, for example) more often than in other disciplines. Because writers in the humanities are studying texts so closely, they often pay similarly close attention to the text they're creating, and they take great care to choose precise, and sometimes artistic, language. In many cases, the language not only conveys information; it also engages in rhetorical activity of its own.

Active Voice

Writing in the humanities tends to privilege the use of the active voice rather than the passive voice. Sentences written in the **active voice** clearly state the subject of the sentence, the agent, as the person or thing doing the action. By contrast, the **passive voice** inverts the structure of the sentence, obscuring or eliminating mention of the agent. Let's look at three simple examples.

> **Active Voice:** The girl chased the dog.
>
> **Passive Voice (agent obscured):** The dog was chased by the girl.
>
> **Passive Voice (agent not mentioned):** The dog was chased.

In the first example, the girl is the subject of the sentence and the person (the agent) doing the action — chasing. In the second sentence, the girl is still there, but her presence is less prominent because the dog takes the subject's position at the beginning of the sentence. In the final sentence, the girl is not mentioned at all.

Now let's look at an example from a student paper in the humanities to understand why active voice is usually preferred. In Sarah Ray's interpretation of "The Story of an Hour" (printed in full on pp. 143–49), she writes this sentence in the introduction, using active voice:

> **Active Voice:** Kate Chopin presents a completely different view of marriage in "The Story of an Hour," published in 1894.

If Sarah were to write the sentence in the passive voice, eliminating the agent, it would look like this:

> **Passive Voice:** A completely different view of marriage is presented in "The Story of an Hour," published in 1894.

In this case, the active voice is preferred because it gives credit to the author, Kate Chopin, who created the story and the character. Scholars in the humanities value giving credit to the person doing the action, conducting the study, or creating a text. Active voice also provides the clearest, most transparent meaning—another aspect of writing that is valued in the humanities. In Chapters 7 and 8, we'll discuss why the passive voice is sometimes preferable in the social sciences and the natural sciences.

Hedging

In the humanities, writers sometimes hedge the claims that they make when interpreting a text, even though they are generally quite fervent about defending their arguments once established. In fact, the sentence that you just read contains not one but three **hedges**, or qualifiers. Take a look:

> In the humanities, writers tend to hedge the claims that they make when interpreting a text.

Each highlighted phrase limits the scope of the claim in a way that is important to improve accuracy and to allow for other possibilities. In contrast, consider the next claim:

> Writers hedge the claims that they make.

If we had stated our claim that way, not only would it not be true, but you would immediately begin to think of exceptions. Even if we had limited the claim to writers in the humanities, you still might find exceptions to it. As the original sentence is written, we've allowed for other possibilities while still identifying a predominant trend in humanities writing.

Humanistic scholars hedge their claims for several reasons. The disciplines of the humanities don't tend to claim objectivity or neutrality in their research (for more detail, see Chapters 7 and 8), so they allow for other interpretations of and perspectives on texts. As an example, take a look at the first sentence of Dale Jacobs's Conclusion from his article printed earlier in the chapter:

> My process of making meaning from these pages of *Polly and the Pirates* is one of many meanings within the matrix of possibilities inherent in the text. (par. 16)

In this example, Jacobs not only hedges the interpretation he has offered, but he explicitly states that there are many possible meanings in the text he has just analyzed.

REFERENCE CONVENTIONS IN THE HUMANITIES

Scholars in the humanities frequently cite the work of others in their scholarship, especially when supporting an interpretation of a text. They often quote the language from their primary sources exactly instead of summarizing or paraphrasing, because the exact words or details included in the primary source might be important to the argument.

Engagement with Other Scholars

When humanistic scholars cite the work of other scholars, they show how their research contributes to ongoing conversations about a subject—whether they're agreeing with a previous interpretation, extending someone else's interpretation, or offering an alternative one. These citations can strengthen their own argument and provide direct support by showing that another scholar had a similar idea or by demonstrating how another scholar's ideas are incorrect, imprecise, or not fully developed.

As we mentioned in Chapter 4, you can integrate the work of others into your writing by paraphrasing, summarizing, or quoting directly. Scholars in the humanities use all these options, but they quote directly more often than scholars in other disciplines because the exact language or details from their primary sources are often important to their argument.

Take a look at this example from Zenia Kish's article "'My FEMA People': Hip-Hop as Disaster Recovery in the Katrina Diaspora." She situates her argument about the message of hip-hop music after Hurricane Katrina within the work of another scholar, Hazel Carby, who had written about the cultural meaning of the blues. Although Carby was writing about a genre that preceded hip-hop, Kish makes a connection between Carby's interpretation of the blues and her own interpretation of the message of hip-hop at a particular point in history:

> Where the early blues served to "sp[ea]k the desires which were released in the dramatic shift in social relations that occurred in a historical moment of crisis and dislocation," as Hazel Carby observes (36), I would argue that the post-Katrina moment is the first time that mainstream American hip-hop has taken up the thematic of contemporary black migration as a mass phenomenon in any significant way. (p. 674)

Establishing Focus/Stance

Most scholars in the humanities include references to the work of others early in their writing to establish what the focus and stance of their own research will be. Because abstracts appear in humanities scholarship less frequently than in social sciences and natural sciences research, the introduction to an article in the humanities provides a snapshot of how the researcher is positioning himself or herself in the ongoing conversation about an object of study.

As you read scholarship in the humanities, notice how frequently the text references or cites secondary sources in the opening paragraphs. Look at this example from the second page of Dale Jacobs's article on teaching literacy through the use of comics, on page 115 of this chapter. Jacobs situates his work historically among work published about comics in the 1950s, and he also references the research of other scholars who had already written about that history in more detail:

> Prior to their current renaissance, comics were often viewed, at best, as popular entertainment and, at worst, as a dangerous influence on youth. Such attitudes were certainly prevalent in the early 1950s when comics were at their most popular, with critics such as Fredric Wertham voicing the most strenuous arguments against comics in his 1954 book *Seduction of the Innocent* (for an extended discussion of this debate, see Dorrell, Curtis, and Rampal). (par. 3)

In these two sentences, Jacobs positions his work within that of other scholars, showing how it's connected to and distinct from it. Also, by citing the work of Dorrell, Curtis, and Rampal, Jacobs doesn't have to write a lengthy history about a period that's tangentially related to his argument but not central to it.

DOCUMENTATION

A few documentation styles are prevalent in the humanities, and those styles tend to highlight elements of a source that are important in humanistic study. Many scholars in the humanities, especially in literature and languages, follow the documentation style of the Modern Language Association (MLA). Scholars in history and some other disciplines of the humanities follow the *Chicago Manual of Style* (CMS). When using CMS, scholars can choose between two kinds of citations. In the humanities, researchers generally use the footnote style of documentation.

The values of the humanities are most prevalent in the in-text citations of both MLA and CMS. In MLA, in-text citations appear in parenthetical references that include the author's last name and a page number, with no comma in between (Miller-Cochran et al. 139). The page number is included regardless of whether the cited passage was paraphrased, summarized, or quoted from—unlike in other common styles like APA, where page numbers are usually given only for direct quotations. One reason for including the page number in the MLA in-text citation is that humanistic scholars highly value the original phrasing of an argument or passage and might want to look at the original source. The page number makes searching easy for the reader, facilitating the possibility of examining the original context of a quotation or the original language of something that was paraphrased or summarized.

CMS style also supports looking for the information in the original source by giving the citation information in a footnote on the same page as the referenced material. Additionally, CMS allows authors to include descriptive details in a footnote that provides more information about where a citation came from in a source.

INSIDE WORK **Analyzing Scholarly Writing in the Humanities**

Answer the following questions about a scholarly article in the humanities. You might choose to focus on Zenia Kish's article, referenced earlier in this chapter, or find another article on a topic that interests you more.

A. Structural Elements

- **Title**   Does the title of the interpretation seek to entertain, to challenge, or to impress the reader somehow? Does the title reveal anything about the writer and his or her relationship to the intended audience?

- **Thesis**   Can you identify a clear statement of thesis? Where is it located? Does the thesis preview the stages of the claim that will be discussed throughout the paper? In other words, does the thesis explicitly or implicitly provide a "blueprint" for guiding the reader through the rest of the paper? If so, what is it?

- **Paragraphs and Transitions**   Look closely at four successive body paragraphs in the paper. Explain how each paragraph relates to the paper's guiding thesis. How does the writer transition between each of the paragraphs such that his or her ideas in each one stay linked together?

B. Language Elements

- **Descriptive and Rhetorical Language**   Is the language of the text meant only to convey information, or does it engage in rhetorical activity? In other words, do similes, metaphors, or other rhetorical devices demonstrate attempts to be creative with language? If so, what are they?

- **Voice**   Is the voice of the text primarily active or passive?

- **Conviction and Hedging**   Is the writer convinced that his or her interpretation is correct? If so, in what way(s) does specific language convey that conviction? Alternatively, if the writer doesn't seem convinced of the certainty of his or her argument, is there evidence of hedging? That is, does the writer qualify statements with words and phrases such as *tend*, *suggest*, *may*, *it is probable that*, or *it is reasonable to conclude that*? What is the significance of hedging?

C. Reference Elements

- **Engagement with Other Scholars**   Choose two or three examples from the article showing the author's use of another scholar's words or ideas, if appropriate. Explain how the writer uses the words and ideas of another to support his or her own argument. Keep in mind that a writer may use another's word or ideas as direct support by showing that another scholar has the same or similar ideas, or by demonstrating how another scholar's ideas are incorrect, imprecise, or not fully developed. Also, does the writer use block quotations? Does he or she fully integrate others' words and ideas in his or her own sentences? Further, notice the writer's attitude toward other scholars: Does he or she treat other scholars' ideas fully and respectfully? Is there praise for others' ideas? Or are their ideas quickly dismissed? Is there any evidence of hostility in the writer's treatment of other voices?

- **Establishing Focus/Stance**   How frequently does the text reference or cite secondary source materials in the opening paragraphs? What function do such citations or references serve in the article's overall organization?

- **Documentation**   Look closely at examples of internal documentation as well as the writer's Works Cited or References page. What form of documentation applies? Why might the chosen documentation system be appropriate for writing about texts in the humanities? ▶

Genres of Writing in the Humanities

The disciplines included under the umbrella of the humanities vary widely, but several genres occur frequently across disciplines. In her Insider's View response to interview questions, Dr. Shelley Garrigan, an associate professor of Spanish at North Carolina State University, describes the kind of academic writing that she does most frequently.

Similar to scholars in the social sciences and the natural sciences, scholars in the humanities often present their research at conferences and publish their work in journal articles and books. In some fields of the humanities, books are highly valued, and scholars here tend to work individually more frequently than scholars in the social sciences and the natural sciences. Also, many scholars in the humanities engage in creative work and might present it at an art installation, reading, or exhibit.

TEXTUAL INTERPRETATION

One of the primary genres that humanities researchers write is an interpretation of a text or set of texts. The research methods and activities outlined in this chapter provide support for

Insider's View
Academics often write for other academics
SHELLEY GARRIGAN, SPANISH LANGUAGE AND LITERATURE

COURTESY OF SHELLEY GARRIGAN

"I write academic articles and am currently editing a book-length manuscript. The articles that I have are peer-reviewed and published in academic journals, in which the readership is largely limited to other specialists in my field or in fields that touch upon what I study. Although the book has the possibility of inviting a wider range of readers, it is contracted with an academic press, and so the reading public that it may attract will most likely also be associated with or limited to academia."

interpretations of texts in a variety of fields in the humanities. A **textual inter-pretation** makes a clear claim about the object of study and then supports that claim with evidence from the text, and often with evidence drawn from the interpretations of other scholars.

WRITING PROJECT **Interpreting a Text**

In this Writing Project, you'll complete a close reading and offer an interpretation of a text for an audience of your peers. Begin by selecting a text that you find particularly interesting. You may choose from a host of categories, including the ones listed here.

paintings	advertisements
photographs	short stories
sculptures	poems
buildings	music videos or recordings

As a model for reading closely, follow the procedures outlined earlier in this chapter for creating a content/form-response grid. As you read, view, listen to, and/or study the text and make notes, consider the ways you are interacting with the text by creating a form-function diagram: *What* are you learning, and *how* is the text itself shaping your experience of it?

Once your close reading is complete, formulate a thesis (or a claim) about the text. You'll need to provide evidence to support your thesis from the text itself. You might also include evidence from secondary sources as support. (See Chapter 3 for more information on developing a clear thesis and Chapter 4 for gathering secondary sources.) Remember that depending on the scope of your thesis, your interpretation may or may not require you to do additional research beyond your close reading of the text. As you compose your interpretation, also keep in mind the conventions of structure, language, and reference that typically appear in scholarship in the humanities. Integrate them into your interpretation as appropriate.

Insider Example
Student Interpretation of a Text

In the following essay, "Till Death Do Us Part: An Analysis of Kate Chopin's 'The Story of an Hour,'" Sarah Ray offers an interpretation of Chopin's story that relies on close observation of the text for support. Read her essay below, and pay particular attention to her thesis statement and to her use of evidence. Note how her thesis responds to the question, "How does Mrs. Mallard's marriage function in the story?" Sarah didn't use outside scholars to support her interpretation, so you could also consider how secondary sources might have provided additional support for her claim.

Sarah Ray
ENG 101
10 April 201-

Till Death Do Us Part: An Analysis of Kate Chopin's
"The Story of an Hour"

The nineteenth century saw the publication of some of
the most renowned romances in literary history, including the
novels of Jane Austen and the Brontë sisters, Charlotte, Emily,
and Anne. While their stories certainly have lasting appeal,
they also inspired an unrealistic and sometimes unattainable
ideal of joyful love and marriage. In this romanticized vision,
a couple is merely two halves of a whole; one without the
other compromises the happiness of both. The couple's lives,
and even destinies, are so intertwined that neither individual
worries about what personal desires and goals are being
forsaken by commitment to the other. By the end of the
century, in her "The Story of an Hour" (1894), Kate Chopin
presents a completely different view of marriage. Through
the perspective of a female protagonist, Louise Mallard,
who believes her husband has just died, the author explores
the more challenging aspects of marriage in a time when
divorce was rare and disapproved of. Through Mrs. Mallard's
emotional development and the concomitant juxtaposition of
the vitality of nature to the repressive indoors, Chopin explores
marriage as the oppression of one's true self and desires.

"The Story of an Hour" begins its critique of marriage
by ending one, when the news of Brently Mallard's death
is gently conveyed to his wife, Louise. Chopin then follows
Mrs. Mallard's different emotional stages in response to her
husband's death. When the news is initially broken to Louise,
"[s]he did not hear the story as many women have heard the
same, with a paralyzed inability to accept its significance"

FORM: Ray uses a common line from marriage vows to indirectly indicate that she focuses on the role of marriage in her interpretation.

CONTENT: Ray clearly states her thesis and provides a preview about how she will develop and support her claim.

CONTENT: In this paragraph, Ray develops the first part of her thesis, the stages of Mrs. Mallard's emotional development.

(Chopin par. 3). She instead weeps suddenly and briefly, a "storm of grief" that passes as quickly as it had come (par. 3). This wild, emotional outburst and quick acceptance says a great deal about Louise's feelings toward her marriage. "[S]he had loved [her husband]—sometimes" (par. 15), but a reader may infer that Louise's quick acceptance implies that she has considered an early death for her spouse before. That she even envisions such a dark prospect reveals her unhappiness with the marriage. She begins to see, and even desire, a future without her husband. This desire is expressed when Louise is easily able to see past her husband's death to "a long procession of years to come that would belong to her absolutely" (par. 13). Furthermore, it is unclear whether her "storm of grief" is genuine or faked for the benefit of the family members surrounding her. The "sudden, wild abandonment" (par. 3) with which she weeps almost seems like Louise is trying to mask that she does not react to the news as a loving wife would. Moreover, the display of grief passes quickly; Chopin devotes only a single sentence to the action. Her tears are quickly succeeded by consideration of the prospects of a future on her own.

Chopin uses the setting to create a symbolic context for Louise's emotional outburst in response to the news of her husband's death. Louise is informed of Brently's death in the downstairs level of her home: "It was her sister Josephine who told her, in broken sentences; veiled hints that revealed in half concealing" (par. 2). No mention is made of windows, and the only portal that connects to the outside world is the door that admits the bearers of bad news. By excluding a link to nature, Chopin creates an almost claustrophobic environment to symbolize the oppression Louise feels from her marriage. It is no mistake that this setting plays host to Mrs. Mallard's initial

FORM: Ray primarily uses active voice to clarify who is doing the action in her sentences.

emotional breakdown. Her desires have been suppressed throughout her relationship, and symbolically, she is being suffocated by the confines of her house. Therefore, in this toxic atmosphere, Louise is only able to feel and show the emotions that are expected of her, not those that she truly experiences. Her earlier expression of "grief" underscores this disconnect, overcompensating for emotions that should come naturally to a wife who has just lost her husband, but that must be forced in Mrs. Mallard's case.

Chopin continues Mrs. Mallard's emotional journey only after she is alone and able to process her genuine feelings. After her brief display of grief has run its course, she migrates to her upstairs bedroom and sits in front of a window looking upon the beauty of nature. It is then and only then that Louise gives in not only to her emotions about the day's exploits, but also to those feelings she could only experience after the oppression of her husband died with him—dark desires barely explored outside the boundaries of her own mind, if at all. They were at first foreign to her, but as soon as Louise began to "recognize this thing that was approaching to possess her . . . she [strove] to beat it back with her will" (par. 10). Even then, after the source of her repression is gone, she fights to stifle her desires and physical reactions. The habit is so engrained that Louise is unable to release her emotions for fear of the unknown, of that which has been repressed for so long. However, "her bosom rose and fell tumultuously . . . When she abandoned herself a little whispered word escaped her slightly parted lips. She said it over and over under her breath: 'free, free, free!' . . . Her pulses beat fast, and the coursing blood warmed and relaxed every inch of her body" (pars. 10, 11). When she's allowed to experience them, Louise's feelings and desires provide a glimpse into a possible joyous

FORM: Ray uses transitions between paragraphs that indicate her organization and connect different ideas.

future without her husband, a future where "[t]here would be no powerful will bending hers in that blind persistence with which men and women believe they have a right to impose" (par. 14). Her marriage is over, and Louise appears finally to be able to liberate her true identity and look upon the future with not dread but anticipation.

The author's setting for this scene is crucial in the development of not only the plot but also her critique of marriage. Chopin sought to encapsulate the freedom Louise began to feel in her room with this scene's depiction of nature. For example, Chopin describes the view from Louise's bedroom window with language that expresses its vitality: "She could see in the open square before her house the tops of trees that were all aquiver with the new spring life" (par. 5). She goes on to say, "The delicious breath of rain was in the air. In the street below a peddler was crying his wares . . . and countless sparrows were twittering in the eaves" (par. 5). The very adjectives and phrases used to describe the outdoors seem to speak of bustling activity and life. This is in stark contrast to the complete lack of vivacity in the description of downstairs.

The language used in the portrayal of these contrasting settings is not the only way Chopin strives to emphasize the difference between the two. She also uses the effect these scenes have on Mrs. Mallard to convey their meaning and depth. On the one hand, the wild, perhaps faked, emotional outburst that takes place in the stifling lower level of the house leaves Louise in a state of "physical exhaustion that haunted her body and seemed to reach into her soul" (par. 4). On the other hand, Louise "[drank] in a very elixir of life through that open window" (par. 18) of her bedroom through which nature bloomed. Because the author strove to symbolize Mrs. Mallard's marriage with the oppressive downstairs

FORM: When making assumptions about the author's intentions, Ray sometimes uses hedging words—in this case, "seem to."

and her impending life without her husband with the open, healing depiction of nature, Chopin suggests that spouses are sometimes better off without each other because marriage can take a physical toll on a person's well-being while the freedom of living for no one but one's self breathes life into even the most burdened wife. After all, "[w]hat could love, the unsolved mystery, count for in face of this possession of self-assertion" (par. 15) felt by Mrs. Mallard in the wake of her emancipation from oppression?

Chopin goes on to emphasize the healing capabilities and joy of living only for one's self by showing the consequences of brutally taking it all away, in one quick turn of a latchkey. With thoughts of her freedom of days to come, "she carried herself unwittingly like a goddess of Victory. She clasped her sister's waist, and together they descended the stairs" (par. 20). Already Chopin is preparing the reader for Mrs. Mallard's looming fate. Not only is she no longer alone in her room with the proverbial elixir of life pouring in from the window, but also she is once again sinking into the oppression of the downstairs, an area that embodies all marital duties as well as the suffocation of Louise's true self and desires. When Brently Mallard enters the house slightly confused but unharmed, the loss of her newly found freedom is too much for Louise's weak heart to bear. Chopin ends the story with a hint of irony: "When the doctors came they said she had died of heart disease—of joy that kills" (par. 23). It may be easier for society to accept that Mrs. Mallard died of joy at seeing her husband alive, but in all actuality, it was the violent death of her future prospects and the hope she had allowed to blossom that sent Louise to the grave. Here lies Chopin's ultimate critique of marriage: when there was no other viable escape, only death could provide freedom from an oppressive marriage.

By killing Louise, Chopin solidifies this ultimatum and also suggests that even death is kinder when the only other option is the slow and continuous addition of the crushing weight of marital oppression.

In "The Story of an Hour," Kate Chopin challenges the typical, romanticized view of love and marriage in the era in which she lived. She chooses to reveal some of the sacrifices one must make in order to bind oneself to another in matrimony. Chopin develops these critiques of marriage through Louise Mallard's emotional responses to her husband's supposed death, whether it is a quick, if not faked, outburst of grief, her body's highly sexualized awakening to the freedoms to come, or the utter despair at finding that he still survives. These are not typical emotions for a "grieving" wife, and Chopin uses this stark contrast as well as the concomitant juxtaposition of nature to the indoors to further emphasize her critique. Louise Mallard may have died in the quest to gain independence from the oppression of her true self and desires, but now she is at least "[f]ree! Body and soul free!" (par. 16).

CONTENT: Ray provides a broad summary of her argument in the concluding paragraph.

CONTENT: In her last sentence, Ray reveals a portion of the significance of the story to an understanding of marital oppression.

Ray 7

Work Cited

Chopin, Kate. "The Story of an Hour." Ann Woodlief's Web

Study Texts. Web. <http://www.vcu.edu/engweb

/webtexts/hour/>. 10 Apr. 2013.

FORM: Ray cites her source using MLA format.

Discussion Questions

1. Describe how Sarah Ray's thesis is both debatable and significant.
2. How does the author use evidence from the text to support her interpretation?
3. How has she organized her interpretation?
4. How could it help Sarah's interpretation if she looked at the work of other scholars who have studied Chopin's story?

ARTISTIC TEXTS

Many scholars in the humanities are creators of artistic texts. It has been said about artistic texts that when you create them, they're the arts, and when you study them, they're the humanities. This formulation oversimplifies somewhat, but it's helpful as shorthand for thinking about the relationship between arts and humanities. Artistic texts can occur in many different forms and media. Some of the more common artistic texts that students create include the following:

paintings	songs	stories
sculptures	pottery	video games
poems	models	short films

The process that you follow to create an artistic text will vary according to the type of text you create. In a writing class, an instructor might ask you to create an artistic text and then reflect on the process of creating it. Additionally, he or she might ask you to interpret your own text or that of another student.

WRITING PROJECT **Creating an Artistic Text**

In this three-part project, you'll create a text, reflect on the process of creating it, and then develop a preliminary interpretation of the text. Your assessment will be based primarily on your reflection on and close reading of your text. We encourage you to try something new; indeed, you might discover a talent you didn't realize you had, or you might understand something new about the creative process by trying an art form you haven't experimented with before.

PART 1

Choose an art form that you'd like to experiment with for this activity. You might try something that you've done before, or you might want to experiment with something new. Some possibilities are listed below.

- sketching or painting a figure or a landscape
- composing a poem or a song
- using a pottery wheel or sculpting with clay
- writing a short story
- creating an advertisement or Public Service Announcement for an issue important to you
- designing a video game
- directing a (very) short film

PART 2

After completing the creative portion of this project, respond to the following prompts for reflection about the process of creating the text.

- First reflect on the process of creating your text and what you learned from it.
- What was the most challenging part of the project for you?
- What was the most enjoyable part of the project?
- What did you discover about yourself as you participated in this activity?
- Did you find yourself trying to imitate other examples you've seen, heard, or experienced, or were you trying to develop something very different?
- What inspired you as you were working?

PART 3

Once you've reflected on the process of creating your text, examine the text closely and take notes regarding the elements of it that you see as important to its meaning. Once you've developed notes, do the following.

1. Complete a content/form-response grid to highlight the notes you see as most important for constructing meaning from the text. Be sure to articulate responses about why you see each note as important and relevant toward interpreting meaning.

2. Brainstorm a list of *how*, *what*, and *why* questions regarding various aspects of the text related to its meaning(s).

3. Select one or two questions that seem most promising to try and answer. You should be able to draw direct evidence from the text (and your notes) that supports your answer.

4. Select and rewrite the best question that has evidence, and then write a thesis statement.

You should construct the remainder of your interpretation of the text based on the thesis statement. Try to develop an interpretation that's organized with clear reasons and evidence (see Chapter 3). Use examples actually taken from your text as evidence.

tip sheet

Reading and Writing in the Humanities

- **In the humanities, scholars seek to understand and interpret human experience.** To do so, they often create, analyze, and interpret texts.

- **Scholars in the humanities often conduct close readings of texts** to interpret and make meaning from them, and they might draw on a particular theoretical perspective to ask questions about those texts.

- **Keeping a content/form-response grid can help you track important elements of a text** and your response to them as you do a close reading.

- **Writing in the humanities also draws on the interpretations of others,** either as support or to position an interpretation within other prior scholarship.

- **Arguments in the humanities generally begin with a thesis statement** that asserts *what* the author intends to prove, and it may also provide insight into *how* the author will prove it. Each section of the argument should provide support for the thesis.

Reading and Writing
in the Social Sciences

Introduction to the Social Sciences

Social scientists study human behavior and interaction along with the systems and social structures we create to organize our world. Professionals in the fields of the **social sciences** help us understand why we do what we do as well as how processes (political, economic, personal, etc.) contribute to our lives. As the image at the bottom of this page shows, the social sciences encompass a broad area of academic inquiry that comprises numerous fields of study. These include sociology, psychology, anthropology, communication studies, and political science, among others.

Maybe you've observed a friend or family member spiral into addictive or self-destructive behavior and struggled to understand how it happened. Maybe you've spent time wondering how cliques were formed and maintained among students in your high school, or how friends are typically chosen. Perhaps larger social issues like war, poverty, or famine concern you the most. If you've ever stopped to consider any of these kinds of issues, then you've already begun to explore the world of the social sciences.

Social scientist Kevin Rathunde, who teaches at the University of Utah, shares his perspective on the work and writing of social scientists in Insider's View features in this chapter. Excerpts from Dr. Rathunde's paper entitled "Middle School Students' Motivation and Quality of Experience: A Comparison of Montessori and Traditional School Environments," which he wrote and published with a colleague, Mihaly

ANDREA TSURUMI

Csikszentmihalyi, in the *American Journal of Education*, also appear throughout this chapter. Rathunde and Csikszentmihalyi's study investigated the types of educational settings that contribute to the best outcomes for students. Specifically, they compared traditional public school environments with those of Montessori schools to assess how students learn, interact, and perceive the quality of their experiences in these differing environments.

As a social scientist, you might study issues like therapy options for autism, the effects of substance abuse on families, peer pressure, the dynamics of dating, social networking websites, stress, or the communication practices of men and women. You might study family counseling techniques or the effects of divorce on teens. Or perhaps you might wonder (as Rathunde and Csikszentmihalyi do) about the effects of differing educational environments on student satisfaction and success.

Whatever the case may be, if you're interested in studying human behavior and understanding why we do what we do, you'll want to consider further how social scientists conduct research and how they present their results in writing. As in all the academic domains, progress in the social sciences rests upon researchers' primary skills at making observations of the world around them.

INSIDE WORK Observing Behavior

For this activity, pick a place to sit and observe people. You can choose a place that you enjoy going to regularly, but make sure you can observe and take notes without being interrupted or distracted. For example, you might observe people in your school's library or another space on campus. Try to avoid places where you could feel compelled to engage in conversation with people you know.

For ten minutes, freewrite about the people around you and what they're doing. Look for the kinds of interactions and engagements that characterize their behavior. Then draft some questions that you think a social scientist observing the same people might ask about them. For example, if you wrote about behaviors you observed in a college classroom or lecture hall, you might consider questions like the ones listed here.

- How are students arranged around the room? What does the seating arrangement look like? What effect does the room's arrangement have on classroom interaction, if any?

- What are students doing? Are they taking notes? Writing? Sleeping? Typing? Texting? Listening? Doing something else?

- Are students doing different things in different parts of the room, or are the activities uniform throughout the room? Why?

- What is the instructor doing in the classroom? Where is he or she positioned? How are students responding?

- Are students using technology? If so, what kinds of technology? What are they using the technology to do?

- If people are interacting with one another in the classroom, what are they talking about? How are they interacting? How are they positioned when they interact? Are numerous people contributing to the conversation? Is someone leading the conversation? If so, how?

See how many different behaviors, people, and interactions you can observe and how many questions you can generate. You might do this activity in the same place with a partner and then compare notes. What did you or your partner find in common? What did you each observe that was unique? Why do you think you noticed the things you did? What was the most interesting thing you observed? ▶

Research in the Social Sciences

As we've indicated, the social sciences comprise a diverse group of academic fields that aim to understand human behavior and systems. But it may be difficult to see the commonalities among these disciplines that make it possible to refer to them as social sciences. One of the ways we can link these disciplines and the values they share, beyond their basic concern for why and how people do things, is by considering how social scientists conduct and report their research.

THE ROLE OF THEORY

Unlike in the natural sciences, where research often takes place in a laboratory setting under controlled conditions, research in the social sciences is necessarily "messier." The reason is fairly simple: human beings and the systems they organize cannot generally be studied in laboratory conditions, where variables are controlled. For this reason, social scientists do not generally establish fixed laws or argue for absolute truths, as natural scientists sometimes do. For instance, while natural scientists are able to argue, with certainty, that a water molecule contains two atoms of hydrogen and one of oxygen, social scientists cannot claim to know the absolute fixed nature of a person's psychology (why a person does what she does in any particular instance) or that of a social system or problem (why homelessness persists, for instance).

Much social science research is therefore based on **theories of human behavior and human systems**, which are propositions that scholars use to explain specific phenomena. Theories can be evaluated on the basis of their ability to explain why or how or when a phenomenon occurs, and they generally result from research that has been replicated time and again to confirm their accuracy, appropriateness, and usefulness. Still, it's important to understand that theories are not laws; they are not absolute, fixed, or perfect explanations. Instead, social science theories are always being refined as research on particular social phenomena develops. The Rathunde and Csikszentmihalyi study we highlight in the Insider's View boxes with Dr. Rathunde, for instance, makes use of goal theory and optimal experience theory as part of the research design to evaluate the type of middle school environment that best contributes to students' education.

Insider Example
Exploring Social Science Theory

Read the following excerpt from Kalervo Oberg's "Cultural Shock: Adjustment to New Cultural Environments," and then reflect on his theory by answering the questions that follow the selection. Oberg (1901–1973) was a pioneer in economic anthropology and applied anthropology, and his foundational work in this study has been cited hundreds of times by sociologists and anthropologists who are interested in the phenomenon. Oberg himself coined the term *culture shock*.

Excerpt from **Cultural Shock: Adjustment to New Cultural Environments**

KALERVO OBERG

Culture shock is precipitated by the anxiety that results from losing all our familiar signs and symbols of social intercourse. These signs or cues include the thousand and one ways in which we orient ourselves to the situations of daily life: when to shake hands and what to say when we meet people, when and how to give tips, how to give orders to servants, how to make purchases, when to accept and when to refuse invitations, when to take statements seriously and when not. Now these cues which may be words, gestures, facial expressions, customs, or norms are acquired by all of us in the course of growing up and are as much a part of our culture as the language we speak or the beliefs we accept. All of us depend for our peace of mind and our efficiency on hundreds of these cues, most of which we do not carry on the level of conscious awareness.

Now when an individual enters a strange culture, all or most of these familiar cues are removed. He or she is like a fish out of water. No matter how broadminded or full of good will you may be, a series of props have been knocked from under you, followed by a feeling of frustration and anxiety. People react to the frustration in much the same way. First they *reject* the environment which causes the discomfort: "the ways of the host country are bad because they make us feel bad." When Americans or other foreigners in a strange land get together to grouse about the host country and its people—you can be sure they are suffering from culture shock. Another phase of culture shock is *regression*. The home environment suddenly assumes a tremendous importance. To an American everything American becomes irrationally glorified. All the difficulties and problems are forgotten and only the good things back home are remembered. It usually takes a trip home to bring one back to reality.

SYMPTOMS OF CULTURE SHOCK

Some of the symptoms of culture shock are: excessive washing of the hands; excessive concern over drinking water, food, dishes, and bedding; fear of physical contact with attendants or servants; the absent-minded, far-away stare (sometimes called "the tropical stare"); a feeling of helplessness and a desire for dependence on long-term residents of one's own nationality; fits of anger over delays and other minor frustrations; delay and outright refusal to learn the language of the host country; excessive fear of being cheated, robbed, or injured; great concern over minor pains and irruptions of the skin; and finally, that terrible longing to be back home, to be able to have a good cup of coffee and a piece of apple pie, to walk into that corner drugstore, to visit one's relatives, and, in general, to talk to people who really make sense.

Individuals differ greatly in the degree in which culture shock affects them. Although not common, there are individuals who cannot live in foreign countries. Those who have seen people go through culture shock and on to a satisfactory adjustment can discern steps in the process. During the first few weeks most individuals are fascinated by the new. They stay in hotels and associate with nationals who speak their language and are polite and gracious to foreigners. This honeymoon stage may last from a few days or weeks to six months depending on circumstances. If one is a very important person he or she will be shown the show places, will be pampered and petted, and in a press interview will speak glowingly about progress, good will, and international amity, and if he returns home he may well write a book about his pleasant if superficial experience abroad.

But this Cook's tour type of mentality does not normally last if the foreign visitor remains abroad and has seriously to cope with real conditions of life. It is then that the second stage begins, characterized by a hostile and aggressive attitude towards the host country. This hostility evidently grows out of the genuine difficulty which the visitor experiences in the process of adjustment. There is maid trouble, school trouble, language trouble, house trouble, transportation trouble, shopping trouble, and the fact that people in the host country are largely indifferent to all these troubles. They help but they just don't understand your great concern over these difficulties. Therefore, they must be insensible and unsympathetic to you and your worries. The result, "I just don't like them." You become aggressive, you band together with your fellow countrymen and criticize the host country, its ways, and its people. But this criticism is not an objective appraisal but a derogatory one. Instead of trying to account for conditions as they are through an honest analysis of the actual conditions and the historical circumstances which have created them, you talk as if the difficulties you experienced are more or less created by the people of the host country for your special discomfort. You take refuge in the colony of your countrymen and its cocktail circuit, which often becomes the fountain-head of emotionally charged labels known as stereotypes. This is a peculiar kind of invidious shorthand which caricatures the host country and its people in a negative manner. The "dollar-grasping American" and the "indolent Latin American" are samples of mild forms of stereotypes. The use of stereotypes may salve the ego of someone with a severe case of culture shock but it certainly does not lead to any genuine understanding of the host country and its people. This second stage of culture shock is in a sense a crisis in the disease. If you overcome it, you stay; if not, you leave before you reach the stage of a nervous breakdown.

If the visitor succeeds in getting some knowledge of the language and begins to get around by himself, he is beginning to open the way into the new cultural environment. The visitor still has difficulties but he takes a "this is my cross and I have to bear it" attitude. Usually in this stage the visitor takes a superior attitude to people of the host country. His sense of humor begins to exert itself. Instead of criticizing he jokes about the people and even cracks jokes about his or her own difficulties. He or she is now on the way to recovery. And there is also the poor devil who is worse off than yourself whom you can help, which in turn gives you confidence in your ability to speak and get around.

In the fourth stage your adjustment is about as complete as it can be. The visitor now accepts the customs of the country as just another way of living. You operate within the new milieu without a feeling of anxiety although there are moments of strain. Only with a complete grasp of all the cues of social intercourse will this strain disappear. For a long time the individual will understand what the national is saying but he is not always sure what the national means. With a complete adjustment you not only accept the foods, drinks, habits, and customs, but actually begin to enjoy them. When you go on home leave you may even take things back with you and if you leave for good you generally miss the country and the people to whom you have become accustomed.

Discussion Questions

1. In your own words, define what you think Kalervo Oberg means by *culture shock*.

2. What are the four stages of culture shock, according to Oberg?

3. Oberg's essay was written more than half a century ago. In what ways does it seem dated? In what ways does it strike you as still valid or relevant?

INSIDE WORK **Tracing a Theory's Development**

As we indicated, theories in the social sciences exist to be developed and refined over time, based on our developing understandings of a social phenomenon as a result of continued research. Conduct a search (using the web or your academic database access) to determine if you can make a rough estimate as to how often Oberg's theory of culture shock has been cited in published research. You might even make a timeline, or another visual representation, of what you find. As you look at the research, identify any evidence or indicators that the theory has been updated or altered since its first appearance. In what ways has the theory been refined? ❱

RESEARCH QUESTIONS AND HYPOTHESES

As we've noted throughout this book, research questions are typically formulated on the basis of observations. In the social sciences, such observations focus on human behavior, human systems, and/or the interactions between the two. Observations of a social phenomenon can give rise to questions about how a phenomenon operates or what effects it has on people or, as Rathunde suggests, how it could be changed to improve individuals' well-being. For example, in their social science study, "'Under the Radar': Educators and Cyberbullying in Schools," W. Cassidy, K. Brown, and M. Jackson (2012) offer the following as guiding research questions for their investigation:

> Our study of educators focused on three research questions: Do they [educators] consider cyberbullying a problem at their school and how familiar are they with the extent and impact among their students? What policies and practices are in place to prevent or counter cyberbullying? What solutions do they have for encouraging a kinder online world? (p. 522)

Research that is designed to inform a theory of human behavior or to provide data that contributes to a fuller understanding of some social or political structure (i.e., to answer a social science research question) also often begins with the presentation of a *hypothesis*. As we saw in Chapter 3, a hypothesis is a testable proposition that provides an answer or predicts an outcome in response to the research question(s) at hand. It's important to note that not all social science reports include a statement of hypothesis. Some social science research establishes its focus by presenting the questions that guide researchers' inquiry into a particular phenomenon instead of establishing a hypothesis. C. Kern and K. Ko (2010) present the following hypothesis, or predicted outcome, for their social science study, "Exploring Happiness and Performance at Work." The researchers make a prediction concerning what they believed their research would show before presenting their findings later in their research report:

> The intent of this analysis was to review how happiness and performance related to each other in this workplace. It is the authors' belief that for performance to be sustained in an organization, individuals and groups within that organization need to experience a threshold level of happiness. It is difficult for unhappy individuals and work groups to continue performing at high levels without appropriate leadership intervention. (p. 5)

Hypotheses differ from *thesis statements*, which are more commonly associated with arguments in the humanities. While thesis statements offer researchers' final conclusions on a topic or issue, hypothesis statements offer a predicted outcome. The proposition expressed in a hypothesis may be either accepted or rejected based on the results of the research. For example, an educational researcher might hypothesize that teachers' use of open-ended questioning increases students' level of participation in class. However, the researcher wouldn't be able to confirm or reject such a hypothesis until the end of his or her research report.

INSIDE WORK) **Developing Hypotheses**

1. For five minutes, brainstorm *social science* topics or issues that have affected your life. One approach is to consider issues that are causing you stress in your life right now. Examples might include peer pressure, academic performance, substance abuse, dating, or a relative's cancer treatment.

2. Once you have a list of topics, focus in on two or three that you believe have had the greatest impact on you personally. Next, generate a list of possible *research questions* concerning the topics that, if answered, would offer you a greater understanding of them. Examples: *What triggers most people to try their first drink of alcohol? What types of therapies are most effective for working with children on the autism spectrum? What kinds of technology actually aid in student learning?*

3. When you've reached the stage of proposing a possible answer to one or more of your questions, then you're ready to state a hypothesis. Try proposing a *hypothesis*, or testable proposition, as an answer to one of the research questions you've posed. For example, if your research question is *What triggers most people to try their first drink of alcohol?* then your hypothesis might be *Peer pressure generally causes most people to try their first drink of alcohol, especially for those who try their first drink before reaching the legal drinking age.* ◗

METHODS

Research in the diverse fields of the social sciences is, as you probably suspect, quite varied, and social scientists collect data to answer their research questions or test their hypotheses in several different ways. Their choice of methods is directly influenced by the kinds of questions they ask in any particular instance, as well as by their own disciplinary backgrounds. In his Insider's View on page 161, Kevin Rathunde highlights the connection between the kinds of research questions a social scientist asks and the particular methods the researcher uses to answer those questions.

We can group most of the research you're likely to encounter in the fields of the social sciences into three possible types: quantitative, qualitative, and mixed methods. Researchers make choices about which types of methods they'll employ in any given situation based on the nature of their line of inquiry. A particular research question may very well dictate the methods used to answer that question. If you wanted to determine the number of homeless veterans in a specific city, for instance, then collecting numerical, or quantitative, data would likely suffice to answer that question. However, if you wanted to know what factors affect the rates of homelessness among veterans in your community, then you would need to do more than tally the number of homeless veterans. You'd need to collect a different type of data to help construct an answer—perhaps responses to surveys or interview questions.

Quantitative Methods

Quantitative studies include those that rely on collecting numerical data and performing statistical analyses to reveal findings in research. Basic statistical data, like those provided by *means* (averages), *modes* (most often occurring value), and *medians* (middle values), are fundamental to quantitative social science research. More sophisticated statistical procedures commonly used in professional quantitative studies include correlations, chi-square tests, analysis of variance (ANOVA), and multivariate analysis of variance (MANOVA), as well as regression model testing, just to name a few. Not all statistical procedures are appropriate in all situations, however, so researchers must carefully select procedures based on the nature of their data and the kinds of findings

they seek. Researchers who engage in advanced statistical procedures as part of their methods are typically highly skilled in such procedures. At the very least, these researchers consult or work in cooperation with statisticians to design their studies and/or to analyze their data.

You may find, in fact, that a team of researchers collaborating on a social science project often includes individuals who are also experienced statisticians. Obviously, we don't expect you to be familiar with the details of statistical procedures, but it's important that you be able to notice when researchers rely on statistical methods to test their hypotheses and to inform their results.

Also, you should take note of how researchers incorporate discussion of such methods into their writing. In the following example, we've highlighted a few elements in the reporting that you'll want to notice when reading social science studies that make use of statistical procedures:

- **Procedure**   What statistical procedures are used?
- **Variables**   What variables are examined in the procedures?
- **Results**   What do the statistical procedures reveal?
- **Participants**   From whom are the data collected, and how are those individuals chosen?

In their study, "Middle School Students' Motivation and Quality of Experience: A Comparison of Montessori and Traditional School Environments,"

Rathunde and Csikszentmihalyi report on the statistical procedures they used to examine different types of schools:

The first analysis compared the main motivation and quality-of-experience variables across school type (Montessori vs. traditional) and grade level (sixth vs. eighth) using a two-way MANCOVA with parental education, gender, and ethnic background as covariates. Significant differences were found for school context (Wilks's lambda = .84, $F(5, 275) = 10.84$, $p < .001$), indicating that students in the two school contexts reported differences in motivation and quality of experience. After adjusting for the covariates, the multivariate eta squared indicated that 17 percent of the variance of the dependent variables was associated with the school context factor. The omnibus test for grade level was not significant (Wilks's lambda = .99, $F(5, 275) = .68$, $p = .64$), indicating that students in sixth and eighth grade reported similar motivation and quality of experience. Finally, the omnibus test for the interaction of school context x grade level was not significant (Wilks's lambda = .97, $F(5, 275) = 2.02$, $p = .08$). None of the multivariate tests for the covariates—parental education, gender, and ethnic background—reached the .05 level. (p. 357)

In the left margin, aligned with the quoted passage above:

> Variables examined, participants or populations involved in the study, and statistical procedure employed—MANCOVA, or a multivariate analysis of covariance—are identified.

> Results of the statistical procedure are identified.

Qualitative Methods

Qualitative studies generally rely on language, observation, and reporting of individual human experiences to reveal findings in research. Research reports often communicate these methods through the form of a study's results, which rely on in-depth narrative reporting. Methods for collecting data in qualitative studies include interviews, document analysis, surveys, and observations.

We can see examples of these methods put into practice in Barbara Allen's "Environmental Justice, Local Knowledge, and After-Disaster Planning in New Orleans" (2007), published in the academic social science journal *Technology and Society*. In this example, we've highlighted a few elements in the reporting that you'll want to notice when reading qualitative research methods:

- **Method** What method of data collection is used?
- **Data** What data is gathered from that method?
- **Results** What are the results? What explanation do the researchers provide for the data, or what meaning do they find in the data?
- **Participants** From whom is the data collected, and how are these individuals chosen?

In the left margin, aligned with the passage below:

> Participants

> Data-collection method: interview

> Data, followed by explanation or meaning of data

Six months after the hurricane I contacted public health officials and researchers, many of whom were reluctant to talk. One who did talk asked that I did not use her name, but she made some interesting observations. According to my informant, health officials were in a difficult position. Half a year after the devastation, only 25% of the city's residents had returned; a year after the storm, that number rose to about 40%. Negative publicity regarding public health issues would deter such repatriation, particularly families with children who had not returned in any large numbers to the city. The informant also told me to pursue the state public health websites where the most prominent worries were still smoking and obesity, not Hurricane Katrina. While the information on various public health websites did eventually reflect concerns about mold, mildew, and other contamination, it was never presented as the health threat that independent environmental scientists, such as Wilma Subra, thought it was. (pp. 154–55)

— Data

. . .

About five months after Hurricane Katrina, I received an e-mail from a high school student living in a rural parish west of New Orleans along the Mississippi River (an area EJ advocates have renamed Cancer Alley). After Hurricane Katrina, an old landfill near her house was opened to receive waste and began emitting noxious odors. She took samples of the "black ooze" from the site and contacted the Louisiana Department of Environmental Quality, only to be told that the landfill was accepting only construction waste, and the smell she described was probably decaying gypsum board. I suspect her story will be repeated many times across south Louisiana as these marginal waste sites receive the debris from homes and businesses ruined by the hurricane. The full environmental impact of Hurricane Katrina's waste and its hastily designated removal sites will not be known for many years. (p. 155)

— Participant

— Explanation or meaning of data

Mixed Methods

Studies that make use of both qualitative and quantitative data-collection techniques are generally referred to as **mixed-methodology studies**. Rathunde and Csikszentmihalyi's study, "Middle School Students' Motivation and Quality of Experience: A Comparison of Montessori and Traditional School Environments," used mixed methods: the authors report findings from both qualitative and quantitative data. In this excerpt, they share results from qualitative data they collected as they sought to distinguish among the types of educational settings selected for participation in their study:

> After verifying that the demographic profile of the two sets of schools was similar, the next step was to determine if the schools differed with respect to the five selection criteria outlined above. We used a variety of qualitative sources to verify contextual differences, including observations by the research staff; teacher and parent interviews; school newsletters, information packets, mission statements, and parent teacher handbooks; summaries from board of education and school council meetings; and a review of class schedules and textbook choices discussed in strategic plans. These sources also provided information about the level of middle grade reform that may or may not have been implemented by the schools and whether the label "traditional" was appropriate. (p. 64)

However, Rathunde and Csikszentmihalyi's central hypothesis, "that students in Montessori middle schools would report more positive perceptions of their school environment and their teachers, more often perceive their class-mates as friends, and spend more time in collaborative and/or individual work rather than didactic educational formats such as listening to a lecture" (p. 68), was tested by using quantitative methods:

> The main analyses used two-way multivariate analysis of covariance (MANCOVA) with school type (Montessori vs. traditional) and grade level (sixth vs. eighth) as the two factors. Gender, ethnicity, and parental education were covariates in all of the analyses. Overall multivariate F tests (Wilks's lambda) were performed first on related sets of dependent variables. If an overall F test was significant, we performed univariate ANOVAs as follow-up tests to the MANCOVAs. If necessary, post hoc analyses were done using Bonferroni corrections to control for Type I errors. Only students with at least 15 ESM signals were included in the multivariate analyses, and follow-up ANOVAs used students who had valid scores on all of the dependent variables. (p. 68)

Addressing Bias

LaunchPadSolo

A political scientist weighs in on avoiding bias.

Because social scientists study people and organizations, their research is considered more valuable when conducted within a framework that minimizes the influence of personal or researcher bias on the study's outcome(s). When possible, social scientists strive for **objectivity** (in quantitative research) or **neutrality** (in qualitative research) in their research. This means that research-ers undertake all possible measures to reduce the influence of biases on their research. Bias is sometimes inevitable, however, so social science research places a high value on honesty and transparency in the reporting of data. Each of the methods outlined above requires social scientists to engage in rigorous procedures and checks (e.g., ensuring appropriate sample sizes and/or using multiple forms of qualitative data) to ensure that the influence of any biases is as limited as possible.

INSIDE WORK **Considering Research Methods**

In the previous activity, we asked you to consider possible hypotheses, or testable propositions, to the research questions you posed. Now choose one of your hypothesis statements, and consider the types of methods that might be appropriate for testing the hypothesis. Think about the kinds of data you'll generate from the different methods.

- Would quantitative, qualitative, or mixed research methods be the most appropriate for testing your hypothesis? Why?

- What specific methods would you use—statistical procedures, surveys, observations, interviews? Why?

- Who would you want to have participate in your research? From whom would you need to collect your data in order to answer your research question? ▶

THE IRB PROCESS AND USE OF HUMAN SUBJECTS

All research, whether student or faculty initiated and directed, must treat its subjects, or participants, with the greatest of care and consider the ethical implications of all its procedures. Although institutions establish their own systems and procedures for verifying the ethical treatment of subjects, most of these include an **institutional review board (IRB)**, or a committee of individuals whose job is to review research proposals in light of ethical concerns for subjects and applicable laws. Such proposals typically include specific forms of documentation that identify a study's purpose; rigorously detail the research procedures to be followed; evaluate potential risks and rewards of a study, especially for study participants; and ensure (whenever possible) that participants are fully informed about a study and the implications of their participation in it.

We encourage you to learn more about the IRB process at your own institution and, when appropriate, to consider your own research in light of the IRB policies and procedures established for your institution. Many schools maintain informational, educational, and interactive websites. You'll notice similarities in the mission statements of institutional review boards from a number of research-intensive universities:

> **Duke University:** To ensure the protection of human research subjects by conducting scientific and ethical review of research studies while providing leadership and education for the research community.
>
> **The George Washington University:** To support [the] research community in the conduct of innovative and ethical research by providing guidance, education, and oversight for the protection of human subjects.
>
> **University of New Mexico:** To promote the safety and protection of individuals involved in human research by providing support, guidance, and education to facilitate ethical and scientifically sound research.

Conventions of Writing in the Social Sciences

In light of the variety of research methods used by social scientists, it's not surprising that there are also a number of ways social scientists report their research findings. In this section, we highlight general conventional expectations of *structure*, *language*, and *reference* that social scientists follow to communicate their research to one another. Understanding these conventions, we believe, can help foster your understanding of this academic domain more broadly.

Aya Matsuda is a linguist and social science researcher at Arizona State University, where she studies the use of English as an international language, the integration of a "World Englishes" perspective into U.S. education, and the ways bilingual writers negotiate identity. In her Insider's View, Dr. Matsuda explains that she learned the conventions of writing as a social scientist, and more particularly as a linguist, "mostly through writing, getting feedback, and revising."

As Dr. Matsuda also suggests, reading can be an important part of understanding the writing of a discipline. Furthermore, reading academic writing

with a particular focus on the rhetorical elements used is a powerful way to acquire insight into the academic discipline itself, as well as a way to learn the literacy practices that professional writers commonly follow in whatever academic domain you happen to be studying.

STRUCTURAL CONVENTIONS AND IMRAD FORMAT

Structural conventions within the fields of the social sciences can vary quite dramatically, but the structure of a social science report should follow logically from the type of study conducted or the methodological framework (quantitative, qualitative, or mixed-methods) it employs. The more quantitative a study is, the more likely its reporting will reflect the conventions for scientific research, using IMRAD format. Qualitative studies, though, sometimes appear in other organizational forms that reflect the particular qualitative methods used in the study. But just as numerous fields within the social sciences rely on quantitative research methods, so too do many social scientists report their results according to the conventional form for scientific inquiry: *IMRAD (Introduction, Methods, Results, and Discussion) format.*

Introduction

The introduction of a social science report establishes the context for a study, providing appropriate background on the issue or topic under scrutiny. The introduction is also where you're likely to find evidence of researchers' review of previous scholarship on a topic. As part of these reviews, researchers typically report what's already known about a phenomenon or what's relevant in the current scholarship for their own research. They may also situate their research goals within some gap in the scholarship—that is, they explain how their research contributes to the growing body of scholarship on the phenomenon under investigation. If a theoretical perspective drives a study, as often occurs in more qualitative studies, then the introduction may also contain an explanation of the central tenets or the parameters of the researchers' theoretical lens. Regardless, an introduction in the social sciences generally builds to a statement of specific purpose for the study. This may take the form of a hypothesis or thesis, or it may appear explicitly as a general statement of the researchers' purpose, perhaps including a presentation of research questions. The introduction to Rathunde and Csikszentmihalyi's study provides an example:

> The difficulties that many young adolescents encounter in middle school have been well documented (Carnegie Council on Adolescent Development 1989, 1995; Eccles et al. 1993; U.S. Department of Education 1991). During this precarious transition from the elementary school years, young adolescents may begin to doubt the value of their academic work and their abilities to succeed (Simmons and Blyth 1987; Wigfield et al. 1991). A central concern of many studies is motivation (Anderman and Maehr 1994); a disturbingly consistent finding associated with middle school is a drop in students' intrinsic motivation to learn (Anderman et al. 1999; Gottfried 1985; Harter et al. 1992).
>
> Such downward trends in motivation are not inevitable. Over the past decade, several researchers have concluded that the typical learning environment in middle school is often mismatched with adolescents' developmental needs (Eccles et al. 1993). Several large-scale research programs have focused on the qualities of classrooms and school cultures that may enhance student achievement and motivation (Ames 1992; Lipsitz et al. 1997; Maehr and Midgley 1991). School environments that provide a more appropriate developmental fit (e.g., more relevant tasks, student-directed learning, less of an emphasis on grades and competition, more collaboration, etc.) have been shown to enhance students' intrinsic, task motivation (Anderman et al. 1999).
>
> The present study explores the issues of developmental fit and young adolescents' quality of experience and motivation by comparing five Montessori middle schools to six "traditional" public middle schools. Although the Montessori educational philosophy is primarily associated with early childhood education, a number of schools have extended its core principles to early adolescent education. These principles are in general agreement with the reform proposals associated with various motivation theories (Anderman et al. 1999; Maehr and Midgley 1991), developmental fit theories (Eccles et al. 1993), as well as insights from various recommendations for middle school reform (e.g., the Carnegie Foundation's "Turning Points" recommendations; see Lipsitz et al. 1997). In addition, the Montessori philosophy is consistent with the theoretical and practical implications of optimal experience (flow) theory (Csikszentmihalyi and Rathunde 1998). The present study places a special emphasis on students' quality of experience in middle school. More specifically, it uses the Experience Sampling Method (ESM) (Csikszentmihalyi and Larson 1987) to compare the school experiences of Montessori middle school students with a comparable sample of public school students in traditional classrooms. (pp. 341–42)

Provides an introduction to the topic at hand: the problem of motivation for adolescents in middle school. The problem is situated in the scholarship of others.

Reviews relevant scholarship: the researchers review previous studies that have bearing on their own aims—addressing the decline in motivation among students.

Identifies researchers' particular areas of interest

Although the introductory elements of Rathunde and Csikszentmihalyi's study actually continue for a number of pages, these opening paragraphs reveal common rhetorical moves in social science research reporting: establishing a topic of interest, reviewing the scholarship on that topic, and connecting the current study to the ongoing scholarly conversation on the topic.

Methods

Social science researchers are very particular about the precise reporting of their methods of research. No matter what the type of study (quantitative, qualitative, or mixed-methods), researchers are very careful not only to identify the methods used in their research but also to explain why they chose certain ones, in light of the goals of their study. Because researchers want to reduce the influence of researcher bias and to provide enough context so others might replicate or confirm their findings, social scientists make sure that their reports thoroughly explain the kinds of data they have collected and the precise procedures they used to collect that data (interviews, document analysis, surveys, etc.). Also, there is often much discussion of the ways the data were interpreted or analyzed (using case studies, narrative analysis, statistical procedures, etc.).

An excerpt from W. Cassidy, K. Brown, and M. Jackson's study on educators and cyberbullying provides an example of the level of detail at which scholars typically report their methods:

Provides highly specific details about data-collection methods, and emphasizes researchers' neutral stance

Each participant chose a pseudonym and was asked a series of 16 in-depth, semi-structured, open-ended questions (Lancy, 2001) and three closed-category questions in a private setting, allowing their views to be voiced in confidence (Cook-Sather, 2002). Each 45- to 60-minute audiotaped interview was conducted by one of the authors, while maintaining a neutral, nonjudgmental stance in regards to the responses (Merriam, 1988).

Provides detailed explanation of procedures used to support the reliability of the study's findings

Once the interviews were transcribed, each participant was given the opportunity to review the transcript and make changes. The transcripts were then reviewed and re-reviewed in a backward and forward motion (Glaser & Strauss, 1967; McMillan & Schumacher, 1997) separately by two of the three researchers to determine commonalities and differences among responses as well as any salient themes that surfaced due to the frequency or the strength of the response (Miles & Huberman, 1994). Each researcher's analysis was then compared with the other's to jointly determine emergent themes and perceptions.

Connects the research to the development of theory

The dominant themes were then reviewed in relation to the existing literature on educators' perceptions and responses to cyberbullying. The approach taken was "bottom-up," to inductively uncover themes and contribute to theory, rather than apply existing theory as a predetermined frame for analysis (Miles & Huberman, 1994). (p. 523)

You'll notice that the researchers do not simply indicate that the data were collected via interviews. Rather, they go to some lengths to describe the kinds of interviews they conducted and how they were conducted, as well as how those interviews were analyzed. This level of detail supports the writers' ethos, and it further highlights their commitment to reducing bias in their research. Similar studies might also report the interview questions at the end of the report in an appendix. Seeing the actual questions helps readers interpret the results on their own and also provides enough detail for readers to replicate the study or test the hypothesis with a different population, should they desire to do so. Readers of the study need to understand as precisely as possible the methods for data collection and analysis.

Results

There can be much variety in the ways social science reports present the results, or findings, of a study. You may encounter a section identified by the title "Results," especially if the study follows IMRAD format, but you may not find that heading at all. Instead, researchers often present their results by using headings and subheadings that reflect their actual findings. As examples, we provide here excerpts from two studies: (1) Rathunde and Csikszentmihalyi's 2005 study on middle school student motivation, and (2) Cassidy, Brown, and Jackson's 2012 study on educators and cyberbullying.

In the Results section of their report, Rathunde and Csikszentmihalyi provide findings from their study under the subheading "Motivation and Quality-of-Experience Differences: Nonacademic Activities at School." Those results read in part:

> Follow-up ANCOVAs were done on each of the five ESM variables. Table 3 summarizes the means, standard errors, and significance levels for each of the variables.

Table 3

Univariate F-Tests for Quality of Experience in Nonacademic Activities at School by School Context

| ESM Measure | School Context | | F-test | p |
	Montessori ($N = 131$)	Traditional ($N = 150$)		
Flow (%)	11.0 (1.7)	17.3 (1.6)	7.19	.008
Affect	.32 (.05)	.14 (.05)	6.87	.009
Potency	.22 (.05)	.16 (.05)	1.90	NS
Motivation	−.03 (.05)	−.12 (.05)	1.70	NS
Salience	−.38 (.04)	−.19 (.04)	11.14	.001

Means are z-scores (i.e., zero is average experience for the entire week) and are adjusted for the covariates gender, parental education, and ethnicity. Standard errors appear in parentheses. Flow percent indicates the amount of time students indicated above-average challenge and skill while doing nonacademic activities.

Consistent with the relaxed nature of the activities, students in both school contexts reported higher levels of affect, potency, and intrinsic motivation in nonacademic activities, as well as lower levels of salience and flow (see table 2). In contrast to the findings for academic work, students in both groups reported similar levels of intrinsic motivation and potency. In addition, students in the traditional group reported significantly more flow in nonacademic activities, although the overall percentage of flow was low.

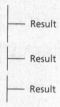
— Result

— Result

— Result

Result

Similar to the findings for academic activities, the Montessori students reported better overall affect, and despite the fact that levels of salience were below average for both student groups, the traditional students reported that their activities were more important. (pp. 360–61)

You'll notice that in this section, the researchers remain focused on reporting their findings. They do not, at this point, go into great detail about what those findings mean or what the implications are.

Cassidy, Brown, and Jackson also report their findings in a Results section, and they subdivide their findings into a number of areas of inquiry (identified in the subheadings) examined as part of their larger study. Only the results are presented at this point in the article; they are not yet interpreted:

RESULTS

Familiarity with technology

Results

Despite the district's emphasis on technology, the educators (except for two younger teachers and one vice-principal) indicated that they were not very familiar with chat rooms and blogs, were moderately familiar with YouTube and Facebook and were most familiar with the older forms of communication—email and cellular phones.

Cyberbullying policies

Result

We asked respondents about specific cyberbullying policies in place at their school and their perceived effectiveness. Despite the district's priorities around technology, neither the school district nor either school had a specific cyberbullying policy; instead educators were supposed to follow the district's bullying policy. When VP17-A was asked if the district's bullying handbook effectively addressed the problem of cyberbullying, he replied: "It effectively addresses the people that are identified as bullying others [but] it doesn't address the educational side of it . . . about what is proper use of the Internet as a tool."

P14-B wanted to see a new policy put in place that was flexible enough to deal with the different situations as they arose. VP19-B thought that a cyberbullying policy should be separate from a face-to-face bullying policy since the impact on students is different. He also felt that there should be a concerted district policy regarding "risk assessment in which you have a team that's trained at determining the level of threat and it should be taken very seriously whether it's a phone threat, a verbal threat, or a cyber threat." Participants indicated that they had not considered the idea of a separate cyberbullying policy before the interview, with several commenting that they now saw it as important. (pp. 524, 526–27)

Result

Visual Representations of Data   The Results section of a report may also provide data sets in the form of charts and/or figures. Figures may appear as photos, images, charts, or graphs. When you find visual representations of data in texts, it's important that you pause to consider these elements carefully. Researchers typically use *tables* when they want to make data sets, or

Table 1

Comparison of Montessori and Traditional Middle School Samples on Various Background Variables

Background Variable	School Context	
	Montessori	Traditional
Ethnicity (%):		
European American	72.6	74.9
Asian American	10.2	7.8
Latino	1.9	3.4
African American	12.7	12.6
Other	2.6	1.2
Parental education	5.5	5.4
Home resources	29.6	29.5
School-related:		
Parental discussion	2.41	2.49
Parental involvement	2.11	2.10
Parental monitoring	1.69	1.66
Number of siblings	1.8	2.0
Mother employment (%)	71.6	74.1
Father employment (%)	83.7	88.1
Intact (two-parent) family (%)	81.0	84.0
Grade point average	1.97	1.93

Note. None of the differences reported in the table was statistically significant.

raw data, available for comparisons. These tables, such as the one Rathunde and Csikszentmihalyi include in "Middle School Students' Motivation and Quality of Experience: A Comparison of Montessori and Traditional School Environments," present variables in columns and rows, as seen above.

In this instance, the "background variable[s]" used to describe the student populations are listed in the column, and the rows identify two "school context[s]," Montessori and Traditional schools, for comparison. The table's title reveals its overall purpose: to compare "Montessori and Traditional Middle School Samples on Various Background Variables." Rathunde and Csikszentmihalyi describe the contents of their table this way:

> Table 1 summarizes this comparison. The ethnic diversity of the samples was almost identical. Both shared similar advantages in terms of high parental education (baccalaureate degree or higher), high rates of two-parent families,

When this occurs, these researchers typically construct a separate Conclusion section in which they address conventional content coverage of their study's limitations, as well as their findings' implications for future research.

Following are some additional structural conventions to consider when you are reading or writing in the fields of the social sciences.

OTHER STRUCTURAL CONVENTIONS

Titles

Research reports in the social sciences, as in the natural sciences, tend to have rather straightforward titles that are concise and that contain key words highlighting important components of the study. Titles in the social sciences tend not to be creative or rhetorical, although there is a greater tendency toward creativity in titles in qualitative studies, which are more typically language driven than numerically driven. The title of Barbara Allen's study reported in the academic journal *Technology in Society*, for instance, identifies the central issues her study examined as well as the study location: "Environmental Justice, Local Knowledge, and After-Disaster Planning in New Orleans." Similarly, the title of Rathunde and Csikszentmihalyi's article is concise in its identification of the study's purpose: "Middle School Students' Motivation and Quality of Experience: A Comparison of Montessori and Traditional School Environments."

Abstracts

Another structural feature of reports in the social sciences is the abstract. **Abstracts** typically follow the title of the report and the identification of the researchers. They provide a brief overview of the study, explaining the topic or issue under study, the specific purpose of the study and its methods, and offering a concise statement of the results. These elements are usually summarized in a few sentences. Abstracts can be useful to other researchers who want to determine if a study might prove useful for their own work or if the methods might inform their own research purposes. Abstracts thus serve to promote collaboration among researchers. Though abstracts appear at the beginning of research reports, they're typically written after both the study and the research report are otherwise completed. Abstracts reduce the most important parts of a study into a compact space.

The following example from Rathunde and Csikszentmihalyi illustrates a number of the conventions of abstracts:

The study's purpose is identified.

Methods are briefly outlined.

This study compared the motivation and quality of experience of demographically matched students from Montessori and traditional middle school programs. Approximately 290 students responded to the Experience Sampling Method (ESM) and filled out questionnaires. Multivariate analyses showed that the Montessori students reported greater affect, potency (i.e., feeling energetic), intrinsic motivation, flow experience, and undivided interest (i.e., the combination of high intrinsic motivation and high salience or importance) while engaged in academic activities at school. The traditional middle school students reported higher salience while doing academic work; however, such responses were often accompanied by low intrinsic motivation. When engaged in informal, nonacademic activities, the students in both school contexts reported similar experiences. These results are discussed in terms of current thought on motivation in education and middle school reform.

Results are provided.

Implications of the research findings are noted.

Acknowledgments

Acknowledgment sections sometimes appear at the end of social science reports. Usually very brief, they offer a quick word of thanks to organizations and/or individuals who have helped to fund a study, collect data, review the study, or provide another form of assistance during the production of the study. This section can be particularly telling if you're interested in the source of a researcher's funding. Barbara Allen's "Environmental Justice, Local Knowledge, and After-Disaster Planning in New Orleans" contains the following Acknowledgments section:

ACKNOWLEDGMENTS

I would like to thank Carl Mitcham, Robert Frodeman, and all the participants of the Cities and Rivers II conference in New Orleans, March 21–25, 2006. The ideas and discussions at this event enabled me to think in a more interdisciplinary manner about the disaster and its impact as well as about my own assumptions regarding environmental justice and citizen participation in science.

    In addition, I would like to thank the American Academy in Rome for giving me the time to think and write about this important topic. Conversations with my colleagues at the academy were invaluable in helping me to think in new ways about historic preservation and rebuilding. (p. 159)

References

The documentation system most often used in the social sciences is the style regulated by the American Psychological Association, which is referred to as **APA format**. (For more details about APA style conventions, see p. 77 of Chapter 4 and the Appendix.) Studies in the social sciences end with a References page that follows APA guidelines—or the formatting style used in the study, if not APA.

Appendices

Social science research reports sometimes end with one or more appendices. Items here are often referenced within the body of the report itself, as appropriate. These items may include additional data sets, calculations, interview questions, diagrams, and images. The materials typically offer context or support for discussions that occur in the body of a research report.

INSIDE WORK   **Observing Structural Conventions**

Although we've discussed a number of structural expectations for reports in the social sciences, we need to stress again that these expectations are conventional. As such, you'll likely encounter numerous studies in the social sciences that rely on only a few of these structural features or that alter the conventional expectations in light of the researchers' particular aims. For this activity, we'd like you to do the following.

- Select a social science topic.

- Locate two articles published in peer-reviewed academic journals that address some aspect of your selected topic.

- Compare and contrast the two articles in terms of their structural features. Note both (1) instances when the articles follow the conventional expectations for social science reporting as explained in this chapter, and (2) instances when the articles alter or diverge from these expectations. Speculate as to the authors' reasoning for following the conventional expectations or diverging from them. ▶

LANGUAGE CONVENTIONS

As with structural conventions, the way social scientists use language can vary widely with respect to differing audiences and/or genres. Nevertheless, we can explore several language-level conventional expectations for writing in the social sciences. In the following sections, we consider the use of both active and passive voice, as well as the use of hedging (or hedge words) to limit the scope and applicability of assertions.

Active and Passive Voice

Many students have had the experience of receiving a graded paper back from an English teacher in high school and discovering that a sentence or two was marked for awkward or inappropriate use of the passive voice. This problem occurs fairly often as students acclimate their writing to differing disciplinary communities. As we discussed in Chapter 6, the passive voice usually appears with less frequency in the fields of the humanities, while writers in the social sciences and natural sciences use it more frequently, and with good purpose. (For a fuller discussion and examples of the differences between active and passive voice constructions, see pp. 136–37 in Chapter 6.)

You may wonder why anyone would want to add words unnecessarily or remove altogether the actor/agent from a sentence. The passive voice is often preferable in writing in the social sciences and natural sciences because, although it may seem wordy or unclear to some readers in some instances, skillful use of the passive voice can actually foster a sense that researchers are acting objectively or with neutrality. This does not mean that natural or social scientists are averse to the active voice. However, in particular instances, the passive voice can go a long way toward supporting an ethos of objectivity, and its use appears most commonly in the Methods sections of social science reports. Consider these two sentences that might appear in the Methods section of a hypothetical social science report:

Active Voice: We asked participants to identify the factors that most influenced their decision.

Passive Voice: Participants were asked to identify the factors that most influenced their decision.

With the agent, *we*, removed, the sentence in passive voice deemphasizes the researchers conducting the study. In this way, the researchers maintain more of a sense of objectivity or neutrality in their report.

Hedging

Another language feature common to writing in the social sciences is hedging. Hedging typically occurs when researchers want to make a claim or propose an explanation but also want to be extremely careful not to overstep the scope of their findings based on their actual data set. Consider the following sentences:

Participants seemed to be anxious about sharing their feelings on the topic.

Participants were anxious about sharing their feelings on the topic.

When you compare the two, you'll notice that the first sentence "hedges" against making a broad or sweeping claim about the participants. The use of *seemed to be* is a hedge against overstepping, or saying something that may or may not be absolutely true in every case. Other words or phrases that are often used to hedge include the following, just to name a handful:

probably	perhaps
some	possibly
sometimes	might
likely	it appears that
apparently	partially

Considering that social scientists make claims about human behavior, and that participants in a study may or may not agree with the conclusions, it's perhaps not surprising that writers in these fields often make use of hedging.

Observing Language Features

Use the two articles you located for the previous Inside Work exercise, in which you compared and contrasted their structural conventions.

- This time, study the language of the articles for instances of the two language conventions we've discussed in this section. Try to determine in what sections of the reports passive voice and hedging occur most frequently.

- Offer a rationale for your findings. If you find more instances of the use of passive voice in the Methods sections than in the Results sections, for instance, attempt to explain why that would be the case. Or, if you find more instances of verbal hedging in the Results sections than in the Methods sections, what do you think explains those findings? ▶

REFERENCE CONVENTIONS

The style guide for writing followed in most (but not all) social science fields is the *Publication Manual of the American Psychological Association* (APA). Many referencing conventions of the social sciences are governed by the APA, and some are worth examining in more detail.

In-Text Documentation

One of the distinguishing features of the APA method for documenting sources that are paraphrased, summarized, or cited as part of a report is the inclusion of a source's year of publication as part of the parenthetical notation in or at the end of a sentence in which a source is used. We can compare this to the MLA documentation system described in Chapter 6 through the following examples:

MLA: The study reports that "in some participants, writing block appears to be tied to exhaustion" (Jacobs 23).

APA: The study reports that "in some participants, writing block appears to be tied to exhaustion" (Jacobs, 2009, p. 23).

Although these examples by no means illustrate all the differences between MLA and APA styles of documentation, they do highlight the elevated importance that social sciences fields place on the year of a source's publication. Why? Imagine that you're reading a sociological study conducted in 2010 that examines the use of tobacco products among teenagers. The study references the finding of a similar study from 1990. By seeing the date of the referenced study in the in-text citation, readers can quickly consider the usefulness of the 1990 study for the one being reported on. Social scientists value recency, or the most current data possible, and their documentation requirements reflect this preference.

Summary and Paraphrase

Another reference distinction among the academic domains concerns how writers reference others' ideas. You've probably had experience writing papers for teachers who required you to cite sources as support for your ideas. You may have done this by copying the language directly from a source. If so, then you noted that these words belonged to another person by putting quotation marks around them and by adding a parenthetical comment identifying the source of the cited language. These practices hold true for writers in the social sciences as well.

However, as you become more familiar with the reference practices of researchers in these fields, you'll discover that social scientists quote researchers in other fields far less frequently than scholars in the humanities do. Why is this so? For humanist scholars, language is of the utmost importance, and how someone conveys an idea can seem almost inseparable from the idea being conveyed. Additionally, for humanists, language is often the "unit of measure"—that is, *how* someone says something (like a novelist or a poet) is actually *what* is being studied. Typically, this is not the case for social science researchers (with the exception of fields such as linguistics and communication, although they primarily address how study participants say something and not how prior research reported its findings). Instead, social scientists tend to be much more interested in other researchers' methodology and findings than they are in the language through which those methods or finding are conveyed. As a result, social scientists are more likely to summarize or paraphrase source materials than to quote them directly.

INSIDE WORK **Observing Reference Features**

In this section, we've suggested that two areas of conventional reference features in social science writing are (1) the elevated position of year of publication in the internal documentation of source material, and (2) the preference among social scientists for summarizing and paraphrasing sources.

- Use the same two studies that you examined for the last two Inside Work activities.

- Based on the principle that social scientists are concerned with the recency of research in their areas, examine the References page (the ending bibliography) for each study. How does the form of entries on the References page reflect the social science concern with the recency of sources?

- Look more closely at the introductions of the two articles, and note the number of times in each article another source is referenced. Count the number of times these sources are paraphrased, summarized, or quoted directly. Based on your findings, what can you conclude about the ways social scientists reference source material? ❭

Genres of Writing in the Social Sciences

Scholars in the social sciences share the results of their research in various ways. As Dr. Matsuda reveals in her Insider's View, social scientists write in a variety of forms for differing venues. They might, for instance, present their work at a conference or publish their research results in a journal or a book.

In this section, we offer descriptions of, and steps for producing, two of the most common types of writing, or genres, required of students in introductory-level courses in the social sciences. These are the literature review and the theory-response paper. As genres, literature reviews and responses to social science theories sometimes appear as parts of other, longer works. Sometimes, though, they stand alone as complete works.

THE LITERATURE REVIEW

The literature review (also referred to as a review of scholarship) is one of the most common genres you will encounter in academic writing. Though this chapter is dedicated to writing in the social sciences, and the literature review genre occurs quite frequently in the social sciences, you can find evidence of reviews of scholarship in virtually every academic field—including the humanities, the natural sciences, and applied fields. The skills required for this genre are thus important to the kinds of inquiry that occur across all the academic disciplines.

At its core, the **literature review** is an analysis of published resources related to a specific topic. The purposes of a literature review may vary: students and researchers may conduct a review of scholarship simply to establish what research has already been conducted on a topic, or the review may make a case for how new research can fill in gaps or advance knowledge about a topic. In the former situation, the resulting literature review may appear as a freestanding piece of writing; in the latter, a briefer review of scholarship may be embedded at the start (usually in the introduction) of a research study.

In fact, most published scholarly articles include a review of literature in the first few pages. Besides serving as a means to identify a gap in the scholarship or a place for new scholarship, a literature review helps to establish researchers' credibility by demonstrating their awareness of what has been discovered about a particular topic or issue. It further respectfully acknowledges the hard work of others within the community of scholarship. Equally as important, the literature review illustrates how previous studies interrelate. A good literature review may examine how prior research is similar and different, or it may suggest how a group of researchers' work developed over several years and how scholars have advanced the work of others.

Insider Example
An Embedded Literature Review

Read the first two paragraphs to "Happiness in Everyday Life: The Uses of Experience Sampling," a social science study reported by Mihaly Csikszentmihalyi and Jeremy Hunter, as an example of a review of scholarship that is embedded within a larger study report. As you read, consider the purposes of a literature review to which it responds, including:

- reviewing what is known on a topic or issue
- identifying a gap in scholarship
- establishing the researchers' ethos

Excerpt from **Happiness in Everyday Life: The Uses of Experience Sampling**

MIHALY CSIKSZENTMIHALYI AND JEREMY HUNTER

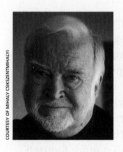

COURTESY OF MIHALY CSIKSZENTMIHALYI

COURTESY OF JEREMY HUNTER. PHOTO BY WILLIAM VASTA

INTRODUCTION

Current understanding of human happiness points at five major effects on this emotion. These are, moving from those most impervious to change to those that are most under personal control: genetic determinants, macro-social conditions, chance events, proximal environment, and personality. It is not unlikely that, as behavioral geneticists insist, a "set level" coded in our chromosomes accounts for perhaps as much as half of the variance in self-reported happiness (Lykken & Tellegen, 1996; Tellegen et al., 1988). These effects are probably mediated by temperamental traits like extraversion, which are partly genetically determined and which are in turn linked to happiness (Myers, 1993). Cross-national

This section of the study's introduction establishes what is known about the topic at hand. It reviews the scholarship of others.

comparisons suggest that macro-social conditions such as extreme poverty, war, and social injustice are all obstacles to happiness (Inglehart & Klingemann, 2000; Veenhoven, 1995). Chance events like personal tragedies, illness, or sudden strokes of good fortune may drastically affect the level of happiness, but apparently these effects do not last long (Brickman et al., 1978; Diener, 2000). One might include under the heading of the proximal environment the social class, community, family, and economic situation—in other words, those factors in the immediate surroundings that may have an impact on a person's well-being. And finally, habits and coping behaviors developed by the individual will have an important effect. Hope, optimism, and the ability to experience flow can be learned and thus moderate one's level of happiness (Csikszentmihalyi, 1997; Seligman, 2002).

> How does this review of previous scholarship affect your view of the writers? What does it say about them?
>
> Reveals the researchers' purpose in the context of the review of scholarship. Identifies a space, or gap, in the scholarship for investigation.

In this paper, we present a method that allows investigators to study the impact of momentary changes in the environment on people's happiness levels, as well as its more lasting, trait-like correlates. Research on happiness generally considers this emotion to be a personal trait. The overall happiness level of individuals is measured by a survey or questionnaire, and then "happy" people—those who score higher on a one-time response scale—are contrasted with less happy ones. Whatever distinguishes the two groups is then assumed to be a condition affecting happiness. This perspective is a logical outcome of the methods used, namely, one-time measures. If a person's happiness level is measured only once, it is by definition impossible to detect intra-individual variations. Yet, we know quite well that emotional states, including happiness, are quite volatile and responsive to environmental conditions.

WRITING A LITERATURE REVIEW

The scope of a freestanding literature review can vary greatly, depending on the knowledge and level of interest of the investigator conducting the review. For instance, you may have very little knowledge about autism, so your review of the scholarship might be aimed at learning about various aspects of the condition and issues related to it. If this is the case, your research would cast a pretty wide net. However, let's say you're quite familiar with certain critical aspects of issues related to autism and are interested in one aspect in particular—for example, the best therapies for addressing autism in young children. If this is the case, then you could conduct a review of scholarship with a more focused purpose, narrowing your net to only the studies that address your specific interest. Regardless of the scope of your research interest, though, literature reviews should begin with a clear sense of your topic. One way to narrow the focus of your topic is by proposing one or more research questions about it. (See Chapter 4 for more support for crafting such research questions.)

Once you've clearly established your topic, the next step is to conduct your research. The research you discover and choose to read, which may be quite substantial for a literature review, is chosen according to the scope of your research interest. (For help in narrowing a search based on key terms in your research question, see Chapter 4.) Here are some tips to conducting research:

- As you search for and review possible sources, pay particular attention to the *abstracts* of studies, as they may help you quickly decide if a study is right for your purposes.

- Unless your review of scholarship targets the tracing of a particular thread of research across a range of years, you should probably focus on the most current research available.

- After you've examined and gathered a range of source materials, determine the best way to keep track of the ideas you discover. Many students find this is a good time to produce an annotated bibliography as a first step in creating a literature review. (See Chapter 4, pp. 77–79, for more help on constructing annotated bibliographies.)

Another useful strategy for organizing your sources is a **source synthesis chart**. We recommend this as a way to visualize the areas of overlap in your research, whether for a broad focus (*What are researchers studying with regard to autism?*) or a more narrow one (*What are the best therapies for addressing autism in young children?*). Here's an abbreviated example of a source synthesis chart for a broad review of scholarship on autism:

| Authors of Study | Topics We Expect to Emerge in Scholarship | | | |
	Issues of Diagnosis	*Treatments*	*Debate over Causes*	*Wider Familial Effects*
Solomon et al. (2012)	pp. 252–55 Notes: emphasizes problems families face with diagnosis	pp. 257–60 Notes: examines and proposes strategies for family therapists	p. 253 Notes: acknowledges a series of possible contributing factors	
Vanderborght et al. (2012)		pp. 359–67 (results) Notes: examines use of robot for storytelling		
Grindle et al. (2012)		pp. 208–313 (results) Notes: school-based behavioral intervention program (ABA)		p. 229 Notes: home-based therapy programs
Lilley (2011)	pp. 135–37 Notes: explores the roles of mothers in diagnosis processes	pp. 143–51 Notes: explores rationales and lived experiences of ABA and non-ABA supporters		

In this case, the studies that we read are named in the column under "Authors of Study." The topics or issues that we anticipated would emerge from our review of the sources are shown in the top row. Based on our reading of a limited number of studies, four at this point, we can already discern a couple of areas of overlap in the scholarship: the diagnosis of autism in children, and intervention programs for children with autism. We can tell which researchers talked about what issues at any given time because we've noted the areas (by page number, along with some detail) where they addressed these issues. The empty cells in the synthesis chart reveal that our review of the sources, thus far at least, suggests there is less concern for those topics. We should note, however, that our review of sources is far from exhaustive. If you're able to create a visual representation of your research such as this one, then you're well on your way to creating a successful literature review. Keep in mind that the more detailed you can make your synthesis chart, the easier your process may be moving forward.

The last step before writing is perhaps the most challenging. You must synthesize the sources. **Synthesizing sources** is the process of identifying and describing the relationships between and among researchers' ideas or approaches: What trends emerge? Does the Grindle et al. study say something similar to the Lilley study about behavioral interventions? Something different? Do they share methods? Do they approach the issue of behavioral interventions similarly or differently? Defining the relationships between the studies and making these relationships explicit is critically important to your success. As you read the sources, you'll likely engage in an internal process of comparing and contrasting the researchers' ideas. You might even recognize similarities and differences in the researchers' approaches to the topic. Many of these ideas will probably be reflected in your synthesis chart, and you might consider color-coding (or highlighting in different colors) various cells to indicate types of relationships among the researchers you note.

A quick review of the abstract to "The Experience of Infertility: A Review of Recent Literature," a freestanding literature review published in the academic journal *Sociology of Health and Illness*, demonstrates the areas of synthesis that emerged from the professionals' examination of recent research on infertility:

Four synthesis points: (1) more recent studies approach the topic of infertility differently; (2) there remains a focus on examining infertility from a clinical viewpoint; (3) there are still questions about research methods, but there have also been "important improvements" in methods; (4) two trends emerged from these scholars' review of the current research.

> About 10 years ago Greil published a review and critique of the literature on the socio-psychological impact of infertility. He found at the time that most scholars treated infertility as a medical condition with psychological consequences rather than as a socially constructed reality. This article examines research published since the last review. More studies now place infertility within larger social contexts and social scientific frameworks, although clinical emphases persist. Methodological problems remain, but important improvements are also evident. We identify two vigorous research traditions in the social scientific study of infertility. One tradition uses primarily quantitative techniques to study clinic patients in order to improve service delivery and to

assess the need for psychological counseling. The other tradition uses primarily qualitative research to capture the experiences of infertile people in a sociocultural context. We conclude that more attention is now being paid to the ways in which the experience of infertility is shaped by social context. We call for continued progress in the development of a distinctly sociological approach to infertility and for the continued integration of the two research traditions identified here.

Presents conclusions reached as a result of the literature review project

Another example, this one a brief excerpt from the introduction to Csikszentmihalyi and Hunter's "Happiness in Everyday Life: The Uses of Experience Sampling," demonstrates the kind of synthesis that typically appears in reviews of scholarship when they're embedded as part of a larger study:

> Cross-national comparisons suggest that macro-social conditions such as extreme poverty, war, and social injustice are all obstacles to happiness (Inglehart & Klingemann, 2000; Veenhoven, 1995). Chance events like personal tragedies, illness, or sudden strokes of good fortune may drastically affect the level of happiness, but apparently these effects do not last long (Brickman et al., 1978; Diener, 2000).

The writers indicate that there is agreement between researchers: both Inglehart & Klingemann (2000) and Veenhoven (1995) have confirmed the finding in "cross-national comparisons."

Again, the writers indicate there is agreement between researchers: both Brickman et al. (1978) and Diener (2000) have confirmed this finding.

WRITING PROJECT Writing a Literature Review

Your goal in this writing project, a freestanding literature review, is to provide an overview of the research that has been conducted on a topic of interest to you.

THE INTRODUCTION
The opening of your literature review should introduce the topic you're exploring and assess the state of the available scholarship on it: What are the current areas of interest? What are the issues or elements related to a particular topic being discussed? Is there general agreement? Are there other clear trends in the scholarship? Are there areas of convergence and divergence?

THE BODY
Paragraphs within the body of your literature review should be organized according to the issues or synthesized areas you're exploring. For example, based on the synthesis chart shown earlier, we might suggest that one of the body sections of a broadly focused review of scholarship on autism concern issues of diagnosis. We might further reveal, in our topic sentence to that section of the literature review, that we've synthesized the available research in this area and that it seems uniformly to suggest that although many factors have been studied, no credible studies establish a direct link between any contributing factor and the occurrence of autism in children. The rest of that section of our paper would explore the factors that have been examined in the research to reiterate the claim in our topic sentence.

Keep in mind that the body paragraphs should be organized according to a claim about the topic or ideas being explored. They should not be organized merely as successive summaries of the sources. Such an organization does not promote effective synthesis.

THE CONCLUSION

Your conclusion should reiterate your overall assessment of the scholarship. Notify your readers of any gaps you've determined in the scholarship, and consider suggesting areas where future scholarship can make more contributions.

TECHNICAL CONSIDERATIONS

Keep in mind the conventions of writing in the social sciences that you've learned about throughout this chapter. Use APA documentation procedures for in-text documentation of summarized, paraphrased, and cited materials, as well as for the References page at the end of your literature review.

Insider Example
Student Literature Review

William O'Brien, a first-year writing student who had a particular interest in understanding the effects of sleep deprivation, composed the following literature review. As you read, notice how William's text indicates evidence of synthesis both between and among the sources he used to build his project. Notice also that he followed APA style conventions in his review.

Effects of Sleep Deprivation: A Literature Review

William O'Brien

North Carolina State University

The findings built upon the idea that sleep deprivation decreases vigilance and that it impairs the "executive control" attentional network, while appearing to leave the other components (alerting and orienting) relatively unchanged (pp. 121-122). These findings help explain how one night of missed sleep negatively affects a person's attention, by distinguishing the effects on each of the three particular attentional networks.

The writer links this study to the continuing discussion of short-term effects of sleep deprivation but also notes a difference.

Research by Giesbrecht, Smeets, Leppink, Jelicic, and Merckelbach (2013) focused on the effects that short-term sleep deprivation has on dissociation. This research is interesting and different from the other research in that it connects sleep deprivation to mental illness rather than just temporarily reduced mental functioning. The researchers used 25 healthy undergraduate students and kept all participants awake throughout one night. Four different scales were used to record their feelings and dissociative reactions while being subjected to two different cognitive tasks (Giesbrecht et al., 2013, pp. 150-152). The cognitive tasks completed before the night of sleep deprivation were used to compare the results of the cognitive tasks completed after the night of sleep deprivation. Although the study was small and the implications are still somewhat unclear, the study showed a clear link between sleep deprivation and dissociative symptoms (pp. 156-158).

This paragraph provides a summative synthesis, or an overview of the findings among the sources reviewed.

It is clear that sleep deprivation negatively affects people in many different ways. These researchers each considered a different type of specific effect, and together they form a wide knowledge base supporting the idea that even a very short-term (24-hour) loss of sleep for a healthy adult may have multiple negative impacts on mental and emotional well-being. These effects include increased anxiety, anger, and stress in response to small stressors (Minkel et al., 2012), inhibited attention—the executive control attentional network more specifically (Jugovac & Cavallero, 2012)—and increased dissociative symptoms (Giesbrecht et al., 2013).

Long-Term Effects of Sleep Deprivation

Although the research on short-term effects of sleep deprivation reveals numerous negative consequences, there may be other, less obvious, implications that studies on short-term effect cannot illuminate. In order to better understand these other implications, we must examine research relating to the possible long-term effects of limited sleep. Unfortunately, long-term sleep deprivation experiments do not seem to have been done and are probably not possible (due to ethical reasons and safety reasons, among other factors). A study by Duggan, Reynolds, Kern, and Friedman (2014) pointed out the general lack of previous research into the long-term effects of sleep deprivation, but it examined whether there was a link between average sleep duration during childhood and life-long mortality risk (p. 1195). The researchers analyzed data from 1,145 participants in the Terman Life Cycle Study from the early 1900s, which measured bedtime and wake time along with year of death. The amount of sleep was adjusted by age in order to find the deviations from average sleep time for each age group. The data were also separated by sex (Duggan et al., 2014, pp. 1196-1197). The results showed that, for males, sleeping either more or less than the regular amount of time for each age group correlated with an increased life-long mortality risk (p. 1199). Strangely, this connection was not present for females. For males, however, this is a very important finding. Since we can surmise that the childhood sleep patterns are independent of and unrelated to any underlying health issues that ultimately cause the deaths later on in life, it is more reasonable to assume causation rather

The writer shifts to an examination of the long-term effects of sleep deprivation and acknowledges a shift in the methods for these studies.

than simply correlation. Thus, the pattern that emerged may demonstrate that too little, or too much, sleep during childhood can cause physiological issues, leading to death earlier in life, which also reaffirms the idea that sleep is extremely important for maintaining good health.

Establishes one of the study's central findings related to long-term effects of sleep deprivation

While this study examined the relationship between sleep duration and death, a study by Kelly and El-Sheikh (2014) examined the relationship between sleep and a slightly less serious, but still very important, subject: the adjustment and development of children in school over a period of time. The study followed 176 third grade children (this number dropped to 113 by the end of the study) as they progressed through school for five years, recording sleep patterns and characteristics of adjustment (Kelly & El-Sheikh, 2014, pp. 1137-1139). Sleep was recorded both subjectively through self-reporting and objectively though "actigraphy" in order to assess a large variety of sleep parameters (p. 1137). The study results indicated that reduced sleep time and poorer-quality sleep are risk factors for problems adjusting over time to new situations. The results also indicate that the opposite effect is true, but to a lesser extent (p. 1146).

From this research, we gain the understanding that sleep deprivation and poor sleep quality are related to problems adjusting over time. This effect is likely due to the generally accepted idea that sleep deprivation negatively affects cognitive performance and emotional regulation, as described in the Kelly and El-Sheikh article (2014, pp. 1144-1145). If cognitive performance and emotional regulation are negatively affected by a lack of sleep, then it makes sense that the sleep-deprived child would struggle to adjust over time as compared to a well-rested child. This hypothesis has important implications. It once again affirms the idea that receiving the appropriate amount of quality sleep is very important for developing children. This basic idea does not go against the research by Duggan et al. (2014) in any way; rather, it complements it. The main difference between each study is that the research by Duggan et al. shows that too much sleep can also be related to a greater risk of death earlier in life. Together, both articles provide evidence that deviation from the appropriate amount of sleep causes very negative long-term effects, including, but certainly not limited to, worse adjustment over time (Kelly & El-Sheikh, 2014) and increased mortality rates (Duggan et al., 2014).

Conclusion

This research provides great insight into the short-term and long-term effects of sleep deprivation. Duggan et al. (2014) showed increased mortality rates among people who slept too much as well as too little. This result could use some additional research. Through the analysis of each article, we see just how damaging sleep deprivation can be, even after a short period of time, and thus it is important to seriously consider preventative measures. While sleep issues can manifest themselves in many different ways, especially in legitimate sleep disorders such as insomnia, just the simple act of not allowing oneself to get enough sleep every night can have significant negative effects. Building on this, there seems to be a general lack of discussion on *why* people (who do not have sleep disorders) do not get enough time to sleep. One possible reason is the ever-increasing number of distractions, especially in the form of electronics, that may lead to overstimulation. Another answer may be that high demands placed on students and adults through school and work, respectively, do not give them time to sleep enough. The most probable, yet most generalized, answer, however, is that people simply do not

Provides a summative synthesis that examines relationships between the sources and considers implications of findings

Conclusion acknowledges what appears as a gap in the scholarship reviewed appropriately manage their time in order to get enough sleep. People seem to prioritize everything else ahead of sleeping, thus causing the damaging effects of sleep deprivation to emerge. Regardless, this research is valuable for anyone who wants to live a healthy lifestyle and function at full mental capacity. Sleep deprivation seems to have solely negative consequences; thus, it is in every person's best interests to get a full night of quality sleep as often as possible.

References

Duggan, K., Reynolds, C., Kern, M., & Friedman, H. (2014).
    Childhood sleep duration and lifelong mortality risk.
    Health Psychology, *33*(10), 1195-1203. doi:10.1037
    /hea0000078

Giesbrecht, T., Smeets, T., Leppink, J., Jelicic, M., &
    Merckelbach, H. (2013). Acute dissociation after one
    night of sleep loss. *Psychology of Consciousness: Theory,
    Research, and Practice*, *1*(S), 150-159. doi:10.1037
    /2326-5523.1.S.150

Jugovac, D., & Cavallero, C. (2012). Twenty-four hours of
    total sleep deprivation selectively impairs attentional
    networks. *Experimental Psychology*, *59*(3), 115-123.
    doi:10.1027/1618-3169/a000133

Kelly, R., & El-Sheikh, M. (2014). Reciprocal relations between
    children's sleep and their adjustment over time.
    Developmental Psychology, *50*(4), 1137-1147. doi:10.1037
    /a0034501

Minkel, J., Banks, S., Htaik, O., Moreta, M., Jones, C.,
    McGlinchey, E., Simpson, N., & Dinges, D. (2012). Sleep
    deprivation and stressors: Evidence for elevated negative
    affect in response to mild stressors when sleep deprived.
    Emotion, *12*(5), 1015-1020. doi:10.1037/a0026871

THEORY RESPONSE ESSAY

Faculty in the fields of the social sciences often ask students to apply a social science theory to their own experiences. Psychology, sociology, and communication professors may ask students to use a psychological, sociological, or communication theory as a lens through which to explain their own or others' behaviors. Assignments like these involve writing a **theory response essay**. These assignments are popular for a number of reasons: (1) they allow students to engage with the fundamental elements of social sciences (theories); (2) they allow students to attend to the basic processes of data collection that are common in the social sciences; and (3) they are often quite engaging for faculty to read and are among the most interesting for students to write.

Whether you're using elements of Freud's dream theories to help understand your own dreams or you're using an interpersonal communication theory to understand why people so easily engage with you, the theory you're working with provides the frame for your analysis of some event or action. The theory is the core of any theory response.

Precisely because the theory is the core of such a writing project, it's crucial that in the beginning stage of such a project, you work with a theory that is actually applicable to the event, action, or phenomenon you want to understand better. You also want to choose a theory that genuinely interests you. Luckily, theories of human behavior and human system interactions abound. If you aren't assigned a theory for the project, then consider the places where you might go about locating a workable theory. Textbooks in the social sciences frequently make reference to theories, and numerous academic websites maintain lists and explanations of social science theories. Here are a few categories of theories that students often find interesting:

birth order theories	friendship theories
parenting style theories	stage theories of grieving
addiction theories	

If you're unable to locate a workable theory that's "ready-made" for application to some experience(s), then consider building a theory based on your reading of a social science study. Though this certainly makes completing the assignment challenging, it is not without rewards.

Personal Experience

Regardless of whether you're working with a particular theory or constructing a theory of behavior based on one or more studies, consider making a list of the "moments" or events in your life that the theory might help you understand further. Your next step might be to write out detailed descriptions of those events as you see or remember them. Capture as much detail as you can, especially if you're writing from memory. Then apply the theory (all of its component parts) to your event or moment to see what it can illuminate for you: Where does it really help you understand something? Where does it fail to help? How might the theory need to change to account for your experiences?

Others' Experiences

Some instructors might ask you to collect and analyze the experiences of others. If you're assigned to do this, then you'll need to consider a data-collection method very carefully and ask your instructor if there are specific procedures at your institution that you should follow when collecting data from other people. We recommend, for now, that you think about the methods most commonly associated with qualitative research: observations, interviews, and open-ended surveys. These rich data-producing methods are most likely to provide the level of detail about others' experiences needed to evaluate the elements of your theory. Trying to understand others' experiences in light of the theory you're working with means considering the same analytical questions that you applied to your own experiences: Where does the theory really help you understand something? Where does it fail to help? How might the theory need to change to account for the experiences of those in your study?

WRITING PROJECT **Writing a Theory Response**

The goal of this writing project is to apply a theoretical framework from an area of the social sciences to your own experiences. The first step is to choose a theoretical framework that has some relevance to you, providing ample opportunity to reflect on and write about your own experiences in relation to the theory.

THE INTRODUCTION
The introduction to your study should introduce readers to the theory and explain all of its essential elements. You should also be clear about whether you're applying the theory to your own experiences or the experiences of others, or to both. In light of the work you did applying the theory, formulate a thesis that assesses the value of the theory for helping to understand the "moments," events, or phenomena you studied.

THE BODY
The body can be organized in a number of ways. If your theory has clear stages or elements, then you can explain each one and apply it to relevant parts of your experiences or those of others. If the theory operates in such a way that it's difficult to break into parts or stages or elements, then consider whether or not it's better to have subheadings that identify either (1) the themes that emerged from your application, or (2) your research subjects (by pseudonym). In this case, your body sections would be more like case studies. Ultimately, the organization strategy you

choose will depend on the nature of the theory you're applying and the kinds of events you apply it to. The body of your project should establish connections among the theory's component elements.

THE CONCLUSION

The conclusion of your study should assert your overall assessment of the theory's usefulness. Reiterate how the theory was useful and how it wasn't. Make recommendations for how it might need to be changed in order to account for the experiences you examined in light of the theory.

TECHNICAL CONSIDERATIONS

Keep in mind the conventions of writing in the social sciences that you've learned about throughout this chapter. Use APA documentation procedures for in-text documentation of summarized, paraphrased, and cited materials, as well as for the References page at the end of your study.

Insider Example
Student Theory Response Paper

Matt Kapadia, a first-year writing student, was interested in understanding the ways people rationalize their own successes and failures. In the following paper, he analyzes and evaluates a theory about the social science phenomenon of attribution (as described at changingminds.org) through the lenses of both his own and others' experiences. As you read Matt's paper, pay close attention to the moments when he offers evaluation of the theory. Ask yourself if his evaluation in each instance makes sense to you, based on the evidence he provides. Notice also that he followed APA style conventions in his paper.

Evaluation of the Attribution Theory
Matt Kapadia
North Carolina State University

Evaluation of the Attribution Theory

In an attempt to get a better sense of control, human beings are constantly attributing cause to the events that happen around them (Straker, 2008). Of all the things people attribute causes to, behavior is among the most common. The attribution theory aims to explain how people attribute the causes of their own behaviors compared to the behaviors of those around them. Behaviors can be attributed to both internal and external causes. Internal causes are things that people can control or are part of their personality, whereas external causes are purely circumstantial and people have no control over the resulting events (Straker, 2008). The attribution theory uses these internal and external causes to explain its two major components: the self-serving bias and the fundamental attribution error. The self-serving bias evaluates how we attribute our own behaviors, whereas the fundamental attribution error evaluates how we attribute the behaviors of those around us (Straker, 2008). This paper evaluates how applicable the attribution theory and its components are, using examples from personal experience as well as data collected from others. Based on the findings of this evaluation, I believe the attribution theory holds true on nearly all accounts; however, the category of the self-serving bias might need revision in the specific area dealing with professionals in any field of study or in the case of professional athletes.

Attribution Theory: An Explanation

The foundation of the attribution theory is based in the nature of the causes people attribute behaviors to, whether it be internal or external. A person has no control over an external cause (Straker, 2008). An example would be a student failing a math test because the instructor used the

The writer establishes a thesis that includes an evaluation of the theory's usefulness in various contexts.

In this paragraph and the next two, the writer reviews and exemplifies the component parts of the theory. That is, the writer offers an explanation of the theory, with examples to illustrate points, as appropriate.

wrong answer key. In this case, the student had no control over the grade he received, and it did not matter how much he had studied. A bad grade was inevitable. A person can also attribute behavioral causes to internal causes. Internal causes are in complete control of the person distributing the behavior and are typically attributed to part of the individual's personality (Straker, 2008). An example would be a student getting a poor grade on his math test because he is generally lazy and does not study. In this case, the student had complete control of his grade and chose not to study, which resulted in the poor grade. These two causes build up to the two major categories within the attribution theory.

The first major category of the attribution theory is that of self-serving bias. This category explores how people attribute causes to their own behaviors. It essentially states that people are more likely to give themselves the benefit of the doubt. People tend to attribute their poor behaviors to external causes and their good behaviors to internal causes (Straker, 2008). An example would be a student saying he received a poor grade on a test because his instructor does not like him. In this case, the student is attributing his poor behavior, making a poor grade on the test, to the external cause of his instructor not liking him. However, following the logic of the theory, if the student had made a good grade on the test, then he would attribute that behavior to an internal cause such as his own good study habits.

The second category of the attribution theory, the fundamental attribution error, states the opposite of the self-serving bias. The fundamental attribution error talks about how people attribute cause to the behaviors of those around them. It states that people are more likely to attribute others' poor behaviors to internal causes and their good behaviors to external causes (Straker, 2008). An example would be a student saying his friend got a better grade on the math test than him because the instructor likes his friend more. The student jumps to the conclusion that his friend's good grade was due to the external cause of the instructor liking the friend more. Moreover, if his friend had done poorly on the test, the student would most likely attribute the poor grade to an internal factor, such as his friend not studying for tests.

Personal Experiences

A situation from my personal experiences that exemplifies the ideas of the attribution theory is my high school golfing career. For my first two years of high school, I performed relatively poorly on the golf course. My team consistently placed last in tournaments, and I ranked nowhere near the top golfers from neighboring high schools. I blamed my performance on factors such as the wind and flat-out bad luck. At the same time, I attributed my teammates' poor performances to factors such as not practicing hard enough to compete in tournament play. In doing this, I became no better a golfer because I was denying that the true cause of my poor scores was the fact that I was making bad swings and not putting in the hours of work needed to perform at a higher level. I finally recognized this during my junior year of high school. I started to realize that blaming everything but myself was getting me nowhere and that the only way to improve was to take responsibility for my own play. I started practicing in areas where my game needed improvement and putting in hours at the driving range to improve my swing memory. In doing this, I became a much better player; by the time my senior season came around, I was ranked one of the top golfers in my conference and one of the best amateur players in the state of North Carolina. However, my team still did not perform

The writer details a particular personal experience that he'll later analyze through the lens of the theory.

well due to my teammates' performance, which I continued to attribute to their poor practice habits.

This experience reflects the attribution theory in several ways. I displayed self-serving bias in my early years of high school golf. I attributed all of my poor performances to external causes, such as the wind, that I could not control. At the same time, I was displaying the fundamental attribution error in attributing my teammates' poor performances to internal causes such as not practicing hard enough. Throughout my high school golf career, I displayed the ideas of the attribution theory's category of the fundamental attribution error. However, during my junior and senior seasons my attributions moved away from the attribution theory's category of the self-serving bias. I began to attribute my poor performance to internal causes instead of the external causes I had previously blamed for my mishaps.

I believe that this is generally true for any athlete or professional seeking improvement in his or her prospective field. If a person continues to follow the ideas discussed in the category of the self-serving bias, he is not likely to improve at what he is trying to do. If Tiger Woods had constantly attributed his bad play to external causes and not taken responsibility for his actions as internal causes, he would have never become the best golfer in the world. Without attributing his poor behaviors to internal causes, he would have never gained the motivation to put in the hours of work necessary to make him the best. This observation can be applied to any other professional field, not only athletics. Personal improvement is only likely to take place when a person begins to attribute his or her poor behaviors to internal causes. I believe athletes and professionals represent problem areas for the theory of self-serving bias. However, the ideas of the fundamental attribution error generally hold true.

In this section, the writer analyzes his experiences through the lens of the theory.

Experiences of Others

The writer provides some insight into his methods for collecting data on the experiences of others.

To evaluate the attribution theory, I conducted an experiment to test both the fundamental attribution error and the self-serving bias. The test subjects were three friends in the same class at North Carolina State University: MEA101, Introduction to Geology. The students were asked to write down if their grades were good or bad on the first test of the semester ("good" meant they received an 80 or higher on the test, and "bad" meant they received below an 80). After the three students had done this for themselves, they were asked to attribute the grades of the others to a cause. This activity provided a clear sample of data that could test the validity of the self-serving bias and the fundamental attribution error. The reason I chose a group of friends versus a group of random strangers was that when people know each other they are more likely to attribute behavioral causes truthfully, without worrying about hurting anyone's feelings.

In this section, the writer provides the results of his data collection.

For the purposes of this experiment, the test subjects will be addressed as Students X, Y, and Z to keep their names confidential. The results of the experiment were as follows. The first student, Student X, received a "bad" grade on the test and attributed this to the instructor not adequately explaining the information in class and not telling the students everything the test would ultimately cover. However, Students Y and Z seemed to conclude that the reason Student X got a "bad" grade was because he did not study enough and is generally lazy when it comes to college test taking. Student Y received a "good" grade on the test and attributed this to studying hard the night before and to the fact that the test was relatively easy if one studied the notes. Students X and Z seemed to conclude that Student Y is a naturally smart student who usually receives good grades on tests regardless of how much he or she studies. Finally, Student Z received a "bad" grade on the test and attributed this to the instructor not covering the material on the test well enough for students to do well, a similar response to Student X. However, Students X and Y attributed Student Z's poor grade to bad study habits and not taking the class seriously.

These results tend to prove the ideas of both of the attribution theory's categories. Student X attributed his poor grade to the external cause of the instructor not covering the material well enough, demonstrating the self-serving bias. Students Y and Z attributed Student X's poor grade to the internal cause of Student X not studying hard enough and being a generally lazy college student, exemplifying the ideas of the fundamental attribution error. Student Y attributed her good grade to the internal cause of good study habits, also exemplifying the self-serving bias. However, Students X and Z felt that the reason for Student Y's success was the external cause of being a naturally good student who does well with or without studying, reflecting the ideas of the fundamental attribution error. Student Z's results also hold true to the theory. Student Z attributed his poor grade to the external cause of the instructor not covering the material adequately, a belief shared by Student X. Also holding true to the fundamental attribution error, both Students X and Y attributed Student Z's failure to the internal cause of poor study habits. Based on the findings of this experiment, I can say that both the fundamental attribution error and the self-serving bias hold true on all accounts.

Conclusion

Overall, I believe the attribution theory's categories of the self-serving bias and the fundamental attribution error are very applicable to everyday life. Based on the data gathered

In this section, the writer discusses the implications of his findings for his overall evaluation of the theory.

The writer concludes his response paper by reviewing his overall evaluation of the theory in light of his own and others' experiences he analyzed.

through personal experiences and the experiences of others through the experiment described in this analysis, I believe the theory holds true in the vast majority of situations where people attribute causes to behaviors and/or actions. The only area needing revisions is the self-serving bias when applied to the specific situations of professionals in a field of study or in the case of professional athletes. In both situations, improvement must occur in order to become a professional, and the only way this is likely to happen is by accepting internal fault for poor behaviors. By accepting internal fault, a person gains the motivation to put in the hours of work necessary to learn and improve at what he or she is trying to do. Without this improvement and learning, the ability to reach the professional level is slim to none. This displays the exact opposite of the attribution ideas that are described in the self-serving bias. With the exception of this small niche of situations that falsify the self-serving bias, the validity of the attribution theory is confirmed on all accounts.

Reference

Straker, D. (2008). *Attribution theory*. Retrieved from
changingminds.org: http://changingminds.org
/explanations/theories/attribution_theory.htm

- **Observation plays a critical role in the social sciences.** The academic fields of the social sciences, including sociology, psychology, anthropology, communication studies, and political science, among others, make observations about human behavior and interactions, as well as the systems and social structures we create to organize the world around us.

- **Social science research rests on theories of human behavior and human systems.** These are propositions that are used to explain specific phenomena. Social science research contributes to the continual process of refining these theories.

- **Researchers in the social sciences typically establish a hypothesis,** or a testable proposition that provides an answer or predicts an outcome in response to the research question(s) at hand, at the beginning of a research project.

- **Social science researchers must make choices about the types of methods they use** in any research situation, based on the nature of their line of inquiry and the kind of research question(s) they seek to answer. They may use a quantitative, qualitative, or mixed-methods research design to collect data for analysis.

- **Social scientists must guard against bias in their research.** As such, they rely on rigorous procedures and checks (e.g., ensuring appropriate sample sizes and/or using multiple forms of qualitative data) to ensure that the influence of any biases is as limited as possible.

- **IMRAD format—Introduction, Methods, Results, and Discussion—is a common *structure* used for the organization of research reports in the social sciences.** Although research reports in the social sciences may appear in any number of forms, much of the scholarship published in these fields appears in the IMRAD format.

- **The passive voice and hedging are uses of *language*** that characterize, for good reason, social scientific writing.

- **APA style is the most common documentation style used for *reference*** in the fields of the social sciences.

- **The genres of the literature review and the theory response paper are often produced in the fields of the social sciences.**

Reading and Writing in the Natural Sciences

Introduction to the Natural Sciences

Each of us has likely observed something peculiar in the natural world and asked, "Why does it do that?" or "Why does that happen?" Perhaps you've observed twinkling stars in the night sky and wanted to know why such distant light seems to move and pulse. Or perhaps you've wondered why, as you drive, trees closer to your car appear to rush by much faster than trees in the distance. Maybe you can recall the first time you looked at a living cell under a microscope in a biology course and wondered about the world revealed on the slide.

For most scientists, observation of natural phenomena is the first step in the process of conducting research. Something in the natural world captures their attention and compels them to pose questions. Some moments of scientific observation are iconic—such as Newton's observation of an apple falling from a tree as inspiration for his theory of gravity.

We interviewed Sian Proctor, a geologist at South Mountain Community College in Phoenix, Arizona, where she teaches classes in physical, environmental, and historical geology. Dr. Proctor has participated in several unique research team experiences, including the Hawaii Space Exploration Analog and Simulation (HI-SEAS) Mars habitat, the NASA Spaceflight and Life Sciences Training Program (she was a finalist for the 2009 NASA Astronaut Program), and the PolarTREC (Teachers and Researchers Exploring and Collaborating) program in Barrow, Alaska. Her work has taken her out of the college/university setting many

ANDREA TSURUMI

Geologists work out in the field, in labs, in educational institutions, and in the corporate world

SIAN PROCTOR, GEOLOGY

COURTESY OF SIAN PROCTOR

"Geology is an extremely diverse discipline encompassing specialties such as planetary geology, geochemistry, volcanology, paleontology, and more. The goal of a general geologist is to develop understanding of Earth processes such as the formation of mineral or energy resources, the evolution of landscapes, or the cause of natural disasters. Geologists work out in the field, in labs, in educational institutions, and in the corporate world. They collect data, analyze samples, generate maps, and write reports. Geology instructors teach students how to conceptualize all the information and processes mentioned above. It is our job to get students to think like a geologist (if you are teaching majors) or gain an appreciation for the Earth and Earth processes (if you are teaching non-majors)."

times. In her Insider's View, she describes the varied places in which scientists conduct observations and collect data as part of their work to understand the natural world.

As Dr. Proctor's description of her field reveals, those who work in the **natural sciences** study observable phenomena in the natural world and search for answers to the questions that spark researchers' interests about these phenomena. The disciplines of the natural sciences include a wide array of fields of academic research, including those in agricultural and life sciences, as well as physical sciences. As Dr. Proctor's own life experiences suggest, the search for understanding of natural phenomena can take scientists to many different places, and there is much variety in the ways they engage in research. One aspect that holds this diverse group of disciplines together, though, is a set of common values and procedures used in conducting research. You're probably already familiar with or at least have heard about the **scientific method**, a protocol for conducting research in the sciences that includes the following elements, or steps:

1. Observe.
2. Ask a research question.
3. Formulate a hypothesis.
4. Test the hypothesis.
5. Explain the results.

In this chapter, we describe the process of writing activities involved in scientific research. We present this strategy, the **scientific writing process**, in terms of a four-step process that maps onto the elements of the scientific method. The process begins with careful observation of natural phenomena and leads to the development of research questions. This step is followed by an investigation that culminates in the reporting or publication of the research:

1. Observe and describe.
2. Speculate.
3. Experiment.
4. Report.

The following table illustrates how the elements of the scientific method map onto the scientific writing process:

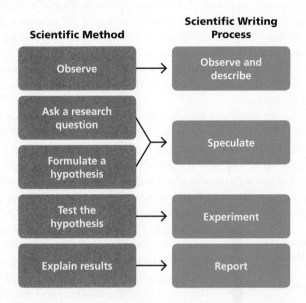

Before we delve too deeply into the research and writing practices of students and scholars of the sciences and how they connect, though, let's consider some of the areas of inquiry that make up the natural sciences.

Astronomy, biology, chemistry, earth science, physics, and mathematics are some of the core disciplinary areas within the natural sciences. Each area of inquiry includes numerous areas of specialty, or fields. For example, quantum physics, acoustics, and thermodynamics are three fields of physics. Conservation biology and marine science are fields of biology. Ecology (the study of organisms and their relationships to their environments) also operates under the umbrella of biology.

Interdisciplinary research is quite common in the natural sciences. An **interdisciplinary field** is an area of study in which different disciplinary perspectives or methods are combined into one. In such instances, methods for data collection often associated with one field may be used within another field of study. Consider biochemistry and biophysics, two interdisciplinary fields. In biochemistry, methods often associated with chemistry research are useful in answering questions about living organisms and biological systems. A biochemist may study aspects of a living organism such as blood alkalinity and its impact on liver function. Likewise, researchers in biophysics may use methods typical of physicists to answer research questions about biological systems. Biophysicists, for instance, might use the methodology of physics to unlock the mysteries of human DNA.

Research in the Natural Sciences

No matter the specific fields in which scientists work, they all collect, analyze, and explain data. Scientists tend to embrace a shared set of values, and as a result they typically share similar desires about how best to conduct research. The importance of any scientific study and its power to explain a natural phenomenon, then, are largely based on how well a researcher or research team designs and carries out a study in light of the shared values and desires of the community's members.

Completing the steps of a research project in a logical order and reporting the results accurately are keys to mastering research and writing in the natural sciences. You must observe and describe an object of study before you can speculate as to what it is or why it does what it does. Once you've described and speculated about a particular phenomenon, and posed a research question and a hypothesis about it, then you're positioned well to construct an experiment (if appropriate) and collect data to test whether your hypothesis holds true. When you report the results of your research, you must describe these steps and the data collected accurately and clearly. These research and writing steps build on one another, and we explore each step in more detail moving forward.

We interviewed biomedical scientist Paige Geiger, who teaches in the Department of Molecular and Integrative Physiology at the University of Kansas Medical Center, where she conducts experimental research in a laboratory on the effects of exercise and age on muscle metabolism and insulin resistance in Type II diabetes. In her Insider's View, she describes the kind of work that natural scientists do in her field and the importance of conducting careful, thorough data collection in the sciences.

Natural scientists collect evidence through systematic observation and experimentation, and they value methods that are quantifiable and replicable. In some instances, the natural sciences are described as "hard" sciences and the social sciences as "soft." This distinction stems from the tendency for natural scientists to value quantitative methods over qualitative methods, whereas social scientists often engage in both forms of data collection and sometimes combine quantitative and qualitative methods in a single

Insider's View
We value innovation, ideas, accurate interpretation of data, and scientific integrity
PAIGE GEIGER, MOLECULAR AND INTEGRATIVE PHYSIOLOGY

COURTESY OF PAIGE GEIGER

"A biomedical scientist performs basic research on questions that have relevance to human health and disease, biological processes and systems. We design scientific studies to answer a particular research question and then report our results in the form of a manuscript for publication. Good science is only as good as the research study design itself. We value innovation, ideas, accurate interpretation of data, and scientific integrity. There is an honor system to science that the results are accurate and true as reported. Manuscripts are peer-reviewed, and there is inherent trust and belief in this system."

study. (See Chapter 7, pp. 160–64, for more discussion of quantitative and qualitative methods.) Natural scientists value experiments and data collection processes that can be repeated to achieve the same or similar results, often for the purposes of generalizing their findings. Social scientists acknowledge the fluidity and variability of social systems and therefore also highly value qualitative data, which helps them to understand more contextual experiences.

INSIDE WORK) **Considering a Natural Science Topic**

Generate a list of natural science topics or issues that interest you. Include any you may have read about or heard about recently, perhaps in a magazine or blog or from a television news report. Then select one for further consideration. Try to focus on a topic in which you're genuinely interested or for which you have some concern. If you're currently taking a natural science course or studying in one of the fields of the natural sciences, you might consider a topic that has emerged from your classroom or laboratory experiences. Answer the following questions.

- What is the topic?

- What do you think scientists are currently interested in discovering about this topic? What would you like to know about the topic?

- Could the topic be addressed by researchers in more than one field of the sciences? Is the topic multidisciplinary in nature? What fields of the natural sciences are currently exploring or could potentially explore the topic?

- How do or could scientists observe and collect data on some aspect of the topic?

- In a broader sense, how does the topic connect with you personally? ▶

OBSERVATION AND DESCRIPTION IN THE NATURAL SCIENCES

Observing in the natural world is an important first step in scientific inquiry. Indeed, the first step of the scientific method is observation, as we show in the table on page 211. Beyond simple observation, though, researchers in the natural sciences conduct **systematic observations** of their objects of study. A systematic approach to observation requires a researcher to follow a regular, logical schedule of observation and to conduct focused and *neutral* observations of the object of study. In other words, the researcher tries to minimize or eliminate any bias about the subject matter and simply records everything he or she experiences, using the five senses. These observations, when written up to share with others as part of a research report, form the basis of description of the object of study. In order to move from observation to description, researchers must keep careful notes about their systematic observations. We discuss one method of tracking those observations, an observation logbook, on pages 227–28.

Read student Kedric Lemon's account of his observations (on pp. 229–39) of various batteries, which he completed between October 11 and October 19, 2013, as part of his observation logbook. Then answer the following questions.

- What do you know about who the author is, based on the language used in this description? Provide at least two specific examples of how the language suggests something about the author's background, knowledge, or frame of reference.

- What can you determine about the observation schedule that the author — the researcher — followed to write this description?

- What kinds of details must the researcher have noted when observing to write this description?

- Did you find any language that seems to reveal bias on the part of the researcher? If so, make a note of this language.

- Based on your answers to the previous questions, what kind of plan for systematic observation would you recommend for the topic you chose in the previous Inside Work activity? ▶

MOVING FROM DESCRIPTION TO SPECULATION

The distinction between description and speculation is a subtle but important one to understand as it relates to scientific inquiry. As we've seen, descriptive writing in the sciences is based on observations. Of course, descriptive writing in the sciences isn't only applicable to a physical space or a stored energy device. A researcher could use similar observational methods to describe, say, the movements of an ant crawling along a sidewalk or tidal erosion along a section of a beach. **Descriptive writing**, then, is the action outcome associated with the first step of the scientific method — observation.

Speculative writing, in contrast, seeks to explain *how* or *why* something behaves the way that it does, and it is most commonly associated with asking a research question and formulating a hypothesis — the second and third steps of the scientific method. In order to speculate about how or why something exists or behaves as it does, a researcher must first observe and describe. Developing a thorough observational strategy and completing a descriptive writing process will help you to lay a solid foundation for speculating about your object of study so that you can later develop a clear research question and formulate a credible hypothesis worthy of testing through experimentation.

To understand the difference between description and speculation, compare the following two zoo memos written by middle school students.* Which

---

* From "Revitalizing Instruction in Scientific Genres: Connecting Knowledge Production with Writing to Learn in the Sciences," *Science Education* 83, no. 2 (1999), 115–30.

one is the better example of descriptive writing? Which one engages more fully in speculative writing?

Middle School Students' Science Memo #1 (12-year-old girls)

On Monday, July 17, DC and I observed the Muntjac. We learned that this animal comes from Asia. And that they eat the bottom part of the grass because it is fresher. We also learned that Muntjacs are very secretive animals. We also observed the difference between a male and female. The male has a [*sic*] earring in his left ear and he has horns. To urinate they stand on three legs. They like to disappear into the bushes. Their habbitat [*sic*] is bushy land.

Another behavior that we observed was the adult Muntjac often moved toward the fence and sniffed. We believe he was sniffing for food. He also rolled back his ears and stuck out his neck. We think he is always alert to protect his family from danger. On one occasion, the male Muntjac came toward the fence. KT [another student] held her shirt toward him. He ran away quickly.

In conclusion, we can say that the Muntjac constantly hunts for food, but is always alert to protect itself and its family.

Middle School Students' Science Memo #2 (13-year-old boys)

Today we went to the Atlanta zoo, where we looked at different animals such as zebras, giraffes, gorilas [*sic*], monkeys, and orangatangs [*sic*]. From my observations of the giraffe I found out that they are rather slow and are always eating. They do many strange things, such as wagging their tails, wiggling their ears, and poking out their tounges [*sic*]. They are very large and I read that they weigh more than a rhinoserous [*sic*], which is close to 2 or 2½ tons, and their necks extend out 7 ft. long. Their tails are 3 ft. long and are sometimes used for swating [*sic*] flies. At times the giraffes will stand completely motionless.

Discussion Questions

1. What similarities and differences do you notice between the two samples?
2. Which sample engages in speculative writing more fully, and which one adheres to mostly descriptive writing?

The process of articulating an explanation for an observed phenomenon and speculating about its meaning is an integral part of scientific discovery.

By collecting data on your own and then interpreting it, you're engaging in the production of knowledge even before you begin testing a proposed hypothesis. In this respect, scientific discovery is similar to writing in the humanities and the social sciences. Scientists interpret data gained through observation, modeling, or experimentation much in the same way that humanists interpret data collected through observation of texts. The ability to *observe systematically* and *make meaning* is the common thread that runs through all academic research.

Descriptive writing seeks to define an object of study, and it functions like a photograph. Speculative writing engages by asking *how* or *why* something behaves the way that it does, and in this sense it triggers a kind of knowledge production that is essential to scientific discovery. Following a writing process that moves a researcher from describing a phenomenon to considering *how* or *why* something does what it does is a great strategy for supporting scientific inquiry.

To this end, we encourage you to collect original data as modeled in the writing projects presented at the end of this chapter—the observation logbook (p. 228), the research proposal (p. 241), and the lab report (p. 248). Your view on the natural world is your own, and the data you collect and how you interpret that data are yours to decide. The arguments you form based on your data and your interpretation of that data can impact your world in small or very large ways.

INSIDE WORK **Practicing Description and Speculation**

For this activity, you should go outdoors and locate any type of animal (a squirrel, bird, butterfly, frog, etc.) as an object of study. Decide beforehand the amount of time you'll spend observing your subject (five minutes may be enough), and write down in a notebook as many observable facts as possible about your subject and its behavior. Consider elements of size, color, weight, distance traveled, and interaction with other animals or physical objects. If you're able to make a video or take a picture (e.g., with a cell phone camera), please do so.

After you've collected your notes and/or video, return to your classroom and write two paragraphs about your subject. Label the first paragraph "Description" and the second paragraph "Speculation," and use the following writing prompt.

Writing Prompt: The director of your local wildlife management agency needs a written report detailing the behaviors that you observed while watching your animal. Be sure to use your notes or video for accuracy. In the first paragraph, write a *description* of the subject and its behavior. Limit your description to observable facts; resist explaining why the subject appears the way it does or behaves the way it does. In the second paragraph, *speculate* about why the animal appears or behaves the way it does. Limit your speculation to the subject's behavior (or appearance) based on the observable data you wrote in your description. Finally, consider writing questions at the end of the second paragraph that might be answered in future research but that cannot be answered on the basis of your observations alone. ❿

Once you've conducted observations and collected data, you can move to speculation, which involves writing research questions and formulating a hypothesis, consistent with the second and third steps of the scientific method. Writing research questions and hypotheses in the natural sciences is a similar process to those activities in the social sciences (see Chapter 7). Devoting time to several days of focused observation, collecting data, and writing and reflecting on your object of study should trigger questions about what you're observing.

As you write research questions, you might consider the difference between open-ended and closed-ended research questions. A **closed-ended question** can be answered by *yes* or *no*. By contrast, an **open-ended question** provokes a fuller response. Here are two examples:

Closed-Ended Question: Is acid rain killing off the Fraser fir population near Mount Mitchell in North Carolina?

Open-Ended Question: What factors contribute to killing off the Fraser fir population near Mount Mitchell in North Carolina?

Scientists use both open-ended and closed-ended questions. Open-ended questions usually begin with *What*, *How*, or *Why*. Closed-ended questions can be appropriate in certain instances, but they can also be quite polarizing. They often begin with *Is* or *Does*. Consider the following two questions:

Closed-Ended Question: Is global warming real?

Open-Ended Question: What factors contribute to global warming?

Rhetorically, the closed-ended question divides responses into *yes* or *no* answers, whereas the open-ended question provokes a more thoughtful response. Neither form of question is better per se, but the forms do function differently. If you're engaging in a controversial subject, a closed-ended research question might serve your purpose. If you're looking for a more complete answer to a complex issue, an open-ended question might serve you better.

Once you've established a focused research question, informed by or derived on the basis of your observation and speculation about a natural science phenomenon, then you're ready to formulate a hypothesis. This will be a testable proposition that provides an answer or that predicts an outcome in response to the research question(s) at hand.

INSIDE WORK   Developing Research Questions and a Hypothesis

Review the observation notes and the descriptions and explanations you produced in the Inside Work activity on page 216. What potential research questions emerged? For example, in an observation logbook about house finches and nesting practices written by one of the authors of this textbook, a question that remained unanswered was why two eggs from the initial brood of five were removed from the nest. Potential research questions for a study might include the one shown here.

> **Research Question: Do female house finches remove eggs from their own nests?**

From such a question, we can formulate a hypothesis.

> **Hypothesis: Our hypothesis is that female house finches do remove eggs from their own nests. Furthermore, our observational data supports other scholars' claims that female house finches cannibalize their brood on occasion.**

Now you try it. Write down at least two research questions that emerged from your observations, and then attempt to answer each question in the form of a hypothesis. Finally, discuss your hypotheses with a classmate or small group, and make the case for which one most warrants further study. Freewrite for five minutes about the evidence you have or additional evidence you could collect that would support your chosen hypothesis. ▶

DESIGNING A RESEARCH STUDY IN THE NATURAL SCIENCES

As we've noted, research in the natural sciences most often relies on quantitative data to answer research questions. While there are many ways to collect and analyze quantitative data, most professional scientists rely on complex statistical procedures to test hypotheses and generate results.

We interviewed Michelle LaRue, a research fellow at the Polar Geospatial Center, a research group based at the University of Minnesota. Her doctorate is in conservation biology, and her research has focused mainly on large-mammal habitat selection and movement—in particular, the phenomenon of potential recolonization of cougars in the American Midwest. In her Insider's View excerpt, Dr. LaRue describes the kinds of questions she asks as a scientist and the kinds of data collection and analysis she typically undertakes as part of her efforts to answer her research questions.

In the previous two sections, we discussed how to conduct systematic observation that leads to description of a phenomenon, and then we explored processes for speculating about what you observed in order to construct a research question and a hypothesis. One way to test a hypothesis is to engage in a systematic observation of the target of your research phenomenon. Imagine that you're interested in discovering factors that affect the migration patterns of bluefin tuna, and you've hypothesized that water temperature has some effect on those patterns. You could then conduct a focused observation to test your hypothesis. You might, for instance, observe bluefin tuna in their migration patterns and measure water temperatures along the routes.

Another way to test a hypothesis, of course, is to design an experiment. Experiments come in all shapes and sizes, and one way to learn about the experimental methods common to your discipline is by reading the Methods sections of peer-reviewed scholarly articles in your field. Every discipline has slightly different approaches to experimental design. Some disciplines, such as astronomy, rely almost exclusively on non-experimental systematic observation, while others rely on highly controlled experiments. Chemistry is a good example of the latter.

One of the most common forms of experimental design is the **comparative experiment**. In a comparative experiment, a researcher tests two or more types of objects and assesses the results. For example, an engineering student may want to test different types of skateboard ball bearings. She may design an experiment that compares a skateboard's distance rolled when using steel versus ceramic bearings. She could measure distances rolled, speed, or the time it takes to cover a preset distance when the skateboard has steel bearings and when it has ceramic bearings.

In some disciplines of the natural sciences, it's common practice to test different objects against a control group. A **control group** is used in a comparative experimental design to act as a baseline with which to compare other objects. For example, a student researcher might compare how subjects score on a memorization test after having consumed (a) no coffee, (b) two cups of decaf coffee, or (c) two cups of caffeinated coffee. In this example, the group of subjects consuming no coffee would function as a control group.

Hear more about the prewriting process from a professional mathematician.

Regardless of a study's design, it is important to realize that academic institutions have very clear policies regarding experimental designs that involve human subjects, whether that research is being conducted by individuals in the humanities, the social sciences, or the natural sciences. Both professional and student researchers are required to submit proposals through an institutional review board, or IRB. In the United States, *institutional review boards* operate under federal law to ensure that any experiment involving humans is ethical. This is often something entirely new to undergraduate students, and it should be taken seriously. No matter how harmless a test involving human subjects may seem, you should determine if you must submit your research plans through an IRB. This can often be done online. Depending on the nature and scope of your research, though, the processes of outlining the parameters of your research for review may be quite labor-intensive and time-consuming. You should familiarize yourself with the protocol for your particular academic institution. An online search for "institutional review board" and the name of your school should get you started. (For more on the role of institutional review boards, see Chapter 7.)

INSIDE WORK) **Freewriting about an Experiment**

Start this activity by writing, in one sentence, what your initial research goal was when you began an observation about a phenomenon that interested you. You might draw on your writing from earlier Inside Work activities to start.

Example: **My goal was to study a bird's nest I discovered on my front porch.**

For many students beginning their inquiry in the sciences, learning about a topic may be the extent of their initial objective. For more advanced students, however, starting an observation from a strong knowledge base may sharpen the objective. The example below draws on prior knowledge of the object of study.

Example: **My goal was to determine whether a female house finch eats her own eggs.**

Once you've written down what your initial objective was, then freewrite for five minutes about what you now know. What are the most important things you learned about your object of study?

Most important, what hypothesis can you make about your object of study?

Hypothesis: **My observational data suggest that female house finches often remove eggs from their nest and may occasionally cannibalize their brood.**

After developing a hypothesis, the next step in the scientific method is to test the hypothesis. Keep in mind data in the sciences to support a hypothesis come from either a systematic observation or an experiment.

Freewrite for five minutes about how you could collect data that would test your hypothesis. As you write, consider feasible methods that you could follow soon, as well as methods that might extend beyond the current semester but that you could develop into a larger project for later use in your under-graduate studies. Consider whether an experiment or a systematic observation would be more useful. Most important, use your imagination and have fun. ▶

After observing and describing, speculating and hypothesizing, and conducting an experimental study or systematic observation, scientists move toward publishing the results of their research. This is the final step of the scientific method and the final stage of the scientific writing process that we introduced at the beginning of the chapter: scientists explain their results by reporting their data and discussing its implications. There are multiple forms through which scientists report their findings, and these often depend on the target audience. For instance, a scientist presenting his research results at an academic conference for the consideration of his peers might report results in the form of a poster presentation. Research results can also be presented in the form of an academic journal article. A scientist who wants to present her results to a more general audience, though, might issue a press release. In the next two sections of this chapter, we discuss conventions for reporting results in the natural sciences and provide examples of common genres that research-ers in the natural sciences produce as a means of reporting their results.

Conventions of Writing in the Natural Sciences

Although the different fields of study that make up the natural sciences have characteristics that distinguish them from one another, a set of core values and conventions connect these areas of inquiry. The values shared among members of the scientific community have an impact on the communication practices and writing conventions of professionals in natural science fields:

- objectivity
- replicability
- recency
- cooperation and collaboration

In this section, we examine each of these commonly held values in more detail. And we suggest that these values are directly linked to many of the conventions that scientists follow when they write, or to the ways scientists communicate with one another more generally.

OBJECTIVITY

In her Insider's View, Michelle LaRue notes the importance of maintaining clarity in the presentation of ideas in science writing. Of course, clarity is a general expectation for all writing, but the desire for clarity in science writing can also be linked to the community's shared value of objectivity. As we noted earlier, **objectivity** (or neutrality) in observation and experimentation are essential to the research that scientists do. Most researchers in the natural sciences believe that bias undermines the reliability of research results. When scientists report their results, therefore, they often use rhetorical strategies that bolster the appearance of objectivity in their work. (Note that our marginal annotations below indicate which parts of the SLR model apply—structure, language, and reference; see Chapter 5.)

Rhetorical Features That Convey Objectivity

Titles may be considered a **language** and/or a **structural** feature of a text.

- **Titles**   Scientists tend to give their reports very clear titles. Rarely will you find a "creative" or rhetorical title in science writing. Instead, scientists prefer non-rhetorical, descriptive titles, or titles that say exactly what the reports are about.

The IMRAD format is a common **structure** used in scientific writing.

- **IMRAD**   Researchers in the sciences generally expect research reports to appear in the IMRAD format (for more detail, see Chapters 5 and 7):

  Introduction

  Methods

  Results

  Discussion

Notice how the structure of IMRAD parallels the ordered processes of the scientific writing process (observe and describe, speculate, experiment, and report). This reporting structure underscores the importance of objectivity because it reflects the prescribed steps of the scientific method, which is itself a research process that scientists follow to reduce or eliminate bias.

- **Jargon**   Scientists often communicate in highly complex systems of words and symbols that hold specific meaning for other members of the scientific community. These words and symbols enable scientists to communicate their ideas as clearly as possible. For example, a scientific researcher might refer to a rose as *Rosa spinosissima*. By using the Latin name, she communicates that the specific type of rose being referenced is actually the one commonly referred to as the Scotch rose. The use of jargon, in this instance, is actually clarifying for the intended audience. Using jargon is a means of communicating with precision, and precision in language is fundamental to objective expression.

  > Jargon is a **language** feature.

- **Numbers**   Scientific reports are often filled with charts and figures, and these are often filled with numbers. Scientists prefer to communicate in numbers because unlike words, which can inadvertently convey the wrong meaning, numbers are more fixed in terms of their ability to communicate specific meaning. Consider the difference between describing a tree as "tall" and giving a tree's height in feet and inches. This represents the difference between communicating somewhat qualitatively and entirely quantitatively. The preference for communicating in numbers, or quantitatively, enables members of the scientific community to reduce, as much as possible, the use of words. As writers use fewer words and more numbers in scientific reports, the reports appear to be more objective.

  > Numbers and other symbol systems function in much the same way as words, so they may be understood as a **language** feature.

INSIDE WORK   **Looking for Conventions of Objectivity**

Although we've discussed a number of writing expectations related to objectivity in the sciences, we need to stress again that these expectations are conventional. As such, you'll likely encounter numerous studies in the sciences that rely on only a few of these features or that alter the conventional expectations in light of a study's particular aims.

- Choose a scientific topic of interest to you, and locate a research article on some aspect of that topic in a peer-reviewed academic journal article.
- Once you've found an appropriate article, look at the features of the article that reflect the writers' desire for objectivity in science reporting. Note evidence of the following in particular:
  - straightforward, descriptive titles
  - IMRAD
  - jargon
  - numbers

- Take notes on instances where the article follows conventional expectations for science reporting as explained in this chapter, as well as instances where the article alters or diverges from these expectations. Speculate as to the authors' reasoning for their decisions to follow the conventional expectations or to diverge from them. ❯

REPLICABILITY

Like objectivity, the **replicability** of research methods and findings is important to the production and continuation of scientific inquiry. Imagine that a scientific report reveals the discovery that eating an orange every day could help prevent the onset of Alzheimer's disease. This sounds great, right? But how would the larger scientific community go about verifying such a finding? Multiple studies would likely be undertaken in an attempt to replicate the original study's finding. If the finding couldn't be replicated by carefully following the research procedures outlined in the original study, then that discovery wouldn't contribute much, if anything at all, to ongoing research on Alzheimer's disease precisely because the finding's veracity couldn't be confirmed.

Several conventional aspects of writing in the natural sciences help ensure the replicability of a study's findings and underscore replicability as an important value shared by members of the scientific community:

Detail may be considered a **language** or a **structural** feature.

- **Detail**   One of the conventional expectations for scientific writing involves the level of detail and specificity, particularly in certain areas of research reporting (e.g., Methods sections). Scientists report their research methods in meticulous detail to ensure that others can replicate their results. This is how scientific knowledge builds. Verification through repeated testing and retesting of results establishes the relative absolute value of particular research findings. It's not surprising, then, that the Methods sections of scientific research reports are typically highly detailed and specific.

Hypotheses are a **structural** feature.

- **Hypotheses**   Hypothesis statements predict the outcome of a research study, but the very nature of a prediction leaves open the possibility of other outcomes. By opening this "space" of possibility, scientists acknowledge that other researchers could potentially find results that differ from their own. In this way, scientists confirm the importance of replicability to their inquiry process.

Precision is a **language** feature of scientific writing.

- **Precision**   Scientific communication must be precise. Just as researchers must choose words and numbers with attention to accuracy and exactness, so too must they present their findings and other elements of scientific communication with absolute precision. As you engage with scientific discourse, you should be able to develop a sense of the precise nature of scientific description and explanation.

RECENCY

Scientific research is an ongoing process wherein individual studies or research projects contribute bits of information that help fill in a larger picture or research question. As research builds, earlier studies and projects become the bases for additional questioning and research. As in other fields, like the social sciences, it's important that scientific researchers remain current on the developments in research in their respective fields of study. To ensure that their work demonstrates **recency**—that is, it is current and draws on knowledge of other recent work—researchers in the sciences may follow numerous conventions in their writing, including those listed here:

- **Reference Selection** Scientific writers typically reference work that has been published recently on their topic. One way to observe the importance of recency is to examine the dates of studies and other materials referenced in a recent scientific publication. If you do this, then you'll likely discover that many studies referenced are relatively recent. By emphasizing recent research in their reports, scientists convey the importance of remaining on top of the current state of research in their areas of expertise. Knowledge production in the natural sciences is highly methodical and builds slowly over time. It's not surprising, then, that the recency of research is important to members of this community.

- **Documentation** The importance of recency is also evident in the methods of documentation most often employed in the fields of the natural sciences, like APA (American Psychological Association), CSE (Council of Science Editors), and others. Unlike MLA, for instance, where only page numbers appear next to authors' names in parenthetical citations—as in (Jacobs 1109)—the APA system requires a date next to authors' names, both for in-text references to research and, often, in parenthetical remarks when this is not provided in text—as in (Jacobs, 2012, pp. 198–199). The fact that the APA method generally requires a date highlights scientists' concern for the recency of the research they reference and on which they build their own research.

LaunchPadSolo

Learn about putting your research in context.

The purposeful selection of resources is a **reference** feature.

Scientific documentation systems of **reference** are often APA or CSE, but they are frequently also specific to the journal in which an article is published.

INSIDE WORK **Looking for Conventions of Replicability and Recency**

Start with the same article that you used in the previous Inside Work activity to search for writing conventions that demonstrate objectivity. If you don't already have an article selected, search for an academic article published in a peer-reviewed journal on a scientific topic of interest to you.

- Look for at least one example of the researchers' use of the following conventions that might demonstrate how much they value replicability and recency. Note evidence of the following:

- details
- precision
- timely reference selection
- choice of documentation style

- Take notes on instances where the article follows conventional expectations for science reporting as explained in this chapter and instances where the article alters or diverges from these expectations. Speculate as to the authors' reasoning for their decisions to follow the conventional expectations or to diverge from them. ▶

COOPERATION AND COLLABORATION

Unlike the clichéd image of the solitary scientist spending hours alone in a laboratory, most scientists would probably tell you that research in their fields takes place in a highly cooperative and collaborative manner. In fact, large networks of researchers in any particular area often comprise smaller networks of scholars who are similarly focused on certain aspects of a larger research question. These networks may work together to refine their research goals in light of the work of others in the network, and researchers are constantly sharing—through publication of reports, team researching, and scholarly conferences—the results of their work. Several common elements in scientific writing demonstrate this value:

The presentation of researchers' names is a **structural** feature.

- **Presentation of Researchers' Names** As you examine published research reports, you'll find that very often they provide a list, prominently, of the names of individuals who contributed to the research and to the reporting of that research. This information usually appears at the top of reports just after the title, and it may also identify the researchers' institutional and/or organizational affiliations. Names typically appear in an order that identifies principal researchers first. Naming all the members of a research team acknowledges the highly cooperative nature of the researching processes that many scientists undertake.

How researchers in the natural sciences treat one another is a feature of **reference**.

- **Treatment of Other Researchers** Another feature you might notice is the way science professionals treat one another's work. In the humanities, where ideas are a reflection of the individuals who present them, researchers and writers often direct commentary toward individuals for their ideas when there's cause for disagreement or dissatisfaction with other researchers' ideas. Conventionally, however, science researchers treat others in their field more indirectly when objections to their research or findings come up. Instead of linking research problems to individuals, scientists generally direct their dissatisfaction with others' work at problems in the research process or design. This approach highlights the importance of cooperation and collaboration as shared values of members of the scientific community.

Genres of Writing in the Natural Sciences

Once again we interviewed Paige Geiger, whom you met earlier in this chapter. She teaches in the Department of Molecular and Integrative Physiology at the University of Kansas Medical Center. In the following Insider's View, she describes two important genres of writing in her discipline.

In this section, we provide descriptions of, and steps for producing, three of the most common genres that writers in the natural sciences produce: an observation logbook, a research proposal, and a lab report. The observation logbook provides a location for carefully recording systematic observations at the beginning of a research process. The research proposal forms the basis for the important grant proposals that Dr. Geiger describes, and it might draw on information gathered during initial observations. It also incorporates other elements such as a careful review of the literature on a subject. Lab reports are the final results of research, and they reflect the form in which a scientist might ultimately publish a scholarly journal article.

AN OBSERVATION LOGBOOK

Systematic and carefully recorded observations can lay a solid foundation for further exploration of a subject. These observations might take place as an initial step in the scientific writing process, or they might be part of the data collection that occurs when testing a hypothesis.

Insider's View
Two different forms serve very different purposes
PAIGE GEIGER, MOLECULAR AND INTEGRATIVE PHYSIOLOGY

COURTESY OF PAIGE GEIGER

"There are two kinds of writing in my discipline—writing manuscripts for publication and writing grant applications. The two different forms serve very different purposes. We must write grant applications to obtain funding to perform our research. The applications are usually for three to five years of funding and are very broad in scope. These applications describe what you plan to do and the results you expect to see. This requires a comprehensive assessment of the literature, an explanation of what is known and what is unknown regarding the specific research question. You must describe how you will design the studies, how you will collect and analyze data, and how you will handle problems or unexpected results. This kind of writing is considered an art form. It is something that you improve upon throughout your career.

"Writing manuscripts for publication is quite different. A manuscript deals with a very specific research question, and you report the direct results of your investigation. There is some background information to place the study in a greater context, but the focus is on the data and the interpretation of the data from this one study. This form of writing is very direct, and overinterpretation of the data is frowned upon. In addition to these two forms of writing, scientists also write review articles and textbook chapters on their area of expertise."

One way to focus and record your observations of a phenomenon is to keep an **observation logbook**. The tools that we discuss over the next few pages parallel the kind of systematic observation that's needed to undertake scientific inquiry, and the observation logbook functions as both a data collection tool and a reflective strategy that becomes useful later in research writing and reporting stages. The observation logbook is a foundational part of the research process that precedes the construction of a formal lab report.

Sometimes observation logbooks include speculation in addition to description, but the two types of writing should be clearly separated from each other to ensure that the more objective observations are not confused with any speculation. Speculation, you'll remember, occurs at the stage of formulating research questions and a hypothesis.

WRITING PROJECT **Keeping an Observation Logbook**

For this project, you'll need to decide on a particular object of study and collect at least five days of observations about it. We encourage you to develop a multi-modal data collection process that includes digital photos and videorecorded evidence. For each daily entry, begin with description before moving into speculation. A natural outgrowth of descriptive writing should include brainstormed research questions that could be answered with further experiments, research, or observation.

For each day, you should do the following.

1. Collect and include photographic evidence.
2. Write a description of your object of study and its status.
3. Generate questions for future research.

At the conclusion of five days, answer the following questions.

1. What did I learn about my object of study?
2. What claims can I now make regarding my object of study?
3. What evidence could I use from my observational logbook to support those claims?

Finally, write a one- to two-page paper that includes two sections.

1. Description
2. Speculation

For the **Description** section, write a description of your object of study. Refrain from explaining or speculating about behavior in this section; simply write the observations that are most important to give a clear picture of what you studied and how you studied it. Make use of time measurements and physical measurements such as weight, size, and distance. For the **Speculation** section, assert suggestions as to why certain behaviors emerged in your object of study. You might begin by deciding which behaviors most surprised you or seem most interesting to you.

You might also use the Speculation section as a place to begin thinking about future questions that could be explored as a follow-up to your observations.

Insider Example
Student Observation Logbook

In the following observation logbook, written using APA style conventions, student Kedric Lemon catalogs his observations concerning the efficiency of several types of batteries over a five-day period. His observations form the basis for his experimental study, which appears later on pages 249–59. You'll notice that he carefully separates his observations and description from any speculation about why he observed what he did.

Running head: THE EFFICIENCY OF BATTERIES 1

Comparing the Efficiency of Various Batteries
Being Used over Time

Kedric Lemon
North Carolina State University

Comparing the Efficiency of Various Batteries
Being Used over Time

Logbook

Introduction

The purpose of this study is to see if some batteries can hold their charge for longer periods of time than others. Also, this observational study will determine if there is an overwhelming difference between generic brand and the top name-brand batteries, or if people are really just paying for the name. I will perform this study by first recording all of the batteries' initial voltages, and then each day I will allow each of the batteries to go on for an hour and a half and then again check the voltage. It is important that I test the voltage immediately after the batteries come out of the flashlight. Otherwise, results could vary. Before putting in the second set of batteries, I will allow the flashlight to cool down for an hour because after being in use for an hour and a half they are likely hot, and I am unsure if this can affect how fast the other batteries will be consumed. I will look first at how much charge was lost over the duration that they were used in the flashlight. Then I will compare them to one another to determine which one has lost the most over a day, and second, which of the batteries still holds the highest voltage. I hypothesize that the Duracell battery will decrease at the slowest rate and that it will have the highest initial voltage.

Establishes the purpose of the study, and outlines an observational protocol

Outlines methods

Establishes a hypothesis

THE EFFICIENCY OF BATTERIES   3

Begins a report on systematic observation of the phenomenon

Friday, October 11, 2013

Today was the first day that I observed results from my batteries. I believe that the first thing is to state the initial voltages of all three types of batteries. (Also, it is important to note that these are the averages of the batteries, as the flashlight demands two AA batteries.)

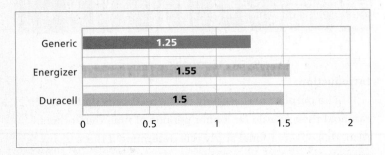

So from these initial observations the Energizer battery has the highest initial voltage.

After allowing all of the batteries to run for an hour and a half, I again took the voltages of the batteries and found this:

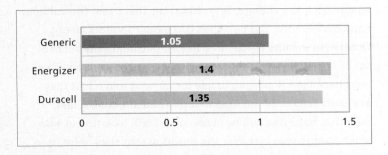

Energizer and Duracell both appear to be decreasing at approximately the same rates thus far in the observation, whereas the generic brand has already dropped much faster than the other two types of batteries. From this observation I have raised the question: What is the composition of the

Observations leading to questions

Duracell and Energizer batteries that allows them to hold a better initial charge than the generic brand of batteries?

Sunday, October 13, 2013

     Today I again put the three sets of batteries into the flashlight, in the same order as the trial prior, to allow them all to have close to the same time between usages, again to try and avoid any variables. Today my data showed similar results after allowing all of the batteries to run in the flashlight for an hour and a half:

Provides evidence of the researcher's attempt to remain systematic in his observations

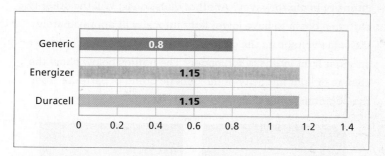

After this day of observing the results I found that the generic brand of batteries did not decrease as significantly as it did after the first trial. This day the generic brand lost close to the same voltage as the other two types of batteries. Another interesting observation I found was that Energizer and Duracell had the same voltages.

Tuesday, October 15, 2013

On this day of observation I again put the batteries into the flashlights for the trial time. The data I found for this day was as follows:

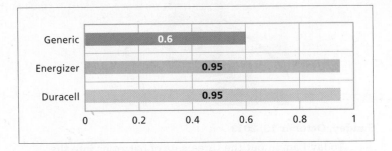

On this day I found that again the generic brand decreased by an amount similar to the other two batteries. Also I found that the generic brand's intensity has begun to decrease. However, both the other two batteries still give off a strong light intensity. This observation raises the question: At what voltage does the light intensity begin to waver? Another question is: Will the other two batteries begin to have lower light intensity at approximately the same voltage as the generic, or will they continue to have a stronger light intensity for longer? The figures below show the change of light intensity of the generic brand of batteries from the beginning until this day's observation.

Student's observations continue to raise questions

Figure 1. Before   *Figure 2.* After

Thursday, October 17, 2013

 Today is my fourth day of observation. The readings for the voltages for this day were:

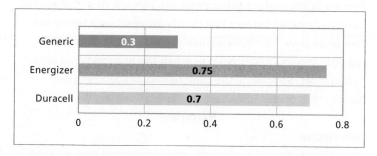

The generic brand is losing even more intensity when it is in the flashlight. It is obvious that it is getting near the end of its battery charge. Today was also the biggest decrease in charge for the generic brand of batteries. This is interesting because it is actually producing less light than before, so why does it lose more voltage toward the end of its life? Also, another thing I observed for this day was that again the Energizer brand holds more voltages than the Duracell, like before. There is still no change in light intensity for the two name brands.

Saturday, October 19, 2013

 Today is my final day of observation. This is the data I collected for this day:

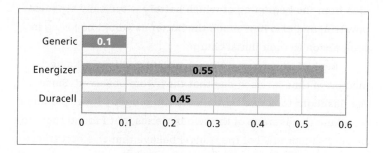

Today the generic battery hardly produced any light out of the flashlight by the end of the time period, although it still didn't drop to 0 voltage, so there are clearly still some electrons flowing in the current throughout the battery. Also, I observed that the Duracell battery has clearly dropped well below the Energizer now. The Duracell has shown a slight decrease in the light intensity compared to when the observational study first started. So what is the composition of the Energizer battery that makes it outlast the Duracell battery?

Narrative

Description

Five days of observations were conducted over an eight-day period. It did not matter what day of the week I took these observations nor the conditions of the environment around my object of study at the time of the observations. The only thing that I made sure that was constant environmentally for all of the batteries in the study was the temperature because more heat results in higher kinetic energy, which causes electrons to move faster. I had to decide on the types of batteries that I wanted to study for the observational study. The batteries I decided on were: Duracell, Energizer, and a generic brand from Wal-Mart. Before I took my first observation I tested each of the batteries that were to be used with the voltmeter to know the initial charge of the battery. Doing this gave me an idea from the beginning of which battery is typically the most powerful and also how much the batteries would be losing in comparison to their initial charge.

Each of these battery types was tested for the same amount of time for each day that they were observed. Since the flashlight took two batteries to run properly I was planning on taking the average of the two batteries, but I found them to be very similar in all of the trials. I believe that this occurrence

The narrative description provides a summary of the student's systematic observation.

is a result of the entire circuit acting at the same time, causing equal electron transfer between the two batteries to occur, thus causing them to have equal voltages.

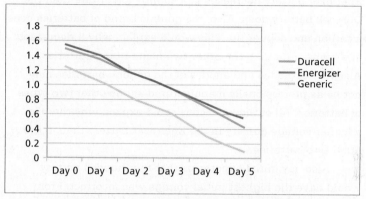

Final Graph from Five Days of Observations

The graph above shows the change in voltage over the five-day period that I took the observations. As you can see, Duracell and Energizer are very similar to one another, with Energizer performing slightly higher than the Duracell brand. The generic has a lower initial voltage than the other two batteries and continues to decrease at a faster rate than the other two batteries. Another thing you can see from this graph is how quickly the generic brand lost its voltage toward the end of its life, whereas the other two batteries seemed to continue to decrease at approximately the same rate throughout.

Speculation

My initial hypothesis that the Duracell battery would decrease at the slowest rate was not supported by this data. I have done a little bit of research on the composition of the cathodes of the Duracell and Energizer batteries. I found that

Evaluates initial hypothesis (speculation) in light of the data the Duracell battery uses a copper tip on the cathode, whereas the Energizer uses a combination of lithium with the copper tip to allow longer battery life. This would explain why the Energizer battery decreases at a slightly lower rate than the Duracell battery does. Also, the generic brand of batteries uses a carbon and copper tip. This would explain why it decreases at a higher rate than the other two name-brand batteries. Also, the cathodes and anodes of the generic batteries may not be as professionally manufactured as the other two types of batteries. All of these reasons could explain why there is a higher voltage density in the Energizer battery than in the other two batteries.

Also, my initial hypothesis that the Duracell battery would have the highest initial voltage was incorrect. From the research that I have gathered, the only explanation for the higher initial voltage in the Energizer battery would be the presence of the alkaline metals that the manufacturer puts into its batteries, whereas the Duracell manufacturer does no such thing. However, there is little information on the Internet about the generic brand of batteries that I used for the experiment, but I was able to find that the reason it has such a lower initial voltage than the other two types of batteries is because it is not packed as well. It takes special equipment to make all the electrons store properly, and the equipment used is not as powerful as the ones that Duracell and Energizer use for their batteries. These ideas all make up my understanding of why there is such a major difference in the rates at which the batteries lose their charge.

For further research into this topic I would recommend using a larger sample, because I used only two batteries for each type of battery. Also, I would recommend looking into the new rechargeable batteries, as that is what a lot of people

Further speculates about factors that contributed to rejection of the hypothesis

Provides suggestions for future research on the subject

are turning to more recently. Another thing that I would try is leaving the batteries on longer because from some of the research that I have done, Duracell does better than Energizer over continuous usage. This means that maybe there is something in the Energizer batteries that causes them to speed up reactions over long periods of use that will cause them to decrease faster over this period. A study like that would be very interesting to compare to my own.

Another interesting topic to follow up on would be the cost of each of the batteries and which battery would be the most cost-effective for users. A lot of people today are buying the generic brand of batteries because they think that this is saving them money. Yes, the generic brand is sold at a lower price, but it is also being used up faster than the other two types of batteries.

RESEARCH PROPOSAL

The research proposal is one of the most common genres of academic writing in the natural sciences. Professional scholars use the **research proposal** to plan out complex studies, to formulate their thoughts, and to submit their research designs to institutional review boards or to grant-funding agencies. The ability to secure grant funding (i.e., to write an effective research proposal and connect it to a realistic, clear budget) is a highly sought-after skill in a job candidate for many academic, government, and private industry positions. In many cases, an effective proposal results from practice with and knowledge of the conventions expected for the genre. No doubt, much of the work of science could not get done without the research proposal, because it is such an important vehicle for securing the funding and materials necessary to conduct research.

Most research proposals include the following sections:

- Title page
- Introduction (and literature review)
- Methods
- References

The *title page* should include (1) the title of your proposal, (2) your name and the names of any co-authors/researchers, and (3) the name of your academic institution. Your instructor may require additional information such as a running header, date, or author's note. Be sure to ask your instructor what documentation and formatting style to use and what information is required in any specific writing context.

The *introduction* of a research proposal explains the topic and purpose of the proposed research. Be sure to include your research question and/or your proposed hypothesis. Additionally, your introduction should contextualize your research by reviewing scholarly articles related to your topic and showing how your proposed research fills a gap in what is already known about the topic. Specifically, the introduction should explain how other researchers have approached your topic (or a closely related one) in the past, with attention to the major overlapping findings in that research. An effective introduction incorporates a literature review that demonstrates your knowledge of other scholars' research. As such, it builds your credibility to conduct your proposed research. (See Chapter 7, pp. 182–85, for more information about writing a literature review.)

The *Methods section* of a research proposal explains exactly what you will do to test your hypothesis (or answer your research question) and how you will do it. It differs from the Methods section of a lab report in several ways: (1) it should be written in future tense, and (2) it should include more detail about your plans. Further, the Methods section should address how long your study will take and should specify how you will collect data (in a step-by-step descriptive manner).

The *references list* for a research proposal is essentially the same as the references list for a lab report or any other academic project. You'll need to include the full citation information for any work you used in your literature review or in planning or researching your topic.

WRITING PROJECT **Developing a Research Proposal**

Drawing on a topic of interest to you, develop a research proposal that outlines a specific research question and/or hypothesis, and describe how you would go about answering the question or testing the hypothesis. Keep in mind that successful research proposals include the elements listed below.

- Title page
- Introduction (and literature review)
- Methods
- References

You might try drawing on the observations you collected while completing an observation logbook to develop your research question and/or hypothesis.

Insider Example
Research Proposal

In the following example of a professional research proposal by Gary Ritchison, a biologist at Eastern Kentucky University, note how the Introduction section begins with a brief introduction to the topic (par. 1) and then proceeds to review the relevant literature on the topic (pars. 1 and 2). As you read, consider how a potential funding entity would likely view both the content and the form in which that content is presented. Also note that the references list is titled "Literature Cited." Minor variations like this are common from discipline to discipline and in various contexts. Here, Ritchison has followed CSE style conventions in his proposal.

Hunting Behavior, Territory Quality, and Individual
Quality of American Kestrels
(*Falco sparverius*)

Gary Ritchison

Department of Biological Sciences
Eastern Kentucky University

Introduction

American Kestrels (*Falco sparverius*) are widely distributed throughout North America. In Kentucky, these falcons are permanent residents and are most abundant in rural farmland, where they hunt over fields and pastures (Palmer-Ball 1996). Although primarily sit-and-wait predators, hunting from elevated perches and scanning the surrounding areas for prey, kestrels also hunt while hovering (Balgooyen 1976). Kellner (1985) reported that nearly 20% of all attacks observed in central Kentucky were made while kestrels were hovering. Habitats used by hunting kestrels in central Kentucky include mowed and unmowed fields, cropland, pastures, and plowed fields (Kellner 1985).

> Establishes the topic and provides background information on American Kestrels

Several investigators have suggested that male and female American Kestrels may exhibit differences in habitat use during the non-breeding period, with males typically found in areas with greater numbers of trees, such as wooded pastures, and females in open fields and pastures (Stinson et al. 1981; Bohall-Wood and Collopy 1986). However, Smallwood (1988) suggested that, when available, male and female kestrels in south-central Florida established winter territories in the same type of habitat. Differential habitat use occurred only because migratory female kestrels usually arrived on wintering areas before males and, therefore, were more likely to establish territories in the better-quality, more open habitats before males arrived (Smallwood 1988).

> Reveals evidence of a review of previous scholarship

In central Kentucky, many American Kestrels are residents. As a result, male and female kestrels would likely have equal opportunity to establish winter territories in the higher-quality, open habitats. If so, habitat segregation should be less apparent in central Kentucky than in areas further south, where wintering populations of kestrels are largely

> Establishes a local context for research

migratory. In addition, territory quality should be correlated with individual quality because higher-quality resident kestrels should be able to defend higher-quality territories.

The objectives of my proposed study of American Kestrels will be to examine possible relationships among and between hunting behavior, territory quality, and individual quality in male and female American Kestrels. The results of this study will provide important information about habitat and perch selection by American Kestrels in central Kentucky in addition to the possible role of individual quality on hunting behavior and habitat use.

Reveals research purposes and identifies significance of the proposed research

Methods

Field work will take place from 15 October 2000 through 15 May 2001 at the Blue Grass Army Depot, Madison Co., Kentucky. During the study period, I will search for American Kestrels throughout accessible portions of the depot. Searches will be conducted on foot as well by automobile.

This section provides a highly detailed description of proposed research procedures, or methods.

An attempt will be made to capture all kestrels observed using bal-chatri traps baited with mice. Once captured, kestrels will be banded with a numbered aluminum band plus a unique combination of colored plastic bands to permit individual identification. For each captured individual, I will take standard morphological measurements (wing chord, tarsus length, tail length, and mass). In addition, 8 to 10 feathers will be plucked from the head, breast, back, and wing, respectively. Plumage in these areas is either reddish or bluish, and the quality of such colors is known to be correlated with individual quality (Hill 1991, 1992; Keyser 1998). Variation in the color and intensity of plumage will be determined using a reflectance spectrometer (Ocean Optics S2000 fiber optic spectrometer, Dunedin, FL), and these values will be used as a measure of individual quality. To confirm that plumage

color and intensity are dependent on condition, we will use
tail feather growth rates as a measure of nutritional condition
during molt. At the time of capture, the outermost tail
feathers will be removed and the mean width of daily growth
bars, which is correlated with nutritional condition (Hill and
Montgomerie 1994), will be determined.

References established
methods, or those
used by other research-
ers, to support his own
method design

Each focal American Kestrel (N = at least 14; 7 males and
7 females) will be observed at least once a week. Observations
will be made at various times during the day, with observation
periods typically 1 to 3 hours in duration. During focal bird
observations, individuals will be monitored using binoculars
and spotting scopes. Information will be recorded on a
portable tape recorder for later transcription. During each
observation, I will record all attacks and whether attacks
were initiated from a perch or while hovering. For perches,
I will note the time a kestrel lands on a perch and the time
until the kestrel either initiates an attack or leaves for another
perch (giving up time). If an attack is made, I will note attack
distances (the distance from a perch to the point where a
prey item was attacked) and outcome (successful or not). If
successful, an attempt will be made to identify the prey (to the
lowest taxonomic category possible).

The activity budgets of kestrels will also be determined
by observing the frequency and duration of kestrel behaviors
during randomly selected 20-min observation periods (i.e., a
randomly selected period during the 1- to 3-hour observation
period). During these 20-minute periods, the frequency of
occurrence of each of the following behaviors will be recorded:
capturing prey, preening, engaging in nonpreening comfort
movements (including scratching, stretching wing or tail,
shaking body plumage, cleaning foot with bill, and yawning),
vocalizing, and flying. The context in which flight occurs,

including pounces on prey, and the duration of flights and of preening bouts will also be recorded.

Territories will be delineated by noting the locations of focal kestrels, and the vegetation in each kestrel's winter territory will be characterized following the methods of Smallwood (1987). Possible relationships among hunting behavior (mode of attack, perch time, attack distance and outcome [successful or unsuccessful], and type of prey attacked), territory vegetation, time budgets, sex, and individual quality will be examined. All analyses will be conducted using the Statistical Analysis System (SAS Institute 1989).

Literature Cited

Balgooyen TG. 1976. Behavior and ecology of the American Kestrel in the Sierra Nevada of California. Univ Calif Publ Zool 103:1-83.

Bohall-Wood P, Collopy MW. 1986. Abundance and habitat selection of two American Kestrel subspecies in north-central Florida. Auk 103:557-563.

Craighead JJ, Craighead FC Jr. 1956. Hawks, owls, and wildlife. Harrisburg (PA): Stackpole.

Hill GE. 1991. Plumage coloration is a sexually selected indicator of male quality. Nature 350:337-339.

Hill GE. 1992. Proximate basis of variation in carotenoid pigmentation in male House Finches. Auk 109:1-12.

Hill GE, Montgomerie R. 1994. Plumage colour signals nutritional condition in the House Finch. Proc R Soc Lond B Biol Sci 258:47-52.

Kellner CJ. 1985. A comparative analysis of the foraging behavior of male and female American Kestrels in central Kentucky [master's thesis]. [Richmond (KY)]: Eastern Kentucky University.

Keyser AJ. 1998. Is structural color a reliable signal of quality in Blue Grosbeaks? [master's thesis]. [Auburn (AL)]: Auburn University.

Mengel RM. 1965. The birds of Kentucky. Lawrence (KS): Allen Press. (American Ornithologists' Union monograph; 3).

Palmer-Ball B. 1996. The Kentucky breeding bird atlas. Lexington (KY): Univ. Press of Kentucky.

SAS Institute. 1989. SAS user's guide: statistics. Cary (NC): SAS Institute.

Smallwood JA. 1987. Sexual segregation by habitat in American Kestrels wintering in southcentral Florida: vegetative structure and responses of differential prey availability. Condor 89:842-849.

Running head: WHICH BATTERY IS MOST EFFECTIVE? 1

The researcher provides a descriptive, non-rhetorical title.

Which Type of Battery Is the Most Effective

When Energy Is Drawn Rapidly?

Kedric Lemon

North Carolina State University

Which Type of Battery Is the Most Effective
When Energy Is Drawn Rapidly?

Introduction

Today batteries are used in many of the products that we
use every day, from the TV remote to the car we drive to work.
AA batteries are one of the most widely used battery types,
but which of these AA batteries is the most effective? Almeida,
Xará, Delgado, and Costa (2006) tested five different types
of batteries in a study similar to mine. They allowed each of
the batteries to run the product for an hour. The product they
were powering alternated from open to closed circuit, so the
batteries went from not giving off energy to giving off energy
very quickly. The researchers then measured the pulse of
the battery to determine the charge. The pulse test is a very
effective way of reading the battery because it is closed circuit,
meaning it doesn't run the battery to find the voltage, and
it is highly accurate. They found that the Energizer battery
had the largest amount of pulses after the experiment. The
energizer had on average 20 more pulses than the Duracell
battery, giving the Energizer battery approximately a half
hour longer in battery life when being used rapidly. Booth
(1999) also performed his experiment using the pulse test.
However, this experiment involved allowing the batteries
to constantly give off energy for two hours, and then Booth
measured the pulse. So his experiment is more comparable
to my observational study because it was constantly drawing
energy from the battery. In this experiment he found that
the Duracell battery was the most effective. The Duracell
battery had over 40 more pulses per minute than the Energizer
battery, which means that the battery could last for an hour
longer than the Energizer battery would.

The report follows the conventional IMRAD format.

The researcher establishes a focus for his research by positing a research question.

Reviews previous research, and connects that research to the current research project

However, in today's market, rechargeable batteries are becoming increasing popular. Zucker (2005) compared 16 different types of rechargeable batteries. Most of these batteries were Nickel Metal Hydride, but a couple of them were the more traditional rechargeable AA battery, the Nickel Cadmium. In his study Zucker was testing how these batteries faired on their second charge after being discharged as closely as they could; rechargeable batteries are not allowed to go to 0 volts because then they cannot be recharged. In the end Zucker found that all but four of the batteries came back up to at least 70% of their initial charge, two of which did not even recharge at all. He found that, not surprisingly, the two most effective rechargeable batteries were Duracell and Energizer, which both came back to 86% of the first charge. However, the Energizer rechargeable battery had the higher initial charge, so Zucker concluded that the Energizer battery was the most effective rechargeable battery. Yu, Lai, Yan, and Wu (1999) looked at the capacity of three different Nickel Metal Hydride (NiMH) rechargeable batteries. They first took three different types of NiMH batteries and found the electrical capacity through a voltmeter. After, they measured the volume of each of the batteries to discover where it fell in the AA battery range of 600 to 660 mAh/cm3. They used this to test the efficiency of the NiMH batteries, as there are slightly different chemical compositions inside the batteries. In the end they concluded that the NiMH battery from the Duracell brand was the most efficient.

Li, Daniel, and Wood (2011) looked at the improvements being made to lithium ion AA batteries. The lithium ion AA batteries are extremely powerful, but in recent years they have become increasingly more popular for studying by many researchers. Li et al. tested the voltage of the lithium ion AA rechargeable battery and found that the starting voltage was

Prominence of dates points to the researcher's concern for the recency of source materials

Continues review of previous scholarship on this topic

on average 3.2 volts. That is more than the average onetime-use AA battery. They further found that what makes modern lithium ion batteries so much more powerful is the cathodes. Research into cathode materials has significantly increased the rate of reactions for lithium ion batteries.

The objective of this study is to determine which brand of batteries is the most efficient and to compare a generic rechargeable battery to these regular AA batteries. My original research question for my logbook was Which brand of AA batteries is the most effective over extended usage? However, for my final study I wanted to look at how batteries reacted when they were being used very quickly, so I formed two research questions for this study: Which type of battery is the most effective for rapid uses? How do regular AA batteries compare to a generic AA rechargeable battery? My hypothesis for this experiment is that the Energizer battery will be the most effective battery when energy is being taken from the battery rapidly.

Establishes specific research questions on the basis of previous observations

Hypothesis

Method

Observation Logbook

In my observation logbook I looked at how different types of batteries compared when they were being tested through a flashlight. The batteries I observed were Duracell, Energizer, and a generic brand. I allowed the flashlight to run for an hour with the set of batteries inside. I did this step for all three types of batteries that I observed in that study. After the hour was up I tested the voltage with a voltmeter. I continued to do this for five consecutive days. For each of the tests I made sure that the temperature was the same for each of the batteries while they were being tested. I also allowed the flashlight to remain off for an hour to let it cool down. These steps were taken to avoid any unknown variables.

Reports on research previously conducted

For my follow-up study, I decided to look at how batteries compare when they are being used in quick bursts, meaning that they quickly change from using no energy to using a lot of energy rapidly. In order to test the battery this way I had to change the flashlight to a strobe light so that it quickly turns on and off automatically. I also decided to add a rechargeable battery to my tests since this is an increasingly popular item today. I found my data by attaching the batteries to a voltmeter immediately after they were taken out of the strobe light. Each of the set of batteries was in the strobe light for 20 minutes.

Variables that I made sure remained constant for this experiment were the temperature of the room as well as the temperature of the strobe light. For this reason I allowed the strobe light a 30-minute cooldown before I put the next set of batteries into it.

Limitations

One of the limitations that I faced in this study was an inability to get the thermocouple that I wanted to measure the temperature of the battery. Also I had a small sample size, so if I had taken more samples, then my results would have been more valid. I could improve on these by getting a thermocouple that would measure the temperature. This would allow me to compare the expected voltage of the battery through the thermocouple and the voltmeter. After

Provides a detailed account of research procedures

The researcher uses technical language, or jargon.

the battery got out of the strobe light I would hook it up to the thermocouple and then measure the voltage by looking at the voltmeter. I could tell what the voltage of the battery is through the thermocouple using a graph that one of my secondary sources provided. Another limitation that I faced in this experiment was that I lacked better equipment that could have made my results more accurate — like a pulse reader or a better voltmeter, as I was using a fairly inexpensive one.

Results

My results from my logbook provided me with primarily quantitative data. For each of the types of batteries I found these results.

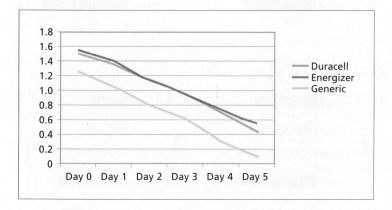

For the Energizer battery I found that it started off with the largest initial charge of 1.55 volts. On average the Energizer battery lost .16 volts for every hour. The Duracell battery had an initial charge of 1.5 volts and lost an average of .18 volts per hour. Last, the generic brand of battery had an initial voltage of 1.25 volts and lost on average .23 volts every hour.

In this experiment I found that the Energizer battery again had the highest starting charge and highest ending charge. The Duracell AA battery was close behind the

The researcher notes limitations he encountered with the methods.

Outlines the major findings of the study. A number of results are also presented visually, in the form of graphs and figures.

The researcher frequently presents results in tables and charts.

Energizer. The generic brand of batteries came next, followed by the rechargeable battery.

This experiment showed similar results to what I had found in my logbook. The Duracell and Energizer batteries were both very similar, while the generic brand lagged behind.

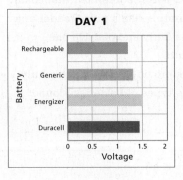

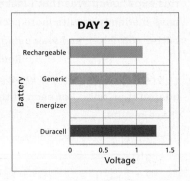

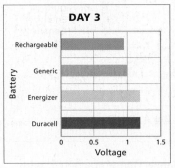

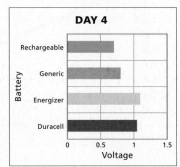

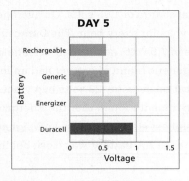

Battery	Initial voltage (volts)	Final voltage (volts)	Average volts lost (volts/20 min)
Energizer	1.60	1.10	0.10
Duracell	1.55	0.95	0.12
Generic	1.40	0.60	0.16
Rechargeable	1.20	0.55	0.13

The table shows that the Energizer battery had the best results in all categories. If I had taken more samples, then I may have found that some of the batteries performed better or worse than they did here, because I could have taken the average of many tests rather than looking at only one. Using a pulse test reader would have been an even more informative way of exploring this experiment because that instrument can estimate the battery life with high precision.

Discussion

Through this experiment I found that the Energizer battery is the most effective battery when used in rapid bursts. Also I found that the rechargeable battery had very bad ratings. Despite the poor ratings, however, it is rechargeable, being a potential reason for its failure. The rechargeable battery is not able to commit as many of its chemicals to solely providing the maximum amount of energy; it has to provide some of the chemicals to the battery's capabilities of recharging. Based on this, the rechargeable battery could be the most effective battery. I found that other studies with similar methods (Booth 1999; Yu, Lai, Yan, & Wu 1999) determined that the Duracell battery was the most effective. However, these studies were conducted years ago.

If I had had more days to conduct this experiment, I could have more accurately represented the usefulness of

Provides an overview of the implications of major findings in light of previous scholarship the rechargeable battery, because after it exhausted its first charge it came back completely recharged for the next day. Another limitation that I faced in this experiment was that I overestimated how fast the battery voltages would decrease in the strobe light, so I was unable to see how the batteries acted near the end of their charge. An area of study for further research would be to compare different types of rechargeable batteries. For instance, I already know that the lithium ion AA rechargeable batteries carry more volts than regular AA batteries, and they are rechargeable.

Discusses limitations of the study overall

If I had had more time to perform this experiment or had allowed the batteries to be in the strobe light for a longer time, I think that I would have found that the rechargeable battery would be ahead of the generic battery in terms of the average voltage lost. Also I think that the gap would have been larger between the Duracell battery and the Energizer battery because looking at my results from the observation logbook shows that the Energizer battery does a lot better than the Duracell battery toward the end of its life. This being said, I think that the Duracell battery does not handle the rapid uses as well as the extended uses.

These results show that the Energizer battery is the most effective battery for rapid use and, from my observation logbook, the most effective for extended use. The rechargeable battery used in this experiment is hard to compare to these regular AA batteries because I wasn't able to exploit its sole advantage, recharging. However, this was just a generic brand of rechargeable batteries, so it would be interesting to see how the Duracell and Energizer rechargeable batteries compare to their regular batteries.

References

Almeida, M. F., Xará, S. M., Delgado, J., & Costa, C. A. (2006). Characterization of spent AA household alkaline batteries. *Waste Management, 26*(5), 466-476. doi:10.1016/j.wasman.2005.04.005

Booth, S. A. (1999). High-drain alkaline AA-batteries. *Popular Electronics, 16*(1), 5.

Li, J., Daniel, C., & Wood, D. (2011). Materials processing for lithium-ion batteries. *Journal of Power Sources, 196*(5), 2452-2460. doi:10.1016/j.jpowsour.2010.11.001

Yu, C. Z., Lai, W. H., Yan, G. J., & Wu, J. Y. (1999). Study of preparation technology for high performance AA size Ni–MH batteries. *Journal of Alloys and Compounds, 293*(1-2), 784-787. doi:10.1016/S0925-8388(99)00463-6

Zucker, P. (2005). AA batteries tested: Rechargeable batteries. *Australian PC User, 17*(6), 51.

Provides a list of sources used in the construction of the lab report

- **Systematic observation plays a critical role in the natural sciences.** The disciplines of the natural sciences rely on methods of observation to generate and answer research questions about how and why natural phenomena act as they do.

- **Many natural scientists work in interdisciplinary fields of study.** These fields, such as biochemistry and biophysics, combine subject matter and methods from more than one field to address research questions.

- **Scientists typically conduct research according to the steps of the scientific method:** observe, ask a research question, formulate a hypothesis, test the hypothesis through experimentation, and explain results.

- **The scientific writing process follows logically from the steps of the scientific method:** observe and describe, speculate, experiment, and report.

- **To test their hypotheses, or their proposed answers to research questions, natural scientists may use multiple methods.** Two common methods are systematic observation and experimentation.

- **Scientific research proposals are typically vetted by institutional review boards (IRB).** Committees that review research proposals are charged with the task of examining all elements of a scientific study to ensure that it treats subjects equitably and ethically.

- **Conventional rhetorical features of the scientific community reflect the shared values of the community's members.** Some of these values are objectivity, replicability, recency, and cooperation and collaboration.

- **Members of the scientific community frequently produce a number of genres.** These include the observation logbook, the research proposal, and the lab report.

Reading and Writing in the Applied Fields

Introduction to the Applied Fields

In this chapter, we explore some of the applied fields that students often encounter or choose to study as part of their college experience. Throughout the chapter, we also look at some of the genres through which writers in these fields communicate to various audiences.

WHAT ARE APPLIED FIELDS?

Applied fields are areas of academic study that focus on the production of practical knowledge and that share a core mission of preparing students for specific careers. Often, that preparation includes hands-on training. Examples of applied fields that prepare students for particular careers include nursing, business, law, education, and engineering, but a somewhat more complete list appears below.

Some Applied Fields

Sports psychology	Counseling
Business	Statistics
Law	Engineering
Education	Speech pathology
Nursing	Public administration
Applied physics	Architecture
Applied linguistics	Broadcast journalism
Social work	

ANDREA TSURUMI

Research in the applied fields typically attempts to solve problems. An automotive engineering team, for example, might start with a problem like consumers' reluctance to buy an all-electric vehicle. The team must first observe and acknowledge that there is a problem, and then it would need to define the scope of the problem. Why does the problem exist? What are the factors contributing to consumers' reluctance to buy an all-electric vehicle? Once a problem has been identified and defined, the team of researchers can then begin to explore solutions to overcome the problem.

Examples of large-scale problems that require practical applications of research are issues such as: racial inequality in the American criminal justice system, the lack of clean drinking water in some non-industrialized nations, obesity and heart disease, and ways to provide outstanding public education to children with behavioral problems. These are all real-world problems scholars and practitioners in the applied fields are working to solve this very moment.

INSIDE WORK **Defining and Solving Problems**

> Describe a time when you conducted research to solve a problem. Start by defining the problem and explaining why you needed to solve it. When did you first identify the problem? What caused you to seek solutions to it? How did you research and understand the problem? What methods did you use to solve it? ❱

Professionals in applied fields often work in collaboration with one another, or in teams, to complete research and other projects, and professors who teach in these areas often assign tasks that require interaction and cooperation among a group of students to create a product or to solve a problem. In the field of business management, for example, teams of professionals often must work together to market a new product. Solid communication and interpersonal skills are necessary for a team to manage a budget, design a marketing or advertising campaign, and engage with a client successfully all at the same time. As such, the ability to work cooperatively—to demonstrate effective interpersonal and team communication skills—is highly valued among professionals in the applied fields. You shouldn't be surprised, then, if you're one day applying for a job in an applied field and an interviewer asks you to share a little about your previous experiences working in teams to successfully complete a project. As you learn more about the applied fields examined in this chapter, take care to note those writing tasks completed by teams, or those moments when cooperation among professionals working in a particular field are highlighted by the content of the genres we explore.

Our purpose in this chapter is to offer a basic introduction to a few of the many applied fields of study and to explore some of the kinds of writing that typically occur in these fields. Because the applied fields vary so much, we've chosen to focus on specific disciplines as examples since we cannot generalize conventions across applied fields. The rest of the chapter examines specific applied fields and examples of writing through a rhetorical approach.

INSIDE WORK **Considering Additional Applied Fields**

Visit your college or university's website, and locate a listing of the majors or concentrations offered in any academic department. In light of the definition of an *applied field* proposed above, consider whether any of the majors or concentrations identified for that particular discipline could be described as applied fields. Additionally, spend some time considering your own major or potential area of concentration: Are you studying an applied field? Are there areas of study within your major or concentration that could be considered applied fields? If so, what are they, and why would you consider them applied fields? ❯

Rhetoric and the Applied Fields

Because applied fields are centrally focused on preparing professionals who will work in those fields, students are often asked to engage audiences associated with the work they'll do in those fields after graduation. Imagine that you've just graduated from college with a degree in business management and have secured a job as a marketing director for a business. What kinds of writing do you expect to encounter in this new position? What audiences do you expect to be writing for? You may well be asked to prepare business analyses or market reports. You may be asked to involve yourself in new product management or even the advertising campaign for a product. All these activities, which call for different kinds of writing, will require you to manage information and to shape your communication of that information into texts that are designed specifically for other professionals in your field—such as boards of directors, financial officers, or advertising executives. As a student in the applied field of business management, you therefore need to become familiar with the audiences, genres, conventions, and other expectations for writing specific to your career path that extend beyond academic audiences. Being mindful of the rhetorical situation in which you must communicate with other professionals is essential to your potential success as a writer in an applied field.

As with more traditional academic writing, we recommend that you analyze carefully any writing situation you encounter in an applied field. You might begin by responding to the following questions:

LaunchPadSolo

Criminal justice instructor Michelle Richter discusses the role of audience.

1. **Who is my audience?** Unlike the audience for a lab report for a chemistry class or the audience for an interpretation of a poem in a literature class, your audience for writing in an applied field is just as likely to be non-academic as academic. Certainly, the writing most students will do in their actual careers will be aimed at other professionals in their field, not researchers or professors in a university. In addition to understanding exactly who your audience is, be sure to consider the specific needs of your target audience.

2. **In light of my purpose and the audience's needs, is there an appropriate genre that I should rely on to communicate my information?** As in the more traditional academic disciplines, there are many genres through which professionals in applied fields communicate. Keeping your purpose for writing in mind, you'll want to consider whether the information you have to share should be reported in a specific genre: Should you write a memorandum, a marketing proposal, or an executive summary, for instance? Answering this question can help you determine if there is an appropriate form, or genre, through which to communicate your information.

3. **Are there additional conventional expectations I should consider for the kind of writing task I need to complete?** Beyond simply identifying an appropriate genre, answering this question can help you determine how to shape the information you need to communicate to your target audience. If the writing task requires a particular genre, then you're likely to use features that conventionally appear as part of that genre. Of course, there are many good reasons to communicate information in other ways. In these situations, we recommend that you carefully consider the appropriateness of the structural, language, and reference features you employ.

Genres in Selected Applied Fields

In the sections that follow, we offer brief introductions to some applied fields of study and provide examples of genres that students and professionals working in these fields often produce. We explore expectations for these genres by highlighting conventional structure, language, and reference features that writers in these fields frequently rely on.

NURSING

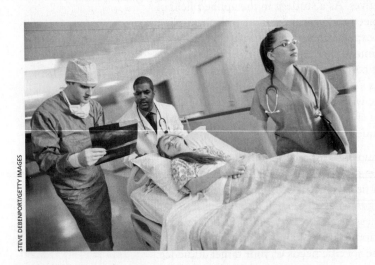

STEVE DEBENPORT/GETTY IMAGES

Most of us have had experiences with nurses, who, along with physicians and other medical professionals, serve on the front lines of preventing and treating illness in our society. In addition to their hands-on engagement with individuals in clinical and community settings, nurses spend a good deal of their time writing—whether documenting their observations about patients in medical charts, preparing orders for medical procedures, designing care plans, or communicating with patients. A student of nursing might encounter any number of additional forms of writing tasks, including nursing care plans for individuals, reviews of literature, and community or public health assessment papers, just to name a few. Each of these forms of communication requires that nurses be especially attuned to the needs of various audiences. A nurse communicating with a patient, for example, might have to translate medical jargon such that the individual can fully understand his or her treatment. Alternatively, a nurse who is producing a care plan for a patient would likely need to craft the document such that other nurses and medical professionals could follow methodically the assessments and recommendations for care. Some nurses, especially those who undertake advanced study or who prepare others to become nurses, often design, implement, or participate in research studies.

We interviewed Dr. Janna Dieckmann, a registered nurse and clinical associate professor in the School of Nursing at the University of North Carolina at Chapel Hill. In her Insider's View, she offers valuable insights into the writing and researching practices of the nursing community.

As Dr. Dieckmann notes, many nurses, especially those working to prepare other nurses, may also participate in various kinds of scholarly research endeavors. In the section that follows, we provide an excerpted look at a 2005 research study published in *Newborn and Infant Nursing Reviews*, a journal of nursing, along with an example of discharge instructions. The latter is a genre of writing that nurses who work in a clinical setting often produce for patients.

Insider's View
Nurses and nursing consider many different areas of research and interest
JANNA DIECKMANN, NURSING

"Research in nursing is varied, including quantitative research into health and illness patterns, as well as intervention to maximize health and reduce illness. Qualitative research varies widely, including research in the history of nursing, which is my focus. There is a wide variety of types of writing demanded in a nursing program. It is so varied that many connections are possible. Cross-discipline collaborations among faculty of various professional schools are valued at many academic institutions today. One of my colleagues conducted research on rats. Another looked at sleep patterns in older adults as a basis for understanding dementia onset. One public health nursing colleague conducts research on out-of-work women, and another examines crosscultural competence. These interests speak to our reasons for becoming nurses—our seeking out of real life, of direct experience, of being right there with people, and of understanding others and their worlds."

Scholarly Research Report

Some nurses are both practitioners and scholars of nursing. As practitioners, they assess and care for patients in cooperation with other medical professionals. As scholars, they may, as Dr. Dieckmann indicates, conduct research on a host of issues, including the history and best practices of nursing. In addition to producing scholarship that advances the field of nursing, these nurses typically work in colleges or universities with programs that prepare individuals for careers in nursing. Such nurses, then, may assume multiple roles as researchers and educators, and as practitioners.

Insider Example
Professional Research Report in Nursing

As you read the following research report, pay particular attention to the structure, language, and reference parallels between the form of the report and those you've encountered already in the fields of the natural sciences and the social sciences. Keep in mind that the text presented here is made up of a series of excerpts from a much lengthier and more substantial research report.

Rural African-American Mothers Parenting Prematurely Born Infants: An Ecological Systems Perspective

MARGARET SHANDOR MILES, PhD, FAAN; DIANE HOLDITCH-DAVIS, PhD, FAAN;
SUZANNE THOYRE, PhD; LINDA BEEBER, PhD

The abstract provides an overview of the report, including a description of the study's purpose, its methods, and its central findings.

ABSTRACT

This qualitative descriptive study describes the concerns and issues of rural African-American mothers with prematurely born infants. Mothers were part of a larger nurse-parent support intervention. The 18 mothers lived in rural areas in the Southeast, and their infants were younger than 35 weeks gestational age at birth and at high risk for developmental problems because they either weighed less than 1500 grams at birth or required mechanical ventilation. Field notes written by the intervention nurses providing support to the mothers after discharge from the hospital were analyzed using methods of content analysis. Concerns of the mothers related to the infant's health and development, the maternal role in parenting the infant, personal aspects of their lives, and relationship issues particularly with the fathers. Findings support the importance of an ecological systems perspective when designing research and caring for rural African-American mothers with prematurely born children.

The review of the literature begins with a synthesis point: mothers experience a period of transitioning. Both McHaffie and May confirm this conclusion.

REVIEW OF THE LITERATURE

Although mothers are excited about taking the preterm infant home, a number of studies have noted that they are also anxious during this important transition. McHaffie[1] found mothers insecure and lacking in confidence at first, followed by a period of accommodation as they learned about the infant's behavioral cues and needs. During this period, mothers became overwhelmed with responsibilities, and fatigue resulted. As the infants settled into their new surroundings and the mothers felt the rewards of caregiving, they became confident in their maternal role. May[2] also found that mothers went through a process of learning about the added responsibilities of caregiving, and this resulted in strains on their time and energy. Mothers were vigilant about looking for changes in the infant's status and for signs of progress through improved physical health and development. During this process, they looked for signs that their child was normal and sought support from others. . . .

METHOD

This study used a qualitative descriptive design[3] to identify the concerns and issues of the mothers based on field notes written by the intervention nurses providing support to the mothers after discharge from the hospital.[4] The Nursing Support Intervention was an 18-month in-person and telephone intervention provided by master's-prepared nurses starting around the time of discharge of the infant and ending when the infants were around 18 months old corrected for prematurity. The nurses helped the mothers to process the mothering experience and resolve emotional distress that is caused by prematurity, identify and reduce parenting and other life stresses, develop relationships with their infants, and identify and use acceptable resources to meet needs of the infant and the mother. . . .

Qualitative research methods are explained.

RESULTS

The concerns and issues raised by the mothers with the intervention nurses fell into four major categories: infant health and development, parenting, personal concerns, and relationship issues (Table 1).

Results of the study, or categories of concerns identified among mothers, are presented in the form of a summary table. The researchers explore these results in more detail in a number of additional paragraphs.

Table 1.
Maternal concerns of rural African-American mothers in parenting prematurely born infants

Infant health and development	Establishing feeding and managing gastrointestinal tract distress
	Managing medical technologies
	Preventing and managing infections
	Establishing sleep patterning
	Learning developmental expectations
Parenting	Learning the infant's needs
	Establishing daily patterns
	Balancing roles
Personal concerns	Coping with financial problems
	Managing stressful jobs while securing appropriate childcare
	Losing and trying to regain educational opportunities toward a better life
	Working toward securing a home of one's own
	Managing depressive symptoms
Relationship issues	Working through relationship with infant's father

The study's Discussion section connects findings to potential changes in support that could improve outcomes for mothers and their children.

DISCUSSION

Findings from this study provide insight into the needs of mothers of prematurely born infants after discharge from the hospital. In the early months after discharge, support is needed related to caring for the infant. As their infants grow, mothers may need help in identifying and getting resources for developmental problems. Agencies that provide services to mothers need to consider the complex lives of the mothers, especially those who are single and living in poverty. Of utmost importance is helping the mothers to manage issues related to finding a job, managing work, and care of their infant. Finding acceptable day care is a particularly important need. Furthermore, community programs are needed to help the mothers achieve their dreams of furthering their education and finding acceptable homes for themselves and their children.

REFERENCES

1. McHaffie HE. Mothers of very low birthweight babies: how do they adjust? J Adv Nurs. 1990;15:6–11.

2. May KM. Searching for normalcy: mothers' caregiving for low birthweight infants. Pediatr Nurs. 1997;23:17–20.

3. Sandelowski M. Whatever happened to qualitative description? Res Nurs Health. 2000;23: 334–340.

4. Holditch-Davis D. A nursing support intervention for mothers of preterm infants. Grant funded by the National Institute of Nursing Research (NR05263). 2001.

Discharge Instructions

If you've ever been hospitalized, then you probably remember the experience quite vividly. It's likely that you interacted with a nurse, who perhaps assessed your health upon arrival. You were also likely cared for by a nurse, or a particular group of nurses, during your stay. Nurses also often play an integral role in a patient's discharge from a hospital. Typically, before a patient is released from a hospital, a nurse provides, in written form, and explains to the patient (and perhaps a family member or two, or another intended primary caregiver) a set of instructions for aftercare. This constitutes the **discharge instructions**.

This document, or series of documents, includes instructions for how to care for oneself at home. The instructions may focus on managing diet and medications, as well as caring for other needs, such as post-operative bandaging procedures. They may also include exercise or diet management plans recommended for long-term recovery and health maintenance. Often presented in bulleted series of items or statements, these lists are usually highly generic; that is, the same instructions frequently apply for patients with the same or similar health conditions. For this reason, discharge instruction forms may include spaces for nurses or other healthcare professionals to write in more specific information relating to a patient's individual circumstances. As well, discharge instructions frequently include information about a patient's follow-up care with his or her doctor or primary caregiver. This could take the form of a future appointment time or directions to call for a follow-up appointment or to consult with another physician. An additional conventional element of discharge instructions is a list of signs of a medical emergency and directions concerning when and how to seek medical attention immediately, should certain signs or symptoms appear in the patient. Finally, discharge instructions are typically signed and dated by a physician or nurse, and they are sometimes signed by the patient as well.

Many patients are in unclear states of mind or are extremely vulnerable at the time of release from a hospital, so nurses who provide and explain discharge instructions to patients are highly skilled at assessing patients' understanding of these instructions.

Insider Example
Discharge Instructions

The following text is an example of a typical set of discharge instructions. As you read the document, consider areas in the instructions that you think a nurse would be more likely to stress to a patient in a discharge meeting: What would a nurse cover quickly? What would he or she want to communicate most clearly to a patient?

FIRST HOSPITAL
Where Care Comes First

Patient's Name:	John Q. Patient
Healthcare Provider's Name:	First Hospital
Department:	Cardiology
Phone:	617-555-1212
Date:	Thursday, May 8, 2014
Notes:	**Nurses can write personalized notes to the patient here.**

Discharge Instructions for Heart Attack

A heart attack occurs when blood flow to the heart muscle is interrupted. This deprives the heart muscle of oxygen, causing tissue damage or tissue death. Common treatments include lifestyle changes, oxygen, medicines, and surgery.

Steps to Take

Home Care

- Rest until your doctor says it is okay to return to work or other activities.
- Take all medicines as prescribed by your doctor. Beta-blockers, ACE inhibitors, and antiplatelet therapy are often recommended.
- Attend a cardiac rehabilitation program if recommended by your doctor.

Diet

Eat a heart-healthy diet:

- Limit your intake of fat, cholesterol, and sodium. Foods such as ice cream, cheese, baked goods, and red meat are not the best choices.
- Increase your intake of whole grains, fish, fruits, vegetables, and nuts.
- Consume alcohol in moderation: one to two drinks per day for men, one drink per day for women.
- Discuss supplements with your doctor.

Your doctor may refer you to a dietician to advise you on meal planning.

Physical Activity

The American Heart Association recommends at least 30 minutes of exercise daily, or at least 3–4 times per week, for patients who have had a heart attack. Your doctor will let you know when you are ready to begin regular exercise.

- Ask your doctor when you will be able to return to work.
- Ask your doctor when you may resume sexual activity.
- Do not drive unless your doctor has given you permission to do so.

Medications

The following medicines may be prescribed to prevent you from having another heart attack:

- Aspirin, which has been shown to decrease the risk of heart attacks
  - Certain painkillers, such as ibuprofen, when taken together with aspirin, may put you at high risk for gastrointestinal bleeding and also reduce the effectiveness of aspirin.
- Clopidogrel or prasugrel
  - Avoid omeprazole or esomeprazole if you take clopidogrel. They may make clopidogrel not work. Ask your doctor for other drug choices.
- ACE inhibitors
- Nitroglycerin
- Beta-blockers or calcium channel blockers

- Cholesterol-lowering medicines
- Blood pressure medicines
- Pain medicines
- Anti-anxiety or antidepressant medicines

If you are taking medicines, follow these general guidelines:

- Take your medicine as directed. Do not change the amount or the schedule.
- Do not stop taking them without talking to your doctor.
- Do not share them.
- Ask what the results and side effects are. Report them to your doctor.
- Some drugs can be dangerous when mixed. Talk to a doctor or pharmacist if you are taking more than one drug. This includes over-the-counter medicine and herbal or dietary supplements.
- Plan ahead for refills so you do not run out.

Directions are provided in as few words as possible.

Lifestyle Changes and Prevention

Together, you and your doctor will plan proper lifestyle changes that will aid in your recovery. Some things to keep in mind to recover and prevent another heart attack include:

- If you smoke, talk to your doctor about ways to help you quit. There are many options to choose from, like using nicotine replacement products, taking prescription medicines to ease cravings and withdrawal symptoms, participating in smoking cessation classes, or doing an online self-help program.
- Have your cholesterol checked regularly.
- Get regular medical check-ups.
- Control your blood pressure.
- Eat a healthful diet, one that is low in saturated fat and rich in whole grains, fruits, and vegetables.
- Have a regular, low-impact exercise program.
- Maintain a healthy weight.
- Manage stress through activities such as yoga, meditation, and counseling.
- If you have diabetes, maintain good control of your condition.

Follow-Up

Since your recovery needs to be monitored, be sure to keep all appointments and have exams done regularly as directed by your doctor. In addition, some people have feelings of depression or anxiety after a heart attack. To get the help you need, be sure to discuss these feelings with your doctor.

Schedule a follow-up appointment as directed by your doctor.

Provides directions for how to "follow up" with medical provider(s)

Call for Medical Help Right Away If Any of the Following Occurs

Call for medical help right away if you have symptoms of another heart attack, including:

- Chest pain, which may feel like a crushing weight on your chest
- A sense of fullness, squeezing, or pressure in the chest
- Anxiety, especially feeling a sense of doom or panic without apparent reason
- Rapid, irregular heartbeat
- Pain, tingling, or numbness in the left shoulder and arm, the neck or jaw, or the right arm
- Sweating
- Nausea or vomiting
- Indigestion or heartburn
- Lightheadedness, weakness, or fainting
- Shortness of breath
- Abdominal pain

If you think you have an emergency, call for medical help right away.

Identifies emergency indicators

INSIDE WORK) **Nurse for a Day**

In Table 1 on page 267, the authors of the qualitative research report "Rural African-American Mothers Parenting Prematurely Born Infants: An Ecological Systems Perspective" identify a number of "concerns and issues" among rural mothers with premature infants. Choose one of these "concerns and issues," and develop a discharge plan for a mother and child in response. Using "Discharge Instructions for Heart Attack" as a model for your own set of discharge instructions, complete the following.

- Provide a brief introduction in which you offer a quick overview of the concern or issue.

- Provide supporting instructions for patients in three central areas: Steps to Take, Follow-Up, and Emergency Response. Note that many, or all, of the directives or recommendations that make up your instructions may be non-medical treatments, interventions, or therapies. You may consult additional sources for support, as needed.

- Authorize the discharge orders by signing and dating your document.

Once you've completed the discharge instructions, spend some time reflecting on the challenges you faced in the process of devising your instructions: What were the least and most challenging parts of writing the instructions? ▶

EDUCATION

When your teachers tell you that writing is important, they're probably conveying a belief based on their own experiences. Professional educators do a lot of writing. As students, you're aware of many contexts in which teachers write on a daily basis. They have project assignment sheets to design, papers

to comment on and grade, websites to design, and e-mails to answer, just to name a few. However, educators also spend a great deal of time planning classes and designing lesson plans. Though students rarely see these written products, they are essential, if challenging and time-consuming, endeavors for teachers. We provide examples and discussion of two forms of writing frequently produced by professionals in the various fields of education: the lesson plan and the Individualized Education Plan (IEP).

When designing a **lesson plan**, teachers must consider many factors, including their goals and objectives for student learning, the materials needed to execute a lesson, the activities students will participate in as part of a lesson, and the methods they'll use to assess student learning. Among other considerations, teachers must also make sure their lesson plans help them meet prescribed curricular mandates.

Insider Example
Student Lesson Plan

The following lesson plan for a tenth-grade English class was designed by Dr. Myra Moses, who at the time of writing the plan was a doctoral candidate in education. In this plan, Dr. Moses begins by identifying the state-mandated curricular standards the lesson addresses. She then identifies the broader goals of her lesson plan before establishing the more specific objectives, or exactly what students will do to reach the broader learning goals. As you read, notice that all the plan's statements of objectives begin with a verb, as they identify actions students will take to demonstrate their learning. The plan ends by explaining the classroom activities the teacher will use to facilitate learning and by identifying the methods the instructor will use to assess student learning. These structural moves are conventional for the genre of a lesson plan.

Educational Standard → Goals → Objectives → Materials → Classroom Activities → Assessment

Lesson Plan

Overview and Purpose
This lesson is part of a unit on Homer's *Odyssey.* Prior to this lesson students will have had a lesson on Greek cultural and social values during the time of Homer, and they will have read the *Odyssey.* In the lesson, students will analyze passages from the *Odyssey* to examine author's and characters' point of view. Students will participate in whole class discussion, work in small groups, and work individually to identify and evaluate point of view.

Education Standards Addressed
This lesson addresses the following objectives from the NC Standard Course of Study for Language Arts: English II:

1.02 Respond reflectively (through small group discussion, class discussion, journal entry, essay, letter, dialogue) to written and visual texts by:

Identifies the state-mandated curricular elements, or the educational objectives, the lesson addresses. Notice that these are quite broad in scope.

- relating personal knowledge to textual information or class discussion.
- showing an awareness of one's own culture as well as the cultures of others.
- exhibiting an awareness of culture in which text is set or in which text was written.

1.03 Demonstrate the ability to read, listen to, and view a variety of increasingly complex print and non-print expressive texts appropriate to grade level and course literary focus, by:

- identifying and analyzing text components (such as organizational structures, story elements, organizational features) and evaluating their impact on the text.
- providing textual evidence to support understanding of and reader's response to text.
- making inferences, predicting, and drawing conclusions based on text.
- identifying and analyzing personal, social, historical, or cultural influences, contexts, or biases.

5.01 Read and analyze selected works of world literature by:

- understanding the importance of cultural and historical impact on literary texts.

Teacher identifies specific goals for the lesson. These goals fit well within the broader state-mandated curricular standards.

Objectives identify what students will do as part of the lesson. Notice that the statements of objectives begin with verbs.

Goals

1. To teach students how to identify and evaluate an author's point of view and purpose by examining the characters' point of view.
2. To teach students to critically examine alternate points of view.

Objectives

Students will:

1. Identify point of view in a story by examining the text and evaluating how the main character views his/her world at different points in the story.
2. Demonstrate that they understand point of view by using examples and evidence from the text to support what they state is the character's point of view.
3. Apply their knowledge and understanding of point of view by taking a passage from the text and rewriting it from a supporting character's point of view.

4. Evaluate the rationality of a character's point of view by measuring it against additional information gathered from the text, or their own life experience.

Materials, Resources

Identifies materials needed for the lesson

- Copies of *The Odyssey*
- DVD with video clips from television and/or movies
- Flip chart paper
- Markers
- Directions and rubric for individual assignment

Activities

Outlines classroom procedures for the two-day lesson plan

Session 1

1. Review information from previous lesson about popular cultural and social views held during Homer's time (e.g., Greek law of hospitality). This would be a combination of a quiz and whole class discussion.
2. Teacher-led class discussion defining and examining point of view by viewing clips from popular television shows and movies.
3. Teacher-led discussion of 1 example from *The Odyssey*. E.g., Examine Odysseus's point of view when he violates Greek law of hospitality during his encounter with the Cyclops, Polyphemus. Examine this encounter through the lens of what Homer might be saying about the value Greeks placed on hospitality.
4. In small groups the students will choose 3 places in the epic and evaluate Odysseus's point of view. Students will then determine what Odysseus's point of view might reflect about Homer's point of view and purpose for that part of the epic.
5. Groups will begin to create a visual using flip chart paper and markers to represent their interpretations of Odysseus's point of view to reflect about Homer's point of view and purpose.

Session 2

1. Groups will complete visual.
2. Groups will present their work to the rest of the class.
3. The class will discuss possible alternate interpretations of Homer's point of view and purpose.
4. Class will review aspects of point of view based on information teacher provided at the beginning of the class.

INDIVIDUALIZED EDUCATION PROGRAM (IEP)

Duration of Special Education and Related Services: From: 06/05/2008 To: 06/04/2009

Student: Joey Smith   **DOB: 08/21/1992**

School: ABC High School   **Grade: 10**

Consideration of Transitions

> If a transition (e.g., new school, family circumstances, etc.) is anticipated during the life of this IEP/IFSP, what information is known about the student that will assist in facilitating a smooth process?   ☒ N/A
>
> The student is age 14 or older or will be during the duration of the IEP.
>   ☒ Yes   ☐ No

Consideration of Special Factors (Note: If you check yes, you must address in the IEP.)

> Does the student have behavior(s) that impede his/her learning or that of others?
>   ☒ Yes   ☐ No
>
> Does the student have Limited English Proficiency?   ☐ Yes   ☒ No
>
> If the student is blind or partially sighted, will the instruction in or use of Braille be needed?   ☐ Yes   ☐ No   ☒ N/A
>
> Does the student have any special communication needs?   ☐ Yes   ☒ No
>
> Is the student deaf or hard of hearing?   ☐ Yes   ☒ No
> ☐ The child's language and communication needs.
> ☐ Opportunities for direct communications with peers and professional personnel in the child's language and communication mode.
> ☐ Academic level.
> ☐ Full range of needs, including opportunities for direct instruction in the child's language, and
> ☐ Communication mode.
> (Communication Plan Worksheet available at www.ncpublicschools.org/ec/policy /forms.)
>
> Does the student require specially designed physical education?   ☐ Yes   ☒ No

Present Level(s) of Academic and Functional Performance
Include specific descriptions of what the student can and cannot do in relationship to this area. Include current academic and functional performance, behaviors, social/emotional development, other relevant information, and how the student's disability affects his/her involvement and progress in the general curriculum.

> Joey consistently reads at grade level. He can answer comprehension questions accurately if given additional time. He does well on tests and assignments that require reading if given additional time and if allowed to be in a separate setting with minimized distractions during longer tests.

INDIVIDUALIZED EDUCATION PROGRAM (IEP)

Duration of Special Education and Related Services: From: 06/05/2008 To: 06/04/2009

Student: Joey Smith   **DOB: 08/21/1992**

School: ABC High School   **Grade: 10**

Annual Goal

☒ Academic Goal   ☐ Functional Goal

> Joey will continue to learn and demonstrate functional reading skill at grade level.

The academic goal for the student is identified here.

Does the student require assistive technology devices and/or services?   ☐ Yes   ☒ No
If yes, describe needs:

(Address after determination of related services.) Is this goal integrated with related service(s)?   ☐ Yes*   ☒ No
*If yes, list the related service area(s) of integration:

Competency Goal

> **Required for areas (if any) where student participates in state assessments using modified achievement standards.**
> **Select Subject Area:** ☐ Language Arts   ☐ Mathematics   ☐ Science
> **List Competency Goal from the *NC Standard Course of Study*:**
> *(Standard must match the student's assigned grade.)*
>
> *Note: Selected Grade Standard Competency Goals listed are those identified for specially designed instruction. In addition to those listed, the student has access to grade-level content standards through general education requirements.*

Benchmarks or Short-Term Objectives (if applicable)

(Required for students participating in state alternate assessments aligned to alternate achievement standards)

> 1) Joey will recognize and use vocabulary appropriate for grade level with 90% accuracy.
> 2) Joey will recognize the author's point of view and purpose with 85% accuracy.
> 3) Joey will apply decoding strategies to comprehend grade-level text with 85% accuracy.

The IEP identifies specific objectives the student will achieve toward reaching the academic goal.

Describe how progress toward the annual goal will be measured

> Progress toward this annual goal will be measured by work samples and tests or quizzes.

The IEP identifies ways the student's progress will be measured.

INDIVIDUALIZED EDUCATION PROGRAM (IEP)

Duration of Special Education and Related Services: From: 06/05/2008 To: 06/04/2009

Student: Joey Smith   **DOB:** 08/21/1992

School: ABC High School   **Grade:** 10

Present Level(s) of Academic and Functional Performance
Include specific descriptions of what the student can and cannot do in relationship
to this area. Include current academic and functional performance, behaviors, social/
emotional development, other relevant information, and how the student's disability
affects his/her involvement and progress in the general curriculum.

> Joey does well getting back on task with assistance and when he implements
> attention-focusing strategies. He needs to improve working on his ability to self-
> monitor and keep himself on task.

Annual Goal
☐ Academic Goal   ☒ Functional Goal

> Joey will continue learning to identify situations where he is more likely to lose
> focus. He will learn to identify and apply appropriate attention-focusing strategies
> in a variety of situations.

Does the student require assistive technology devices and/or services? ☐ Yes   ☒ No
If yes, describe needs:

(Address after determination of related services.) Is this goal integrated with related
service(s)?   ☐ Yes*   ☒ No
*If yes, list the related service area(s) of integration:

Competency Goal

> **Required for areas (if any) where student participates in state assessments using
> modified achievement standards.**
> **Select Subject Area:** ☐ Language Arts   ☐ Mathematics   ☐ Science
> **List Competency Goal from the *NC Standard Course of Study*:**
> *(Standard must match the student's assigned grade.)*
>
> *Note: Selected Grade Standard Competency Goals listed are those identified for
> specially designed instruction. In addition to those listed, the student has access to
> grade-level content standards through general education requirements.*

The functional goal
for the student is
identified here.

INDIVIDUALIZED EDUCATION PROGRAM (IEP)

Duration of Special Education and Related Services: From: 06/05/2008 To: 06/04/2009

Student: Joey Smith   **DOB: 08/21/1992**

School: <u>ABC High School</u>   **Grade: <u>10</u>**

Benchmarks or Short-Term Objectives (if applicable)
(Required for students participating in state alternate assessments aligned to alternate achievement standards)

> 1) Joey will be able to articulate how he feels when he becomes frustrated when work gets difficult on 4 trials over a 2-week period as evaluated by structured observations every 6 weeks.
> 2) By January, Joey will independently request a break from work when he needs it to prevent class disruptions and allow himself to refocus.

The IEP identifies specific objectives the student will achieve toward reaching the functional goal.

Describe how progress toward the annual goal will be measured

> Progress will be monitored through documented teacher observation, student self-monitoring checklist, and anecdotal logs.

The IEP identifies ways that the student's progress will be measured.

Teacher for a Day

For this exercise, imagine that you've just taken a job teaching in your major area of study. Identify a specific concept or skill you can see yourself teaching to a group of students. Consider the background and previous knowledge of your target audience. Then, with the concept or skill in mind, design a single-day lesson plan that addresses each of the following elements of a typical lesson plan.

- **Goal(s)** State the specific goal(s) for the skill you want to teach.
- **Objectives** Identify what students will do to better understand the concept or learn the target skill.
- **Materials** Identify the materials needed to carry out the lesson plan successfully.
- **Classroom Activities** Outline the procedures, in chronological order, for the day's lesson.
- **Assessment** Explain how you will assess your students' mastery of the concept or skill. ❱

BUSINESS

Communication in businesses takes many forms, and professionals writing in business settings may spend substantial amounts of time drafting e-mails and memos, or writing letters and proposals. In some instances, businesses may hire individuals solely for their expertise in business communication practices. Such individuals are highly skilled in the analysis and practice of business communication, and their education and training are often aimed at these purposes. Still, if your experiences lead you to employment in a business setting, you're likely to face the task of communicating in one or more of the genres frequently used in those settings. It's no surprise, then, that schools of business, which prepare students to work in companies and corporations, often require their students to take classes that foster an understanding of the vehicles of communication common to the business setting. In the following section, we provide some introductory context and annotated examples of a couple of the more common forms of communication you're likely to encounter in a business setting: the memorandum and the business plan.

Memorandum

The **memorandum**, or memo, is a specialized form of communication used within businesses to make announcements and to share information among colleagues and employees. Although memos serve a range of purposes, like sharing information, providing directives, or even arguing a particular position, they are not generally used to communicate with outside parties, like other companies or clients. While they may range in length from a couple of

paragraphs to multiple pages, they're typically highly structured according to conventional expectations. In fact, you'd be hard pressed to find an example of a professional memo that didn't follow the conventional format for identifying the writer, the audience, the central subject matter, and the date of production in the header. Also, information in memos typically appears in a block format, and the content is often developed from a clear, centralized purpose that is revealed early on in the memo itself.

Insider Example
Student Memorandum

The following is an example of a memo produced by a student in a professional writing class. His purpose for writing was to share his assessment of the advantages and drawbacks of a particular company he's interested in working for in the future. As you read, notice how the information in the opening paragraphs forecasts the memo's content, along with how the memo summarizes its contents in the concluding passages. We've highlighted a number of the other conventional expectations for the memo that you'll want to notice.

MEMO

To: Jamie Larsen
         Professor, North Carolina State University

From: James Blackwell
         Biological Engineering, North Carolina State University

Date: September 2, 2014

Subject: Investigative Report on Hazen and Sawyer

I plan on one day using my knowledge gained in biological engineering to help alleviate the growing environmental problems that our society faces. Hazen and Sawyer is a well-known environmental engineering firm. However, I need to research the firm's background in order to decide if it would be a suitable place for me to work. Consequently, I decided to research the following areas of Hazen and Sawyer engineering firm:

- Current and Past Projects
- Opportunities for Employment and Advancement
- Work Environment

The purpose of this report is to present you with my findings on Hazen and Sawyer, so that you may assist me in writing an application letter that proves my skills and knowledge are worthy of an employment opportunity.

Current and Past Projects

Founded in 1951, Hazen and Sawyer has had a long history of providing clean drinking water and minimizing the effects of water pollution. The company has undertaken many projects in the United States as well as internationally. One of its first projects was improving the infrastructure of Monrovia, Liberia, in 1952. I am interested in using my knowledge of environmental problems to promote sustainability. Designing sustainable solutions for its clients is one of the firm's main goals. Hazen and Sawyer is currently engaged in a project to provide water infrastructure to over one million people in Jordan. Supplying clean drinking water is a problem that is continuously growing, and I hope to work on a similar project someday.

Opportunities for Employment and Advancement

Hazen and Sawyer has over forty offices worldwide, with regional offices in Raleigh, NC, Cincinnati, OH, Dallas, TX, Hollywood, FL, Los Angeles, CA, and its headquarters in New York City. The company currently has over thirty job openings at offices across the United States. I would like to live in the Raleigh area following graduation, so having a regional office here in Raleigh greatly helps my chances of finding a local job with the company. Hazen and Sawyer also has offices in Greensboro and Charlotte, which also helps my chances of finding a job in North Carolina. I am interested in finding a job dealing with stream restoration, and the Raleigh office currently has an opening for a Stream Restoration Designer. The position requires experience with AutoCAD and GIS, and I have used both of these programs in my Biological Engineering courses.

In addition to numerous job openings, Hazen and Sawyer also offers opportunities for professional development within the company. The Pathway Program for Professional Development is designed to keep employees up-to-date on topics in their fields and also stay educated to meet license requirements in different states. Even if I found a job at the Raleigh office, I would most likely have to travel out of state to work on projects, so this program could be very beneficial. I am seeking to work with a company that promotes continuous professional growth, so this program makes me very interested in Hazen and Sawyer.

Work Environment

Hazen and Sawyer supports innovation and creativity, and at the same time tries to limit bureaucracy. I am seeking a company that will allow me to be creative and assist with projects while not being in charge initially. As I gain experience and learn on the job, I hope to move into positions with greater responsibility. The firm offers a mentoring program that places newly hired engineers with someone more experienced. This program would help me adapt to the company and provide guidance as I gain professional experience. I hope to eventually receive my Professional Engineering license, so working under a professional engineer with years of experience would be a great opportunity for me. Hazen and Sawyer supports positive relationships among its employees, by engaging them in social outings such as sporting events, parties, picnics, and other activities.

References

Hazen and Sawyer—Environmental Engineers and Scientists. Web. 2 Sept. 2014.
<http://www.hazenandsawyer.com/home/>.

Many people dream of being their own bosses. One avenue for achieving this dream is to create a successful business, or to own and operate a service or company. Anyone undertaking such a task in the economy today will need a solid business background that includes knowledge of the many forms of written communication required to start and continue the operation of a successful business. Two very important genres for these purposes are the business plan and the business proposal. If you're a business owner looking to raise capital, or if you've got a good idea or product that you want to sell to potential investors, then you're going to need a solid **business plan**, a document that clearly and efficiently describes your business and its essential operations, analyzes your market competition, and assesses the expected expenses and potential for profit. Let's say that you've got a great idea for a new lawn care service, but you need capital to purchase the necessary equipment and to advertise your services to potential customers. To obtain that capital, you're likely going to need a business plan that others can read when deciding whether to invest in your business.

By contrast, the **business proposal** is a form of communication through which a company proposes a relationship of some sort with another entity—often another company. Companies frequently receive unsolicited business proposals. A photocopying company, for instance, may design a proposal to begin a relationship that involves installing and maintaining all the photocopiers owned by a particular city or municipality. At other times, companies request business proposals. Imagine that you're the president of a landscaping service, for example, and you've decided to outsource all work that involves tree removal. To determine whom you want to hire for those jobs, you call for proposals from those companies or individuals to determine whose services best match your needs. In the world of business, effective communication means making money.

Insider Example
Student Business Plan

The following business plan was produced by a student in a writing class that addressed the communication needs of his major. As you read, notice how the student shaped the plan to satisfy the needs of the target audience, a bank, as a potential source of funding.

The Electricity Monitor Company

Daniel Chase Mills

The Electricity Monitor Company

This document is a request for a start-up business loan for a company that will design, manufacture, and sell an electricity-monitoring product that will answer customers' demands for a solution to high power bills.

To: Ms. Jane Harmon Bausch, President

First National Bank

10 Money Street

Raleigh, North Carolina 27695

Prepared By:

Daniel Chase Mills

The Electricity Monitor Company

100 Satellite Lane

City, North Carolina 20000

Email: dcmills@ncsu.edu

Phone: (919) 555-2233

November 21, 2014

In the executive summary, the writer provides a general overview of the plan: identifies a problem, briefly describes the company's unique product and market, and highlights potential customers. The section ends by noting the dollar amount requested from the bank.

In what way is an executive summary like an abstract?

Executive Summary

The Electricity Monitor Company

Prepared by Daniel Chase Mills, November 21, 2014

This document is a start-up business proposal for the Electricity Monitor Company and a request for an investment from First National Bank of Raleigh, North Carolina. The Company will design, manufacture, and sell the Electricity Monitor. Families with a traditional circuit-breaker box often struggle with high power bills, due to their inability to monitor their electricity usage. The Electricity Monitor is a device that will answer this pain point. This device is an adapter that attaches to any existing breaker box with installation simple enough for consumers to perform on their own. The device monitors current electricity usage and determines ways to reduce energy consumption. The device is superior to alternatives in the market in that it is cheaper, easier to install, and more effectively solves the problem of not knowing how much electricity is being used. The overall purpose of the

Electricity Monitor Company is to develop a high-quality product that can generate excitement in the electricity monitor market and turn a profit for its business owners and investors. The total loan request from First National Bank is three hundred and fifty-four thousand dollars ($354,000.00).

Table of Contents

Notice the ordering of elements of the plan. How would you describe the order of these elements?

List of Tables and Figures

Introduction to the Electricity Monitor Company

A. Purpose

The purpose of this document is to request funding from First National Bank for a start-up business called the Electricity Monitor Company. This

Briefly identifies the general purpose of the document and offers a preview of the document's contents

document will contain an overview of the problem that the company will address in the market, how the Electricity Monitor will solve this problem, and a plan for this business.

Explains a problem that consumers face

B. Problem: High Power Bills

In twenty-first century America, and in most first world countries, electricity is a necessity. In the home, electricity is used for a variety of devices. Due to the vast number of devices that use electricity, and no good way of knowing how much power they are consuming on a daily basis, families with a traditional circuit-breaker box often struggle with using too much electricity. The problem is high power bills.

Provides a brief market analysis, and identifies a gap in the market

C. Current Alternatives to High Power Bills

There are three currently available solutions to measuring home energy usage in an attempt to lower power bills: Plug-in Meters, Energy Meter Monitors, and Home Energy Monitors. Plug-in Meters are devices that plug in to individual outlets to measure energy usage of a single device. An

How is this section of the report similar to or different from a review of scholarship?

Energy Meter Monitor attaches to an electricity meter, measures total energy consumption of a home, and estimates what the power bill will be for the month. Neither device is effective in determining energy usage of the entire home across multiple devices. The Home Energy Monitors contain multiple channels to measure energy usage across multiple devices in the home, but these devices are extremely expensive and require detailed installation that increases the cost of the products. Three Home Energy Monitoring Devices are the TED 5000, eGuage, and EnviR, with respective prices of $239, $494, and $129. I have determined that the current solutions in this market are too expensive and do not adequately provide families with an affordable way to monitor their electricity usage. I have developed a better solution to this pain point.

Stresses reasons that support the business's potential for success

D. The Electricity Monitor

The Electricity Monitor is a device that can solve the pain point of high power bills by measuring the electricity usage of each device in the home. This device can easily attach to any existing breaker box. Installation of the device can be performed by any customer with the instructions provided with the device. At a price of $75, this device will be much cheaper than current solutions to monitoring power usage. A price comparison is shown in Figure 1 below. By measuring electricity usage of each device in the home, the Electricity Monitor will be able to accurately estimate the power bill for the month (within 1% error) and update daily with changes to electricity usage trends in the home. All data will be transmitted to a monitoring display. This device is also superior to the competition in that it makes suggestions as to how to decrease energy consumption and provides information on which devices in the home are using the most energy. Using the data from the Electricity Monitor, families will finally have the tool they need to save money on their power bill.

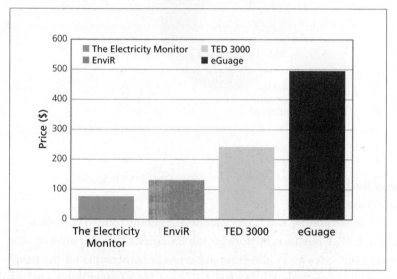

Fig. 1. Price comparison

Charts and figures appear commonly in business documents for clarification of ideas or to explain relationships between variables.

E. Market for This Product

Performs a more detailed market analysis

Industry market research from the IBIS World database shows small household appliance manufacturing to have $3.1 billion in annual revenue with $77.9 million in annual profit. This number alone shows the vastness of this market. In addition, IBIS World estimates 38.4% of this market to account for small household devices similar to the Electricity Monitor. Figure 2 below from IBIS World shows the market breakdown. The main demographic for this product will be families of three or more who are unhappy with their current power bill. The United States Census Bureau estimated there to be 4.4 million households with families of three or more people, accounting for 39% of all households in 2011. IBIS World describes the technology change in this market to be "Medium." This leads me to believe that a new product in this market could really shake the market and attract interest from consumers. Assuming that the current trend for revenue and profit in the small household appliance industry performs as predicted, the market for the Electricity Monitor will be large.

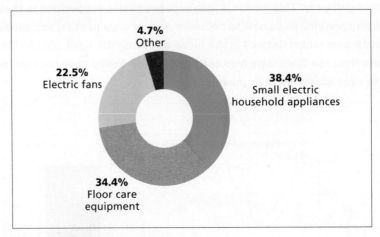

Fig. 2. Market breakdown

Explains governance and operating procedures of the proposed company

Plan of Business

A. Overview

I plan to construct the Electricity Monitor Company to hold complete ownership of all business sectors for the Electricity Monitor product. The Company will have an engineering department responsible for the design of the product, a manufacturing facility where the product will be built, and a marketing department responsible for the marketing and selling of the product. The overall cost for the start-up is analyzed below. This breakdown of cost can also be found in the Attachments section of this document.

Offers a detailed analysis of costs associated with the business start-up

B. Cost Analysis

Table 1
Design Expense

Design Expense	Description	Total Cost
Building	Rented office space	$ 5,000.00
Software	CAD modeling and FEA software license	$ 4,000.00
Total		**$ 9,000.00**

Table 1 is an analysis of the cost for designing the product. The requested loan will need to cover the first month of rent for an office and also a license for software that will be used to design the product. The labor is not included in the cost here because I will be designing the product myself.

Table 2
Manufacturing Expense

Manufacturing Expense (First 500 Products)	Description	Total Cost
Building	Small manufacturing facility	$ 100,000.00
Manufacturing equipment	Laser cutting machine, etc.	$ 200,000.00
Tools	Screwdrivers, socket wrenches, Allen wrenches, etc.	$ 5,000.00
Materials	First 500 monitors (avg cost $20/monitor)	$ 10,000.00
Labor	$25/hr with five employees @ 40 hours a week	$ 20,000.00
Total		$ 335,000.00

Table 2 is an analysis of the cost for manufacturing the product. The building and manufacturing equipment are one-time costs for the initial start-up. The materials and labor will be ongoing costs, but the loan request is only enough to cover the first 500 products manufactured. Five hundred products have been estimated as enough to cover the first month of sales and will allow my company to be self-sufficient after selling the first 500 products.

Table 3
Marketing Expense

Marketing Expense	Description	Total Cost
Commercial	Television ad	$ 5,000.00
Web search	Google AdWords	$ 5,000.00
Total		$ 10,000.00

Table 3 is an analysis of the total marketing expense. I will additionally market this product to retail stores that could also sell this product, but cost for labor of this marketing is not included here because I will do it myself.

Table 4
Total Cost Analysis

Business Sector	Total Cost
Design	$ 9,000.00
Manufacturing	$ 335,000.00
Marketing	$ 10,000.00
Total	$ 354,000.00

Table 4 is a summary of the total cost analysis for this product. The highlighted cell in Table 4 represents the total start-up cost for the Electricity Monitor Company. This is also the total requested loan amount from First National Bank.

C. Summary

The total cost for this start-up was analyzed in Tables 1 through 4 above. The cost of materials was estimated from current market cost of materials and is subject to change with the market. However, my request for the bottom-line loan amount for this start-up is three hundred and fifty-four thousand dollars ($354,000.00), and this request will not change with cost of materials. A sound business plan has been constructed that will allow the Electricity Monitor Company to become self-sufficient after one month. In order for this business plan to work, the product must be successful in attracting customers quickly as projected by the market research.

The conclusion reiterates the proposed product's unique characteristics and potential for success in hopes of securing the capital investment.

Conclusion

The overall purpose of the Electricity Monitor start-up business is to develop a high-quality product that can generate excitement in the electricity monitor market and turn a profit for its business owners and investors. This product will benefit not only its investors, but also its consumers in that it will solve their pain point of not being able to affordably measure their current energy consumption. In comparison to other products in the market that attempt to solve the problem of high power bills, the Electricity Monitor is superior in price, ease of installation, and overall ability to solve the problem. There is nothing quite like this product currently in the market, and this is why it will be successful. The market research has proven that there is a large potential market and that current technology change is not very high. I am excited about starting the Electricity Monitor Company, the potential of this product, and the benefits for all parties involved. Please grant the requested loan amount of three hundred and fifty-four thousand dollars ($354,000.00) and help me make unnecessarily high power bills a thing of the past.

Documents sources consulted in the preparation of the business document

Bibliography

Entrepreneur. "TV Ads." Web. <http://www.entrepreneur.com/article/83108>.

IBIS World. "Vacuum, Fan, & Small Household Appliance Manufacturing in the US." Web. <http://clients1.ibisworld.com.prox.lib.ncsu.edu/reports/us/industry/ataglance.aspx?indid=786>.

Kreider, Rose M. "America's Families and Living Arrangements: 2012."
United States Census Bureau. Web. <https://www.census.gov/prod
/2013pubs/p20-570.pdf>.

Thornton Oliver Keller Commercial Real Estate. "Rental Rate Calculations."
Web. <http://tokcommercial.com/MarketInformation/LearningCenter
/RentalRateCalculations.aspx>.

Attachments

A. Cost Breakdown

Design Expense	Description	Total Cost
Building	Rented office space	$ 5,000.00
Software	CAD modeling and FEA software license	$ 4,000.00
Total		**$ 9,000.00**

Manufacturing Expense (First 500 Products)	Description	Total Cost
Building	Small manufacturing facility	$ 100,000.00
Manufacturing equipment	Laser cutting machine, etc.	$ 200,000.00
Tools	Screwdrivers, socket wrenches, Allen wrenches, etc.	$ 5,000.00
Materials	First 500 monitors (avg cost $20/monitor)	$ 10,000.00
Labor	$25/hr with five employees @ 40 hours a week	$ 20,000.00
Total		**$ 335,000.00**

Marketing Expense	Description	Total Cost
Commercial	Television ad	$ 5,000.00
Web search	Google AdWords	$ 5,000.00
Total		**$ 10,000.00**

Business Sector	Total Cost
Design	$ 9,000.00
Manufacturing	$ 335,000.00
Marketing	$ 10,000.00
Total	**$ 354,000.00**

Compiles the costs associated with the business start-up. See the reference to the attachment on page 290.

For this exercise, imagine that you're the chief financial officer for a company, Music Studio Emporium. Your company has twenty employees, and you've been charged with the task of notifying ten of them that they'll be receiving a 2 percent annual pay increase, effective immediately, based on their sales records. Unfortunately, you must also notify your other ten employees that they will not be receiving raises. Draft a brief memo to each group of employees—one for those receiving raises and one for those who aren't—in which you explain the company's decisions regarding your employees' compensation. Feel free to provide additional reasoning for those decisions, as you see fit.

Refer to the memo on page 284 as a model of the structural features you'll want to employ in constructing your memo. Once you're done, consider how the nature of the news you had to convey to each audience influenced the way you delivered that news. What did you do the same for each of your audiences? What did you do differently in constructing the two memos? ▶

LAW

Most of us probably have clichéd understandings of the law at work. Many of these likely originated from television shows and movies. In these scenarios, there's almost always lots of drama as the lawyers battle in court, parse witnesses' words, and attempt to sway a judge or jury to their side of a case.

In real life, the practice of law may not always be quite as dramatic or enthralling as it appears on the screen. In fact, many lawyers rarely, or maybe never, appear in court. A criminal defense attorney may regularly appear before a judge or jury in a courtroom setting, but a corporate lawyer may spend the

majority of her time drafting and analyzing business contracts. This difference is directly related to the field of law an individual specializes in, be it criminal law, family law, tax law, or environmental law, just to name a few.

Regardless of an attorney's chosen specialization, though, the study of law remains fundamentally concerned with debates over the interpretation of language. This is because the various rules that govern our lives—statutes, ordinances, regulations, and laws, for example—are all constructed in language. As you surely recognize, language can be quite slippery, and rules can often be interpreted in many different ways. We need only briefly to consider current debates over free speech issues or the "right to bear arms" or marriage equality to understand how complicated the business of interpreting laws can become. In the United States, the U.S. Supreme Court holds the authority to provide the final interpretation on the meaning of disputed laws. However, there are lots of legal interpretations and arguments that lower courts must make on a daily basis, and only a tiny portion of cases are ever heard by the U.S. Supreme Court.

As in the other applied fields, there are many common forms of communication in the various fields of law, as lawyers must regularly communicate with different kinds of stakeholders, including clients, other lawyers, judges, and law enforcement officials. For this reason, individuals working in the legal professions are generally expert at composing e-mail messages, memos, letters to clients, and legal briefs, among other genres. The following examples provide a glimpse into two types of writing through which lawyers frequently communicate.

Legal Brief

One of the first forms of writing students of law are likely to encounter in their academic study is the **legal brief**. Briefs can serve any number of functions, but their primary purpose is to outline the critical components of a legal argument to a specified audience. They may be descriptive or argumentative. A typical assignment for a student in law school might include writing a legal brief that describes a particular court's decision and explains how the court reached that decision. Cases that appear before the U.S. Supreme Court are usually accompanied by numerous legal briefs that are written and filed with the Court by parties who are interested in the outcomes of those cases. Many of these briefs are argumentative. Students of law, then, must be familiar with the basic structural components, or the structural conventions, of the legal brief. And law schools regularly instruct their students to produce legal briefs using the generalized form known as **IRAC**—an acronym for **Introduction, Rule, Application, and Conclusion**—as a means to describe past court decisions and/or to present written arguments to a court:

- **Identify the Legal Issue(s) in the Case**

  Introduction   Legal cases can be very complicated. It is a lawyer's task to explore the facts of a case, along with its legal history, to determine which facts are actually relevant and which are irrelevant as they pertain to a legal question or dispute.

- **Identify and Explain the Relevant Law(s) to the Case**

  Rule   Often, many different statutes, regulations, laws, or other court precedents are applicable and need exploration as part of a legal dispute. A lawyer must identify the applicable rules of law and explain their relevance to the legal question or dispute at hand.

- **Apply the Relevant Rules to the Facts of the Case**

  Application The facts of the case are explored through the lens of relevant rules. Arguments are presented in these sections of a brief.

- **Argue for a Particular Decision or Outcome**

  Conclusion Based on the application of relevant rules to the facts of the case, a lawyer makes a recommendation that the judge or court should reach a particular conclusion.

Insider Example
Professional Legal Brief

The following excerpts are from a 55-page legal brief that was filed with the U.S. Supreme Court on behalf of the University of Texas at Austin, et al., which was sued by an applicant after being denied admission to the university. In arguing their case, attorneys writing on behalf of the respondents, or the university, defended its decision to deny admission to the complainant, or the petitioner, Abigail Fisher. As you read the excerpted sections below, try to identify parts of the brief that correspond to the elements of the IRAC structure for presenting legal arguments: Introduction, Rule, Application, and Conclusion.

No. 11-345

In the
Supreme Court of the United States

ABIGAIL NOEL FISHER,
Petitioner,

v.

UNIVERSITY OF TEXAS AT AUSTIN, ET AL.,
Respondents.

ON WRIT OF CERTIORARI TO THE
UNITED STATES COURT OF APPEALS
FOR THE FIFTH CIRCUIT

BRIEF FOR RESPONDENTS

PATRICIA C. OHLENDORF	GREGORY G. GARRE
Vice President for	*Counsel of Record*
Legal Affairs	MAUREEN E. MAHONEY

The University of
Texas at Austin
Flawn Academic Center
2304 Whitis Avenue
Stop G4800
Austin, TX 78712

Douglas Laycock
University of Virginia
School of Law
580 Massie Road
Charlottesville, VA 22903

J. Scott Ballenger
Lori Alvino McGill
Katya S. Georgieva
Latham & Watkins LLP
555 11th Street, NW
Suite 1000
Washington, DC 20004
(202) 637-2207
gregory.garre@lw.com

James C. Ho
Gibson, Dunn &
    Crutcher LLP
2100 McKinney Avenue
Suite 1110
Dallas, TX 75201-6912

Counsel for Respondents

INTRODUCTION

After considering largely the same objections raised by petitioner and her amici here, this Court strongly embraced Justice Powell's controlling opinion in *Regents of the University of California v. Bakke*, 438 U.S. 265 (1978), and refused to prohibit the consideration of race as a factor in admissions at the Nation's universities and graduate schools. *Grutter v. Bollinger*, 539 U.S. 306 (2003); *see id.* at 387 (Kennedy, J., dissenting). And although the Court has made clear that any consideration of race in this context must be limited, it has been understood for decades that "a university admissions program may take account of race as one, non-predominant factor in a system designed to consider each applicant as an individual, provided the program can meet the test of strict scrutiny by the judiciary." *Id.* at 387 (Kennedy, J., dissenting) (citing *Bakke*, 438 U.S. at 289-91, 315-18 (Powell, J.)); *see id.* at 322-23. The University of Texas at Austin (UT)'s highly individualized consideration of race for applicants not admitted under the State's top 10% law satisfies that demand, and meets strict scrutiny under any conception of that test not designed simply to bar the consideration of race altogether.

That conclusion follows *a fortiori* from existing precedent. UT's admissions plan was modeled on the type of plan upheld in *Grutter* and commended by Justice Powell in *Bakke*. Moreover, UT's plan lacks the features criticized in *Grutter* by Justice Kennedy—who agreed with the majority that *Bakke* is the "correct rule." *Id.* at 387 (dissenting). Justice Kennedy concluded that Michigan Law School's admissions plan used race "to achieve numerical goals

Identifies the critical issue at stake, and lays out the respondents' position

Reviews relevant precedents, or earlier conclusions reached by the Court

indistinguishable from quotas." *Id.* at 389. Here, it is undisputed that UT has not set any "target" or "goal" for minority admissions. JA 131a. Justice Kennedy stressed that Michigan's "admissions officers consulted...daily reports which indicated the composition of the incoming class along racial lines." *Grutter*, 539 U.S. at 391 (dissenting). Here, it is undeniable that no such monitoring occurs. JA 398a. And Justice Kennedy believed that race was "a predominant factor" under Michigan's plan. *Grutter*, 539 U.S. at 393 (dissenting). Here, petitioner argues (at 20) that UT's consideration of race is too "minimal" to be constitutional. That paradoxical contention not only overlooks the indisputably meaningful impact that UT's plan has on diversity, *infra* at 36-38, it turns on its head Justice Powell's conception of the appropriately nuanced and modest consideration of race in this special context.

Presents the complainant's central claims, and offers response

Because petitioner cannot dispute that UT's consideration of race is both highly individualized and modest, she is forced to take positions directly at odds with the record and existing precedent. Her headline claim that UT is engaged in "racial balancing" (Pet. Br. 6-7, 19, 27-28, 45-46) is refuted by her own concession that UT has *not* set any "target" for minority admissions. JA 131a. Her argument that the State's top 10% law bars UT from considering race in its holistic review of applicants not eligible under that law is foreclosed by *Grutter*'s holding that percentage plans are not a complete, workable alternative to the individualized consideration of race in full-file review. 539 U.S. at 340. And her argument that, in 2004, UT had already achieved all the diversity that the Constitution allowed is based on "a limited notion of diversity" (*Parents Involved in Cmty. Schs. v. Seattle Sch. Dist. No. 1*, 551 U.S. 701, 723 (2007)) rejected by this Court—one that crudely lumps together distinct racial groups and ignores the importance of diversity among individuals *within* racial groups.

Identifies stakes for the outcome of the decision, and reasserts the respondents' position

In the end, petitioner really is just asking this Court to move the goal posts on higher education in America—and overrule its precedent going back 35 years to *Bakke*. Pet. Br. 53-57. *Stare decisis* alone counsels decisively against doing so. Petitioner has provided no persuasive justification for the Court to reexamine, much less overrule, its precedent, just nine years after this Court decided *Grutter* and eliminated any doubt about the controlling force of Justice Powell's opinion in *Bakke*. And overruling *Grutter* and *Bakke* (or effectively gutting them by adopting petitioner's conception of strict scrutiny) would jeopardize the Nation's paramount interest in educating its future leaders in an environment that best prepares them for the society and workforce they will encounter. Moreover, the question that petitioner herself asked this Court to decide is the constitutionality of UT's policy under *existing* precedent, including *Grutter. See* Pet. i; Pet. Br. i. Because the court of appeals correctly answered that question, the judgment below should be affirmed.

STATEMENT OF THE CASE

. . .

E. Petitioner's Application for Admission

Petitioner, a Texas resident, applied for admission to UT's Fall 2008 freshman class in Business Administration or Liberal Arts, with a combined SAT score of 1180 out of 1600 and a cumulative 3.59 GPA. JA 40a-41a. Because petitioner was not in the top 10% of her high school class, her application was considered pursuant to the holistic review process described above. JA 40a. Petitioner scored an AI of 3.1, JA 415a, and received a PAI score of less than 6 (the actual score is contained in a sealed brief, ECF No. 52). The summary judgment record is uncontradicted that—due to the stiff competition in 2008 and petitioner's relatively low AI score—petitioner would not have been admitted to the Fall 2008 freshman class even if she had received "a 'perfect' PAI score of 6." JA 416a.

> Provides background facts about the case concerning the student's application to UT–Austin

Petitioner also was denied admission to the summer program, which offered provisional admission to some applicants who were denied admission to the fall class, subject to completing certain academic requirements over the summer. JA 413a-14a. (UT discontinued this program in 2009.) Although one African-American and four Hispanic applicants with lower combined AI/PAI scores than petitioner's were offered admission to the summer program, so were 42 Caucasian applicants with combined AI/PAI scores identical to or lower than petitioner's. In addition, 168 African-American and Hispanic applicants in this pool who had combined AI/PAI scores identical to or *higher* than petitioner's were *denied* admission to the summer program.[1]

---

[1]These figures are drawn from UT's admissions data and are provided in response to petitioner's unsupported assertion (at 2) that her "academic credentials exceeded those of many admitted minority applicants." Petitioner presented a subset of this data (admitted minority students) to the district court as Plaintiffs' Exhibits 26 and 27 at the preliminary injunction hearing (the court later returned the exhibits). *See* W.D. Tex. Record Transmittal Letter (July 27, 2012), ECF No. 136. UT summarized additional data in a sealed letter brief after the hearing. ECF No. 52; JA 20a (discussing data and explaining that petitioner had not requested data regarding the applicants "who were *not* admitted to UT"). In denying a preliminary injunction, the district court stated (without citation) that 64 minority applicants with lower AI scores than petitioner were *admitted* to Liberal Arts. *Fisher v. Texas*, 556 F. Supp. 2d 603, 607 & n.2 (W.D. Tex. 2008). That statement is not binding at the merits stage. *University of Texas v. Camenisch*, 451 U.S. 390, 395 (1981). Although the district court did not specify whether it was referring to admissions to the fall class or the summer program, that figure can only encompass admits to the summer program. As explained in the unrebutted summary judgment record, with her AI score, petitioner could not "have gained admission through the fall review process," even with a "perfect" PAI score. JA 415a-16a. Petitioner has submitted no contrary evidence (and UT is aware of none). That leaves the now-defunct summer program. The district court's statement that minority applicants with lower AI scores than petitioner were admitted does not establish that race was a factor in petitioner's

UT did offer petitioner admission to the Coordinated Admissions Program, which allows Texas residents to gain admission to UT for their sophomore year by completing 30 credits at a participating UT System campus and maintaining a 3.2 GPA. JA 414a. Petitioner declined that offer and enrolled at Louisiana State University, from which she graduated in May.

F. Procedural History

Provides a brief history of the case in the courts, explaining decisions by lower courts

Petitioner and another applicant—"no longer involved in this case," Pet. Br. ii—filed suit in the Western District of Texas against UT and various University officials under 42 U.S.C. § 1983, alleging, *inter alia*, that UT's 2008 full-file admissions procedures violate the Equal Protection Clause. JA 38a. They sued only on their own behalf (not on behalf of any class of applicants) and sought a declaratory judgment and injunctive relief barring UT's consideration of race and requiring UT to reconsider their own applications in a race-blind process. JA 39a. They also sought a "refund of [their] application fees and all associated expenses incurred . . . in connection with applying to UT." *Id.*; *see* App. 3a-4a.

The district court denied petitioner's request for a preliminary injunction. The parties filed cross-motions for summary judgment and supporting statements of fact (JA 103a-51a, 363a-403a). Applying strict scrutiny (App. 139a), the court granted judgment to UT, holding that UT has a compelling interest in attaining a diverse student body and the educational benefits flowing from such diversity, and that UT's individualized and holistic review process is narrowly tailored to further that interest. App. 168-69a.

The Fifth Circuit affirmed. Like the district court, the court of appeals found that "it would be difficult for UT to construct an admissions policy that more closely resembles the policy approved by the Supreme Court in *Grutter*." App. 5a. And the court likewise took it as "a given" that UT's policy "is subject to strict scrutiny with its requirement of narrow tailoring." App. 35a. While acknowledging that *Bakke* and *Grutter* call for some deference to a university's "educational judgment," the court emphasized that "the scrutiny triggered by

---

denial from the summer program, because (as noted above) many more minority applicants (168) with identical or *higher* AI/PAI scores were *denied* admission to the summer program. It is thus hard to see how petitioner could establish any cognizable injury for her § 1983 damages claim— the only claim still alive in this case—or, for that matter, standing to maintain that claim. *See Texas v. Lesage*, 528 U.S. 18, 19, 21 (1999) (per curiam); *Lujan v. Defenders of Wildlife*, 504 U.S. 555, 562 (1992). (Petitioner's claims for injunctive relief dropped out of the case at least once she graduated from a different university in May 2012, making this issue pertinent now.) And that is just one apparent vehicle—if not jurisdictional—defect with this case. *See* Br. in Opp. 6-22; *see also* Adam D. Chandler, *How (Not) to Bring an Affirmative-Action Challenge*, 122 Yale L. J. Online (forthcoming Sept. 2012), *available at* http://ssrn.com/abstract_id=2122956 (discussing vehicle defects stemming from, among other things, the unusual manner in which this case was framed).

racial classification 'is no less strict for taking into account' the special circumstances of higher education." App. 34a, 36a. Applying strict scrutiny, the court upheld UT's admissions policy. App. 71a.

Judge Garza concurred. He recognized that the court's opinion was "faithful" to *Grutter*, but argued that *Grutter* was wrongly decided. App. 72a-73a.

SUMMARY OF ARGUMENT

Presents a summary of arguments in defense of the respondents' position in light of the facts of the case

UT's individualized consideration of race in holistic admissions did not subject petitioner to unequal treatment in violation of the Fourteenth Amendment.

I. Racial classifications are subject to strict scrutiny, including in the higher education context. But ever since Justice Powell's opinion in *Bakke*, this Court has recognized that universities have a compelling interest in promoting student body diversity, and that a university may consider the race of applicants in an individualized and modest manner—such that race is just one of many characteristics that form the mosaic presented by an applicant's file.

UT's holistic admissions policy exemplifies the type of plan this Court has allowed: race is only one modest factor among many others weighed; it is considered only in an individualized and contextual way that "examine[s] the student in 'their totality,'" JA 129a; and admissions officers do not know an applicant's race when they decide which "cells" to admit in UT's process. At the same time, UT's policy *lacks* the features that Justice Kennedy found disqualifying in *Grutter*: it is undisputed that UT has not established any race-based target; race is not assigned any automatic value; and the racial or ethnic composition of admits is not monitored during the admissions cycle.

II. Petitioner's arguments that she was nevertheless subjected to unequal treatment in violation of the Fourteenth Amendment are refuted by both the record and existing precedent.

. . .

III. The Court should decline petitioner's far-reaching request to reopen and overrule *Bakke* and *Grutter*. That request is outside the scope of the question presented, which asks the Court to review UT's policy under *existing* precedent, including *Grutter*. In any event, petitioner has failed to identify any special justification for taking the extraordinary step of overruling *Grutter*, just nine years after this Court decided *Grutter* and unequivocally answered any doubt about the validity of Justice Powell's opinion in *Bakke*. Abruptly reversing course here would upset legitimate expectations in the rule of law—not to mention the profoundly important societal interests in ensuring that the future leaders of America are trained in a campus environment in which they are exposed to the full educational benefits of diversity.

. . .

Concludes by asserting
the decision that
respondents believe
the Court should reach

CONCLUSION

The judgment of the court of appeals should be affirmed.

    Respectfully submitted,

PATRICIA C. OHLENDORF	GREGORY G. GARRE
Vice President for	*Counsel of Record*
Legal Affairs	MAUREEN E. MAHONEY
THE UNIVERSITY OF	J. SCOTT BALLENGER
TEXAS AT AUSTIN	LORI ALVINO MCGILL
Flawn Academic Center	KATYA S. GEORGIEVA
2304 Whitis Avenue	LATHAM & WATKINS LLP
Stop G4800	555 11th Street, NW
Austin, TX 78712	Suite 1000
	Washington, DC 20004
DOUGLAS LAYCOCK	(202) 637-2207
UNIVERSITY OF VIRGINIA	gregory.garre@lw.com
SCHOOL OF LAW	
580 Massie Road	JAMES C. HO
Charlottesville, VA 22903	GIBSON, DUNN &
	CRUTCHER LLP
	2100 McKinney Avenue
	Suite 1110
	Dallas, TX 75201-6912
AUGUST 2012	

Counsel for Respondents

E-Mail Correspondence

As you might expect, technological advances can have a profound impact on the communication practices of professionals. There may always be a place for hard copies of documents, but e-mail communication has no doubt replaced many of the letters that used to pass between parties via the U.S. Postal Service. Like most professionals these days, those employed in the legal fields often spend a lot of time communicating with stakeholders via e-mail. These professionals carefully assess each rhetorical situation for which an e-mail communication is necessary, both (1) to make sure the ideas they share with stakeholders (the explanations of legal procedures, or legal options, or applicable precedents, etc.) are accurate, and (2) to make sure they communicate those ideas in an appropriate fashion (with the appropriate tone, clarity, precision, etc.).

Insider Example
E-Mail Correspondence from Attorney

The following example is an e-mail sent from a practicing lawyer to a client. In this instance, the lawyer offers legal advice concerning a possible donation from a party to a foundation. As you read the lawyer's description of the documents attached to his **e-mail correspondence** with the client, pay attention to the ways the attorney demonstrates an acute awareness of his audience, both in terms of the actual legal advice he provides and in terms of the structure and language of his message.

Dear _____

As promised, here are two documents related to the proposed gift of the ABC property to the XYZ Foundation (the "Foundation"). The first document summarizes the recommended due diligence steps (including the creation of a limited liability company) that should take place prior to the acceptance of the property, accompanied by estimated costs associated with each such step. The second document contains a draft "pre-acceptance" agreement that the Foundation could use to recover its documented costs in the event that either the donor or the Foundation backs out of a gift agreement following the due diligence process.

> *Establishes the level of familiarity and tone*

> *Provides transactional advice, explaining what procedure needs to occur between the two parties involved: a donor and a receiving foundation*

You will note that we have limited the Foundation's ability to recover costs in the event that the Foundation is the party that "pulls the plug." In such a scenario, the Foundation could recover costs only if it reasonably determines that either (i) the property would create a risk of material exposure to environmentally related liabilities or (ii) the remediation of environmental issues would impose material costs on the Foundation. We realize that even in light of this limiting language, the agreement represents a fairly aggressive approach with the donor, and we will be glad to work with you if you wish to take a softer stance.

> *Provides additional advice to protect the interests of the parties in the event that either party decides to back out of the transaction*

> *Explains more specific details included in the attached legal documents to protect the interests of the Foundation*

Please don't hesitate to call me with any questions, concerns, or critiques. As always, we appreciate the opportunity to serve you in furthering the Foundation's good work.

> *Communicates a willingness to continue the relationship with the client*

Best regards,

Joe

Joseph E. Miller, Jr.
Partner
joe.miller@FaegreBD.com
Direct: +1 317 237 1415
FaegreBD.com Download vCard
FAEGRE BAKER DANIELS LLP
300 N. Meridian Street
Suite 2700
Indianapolis, IN 46204, USA

> *Provides standard identification and contact information for communication between and among professionals*

INSIDE WORK) **Lawyer for a Day**

Imagine that you're an attorney, and you've just been hired as a consultant by the Board of Governors of a local college that's in the process of designing new guidelines for student admissions. As part of that process, the Board has asked you to review legal briefs presented on behalf of various stakeholders in *Fisher v. University of Texas at Austin, et al.* Additionally, the Board wants you to provide a summary of UT–Austin's response to the charge that its admissions procedures violated the petitioner's rights under the Fourteenth Amendment to the U.S. Constitution.

Read again the section of the legal brief filed with the U.S. Supreme Court entitled "Summary of Argument" (on p. 301), and then draft an e-mail correspondence to your client (the Board of Governors) in which you offer an overview of UT–Austin's response to its possible violation of a prospective student's constitutional rights. As part of your summary, offer your client an assessment of the likely effectiveness of UT–Austin's argument. Be clear and precise in your presentation of UT–Austin's argument in defense of its position. Keep your audience and your relationship to that audience in mind as you compose your e-mail. ❿

WRITING PROJECT) **Discovering Genres of Writing in an Applied Field**

In this chapter, you've read about some of the conventions of writing in the applied fields of nursing, education, business, and law. You might be interested in a field that's not represented in this chapter, though. For this assignment, you will conduct research to discover more about the kinds of writing that are common within a particular applied field—ideally, one you're interested in. You might conduct either primary or secondary research to respond to this assignment. However, you should focus on collecting examples of the kinds of writing done in the field. Consider following the steps below to complete this assignment.

1. Collect examples of the kinds of writing done in the field.

2. Describe the different genres and how they relate to the work of that applied field.

3. Look for comparisons and contrasts across those genres. Do any commonalities point to conventions shared across genres? Are there differences that are important to notice? What do the patterns across the genres tell you about the work and values of that applied field?

Variation: Imagine that your audience is a group of incoming students interested in the same field of study you've researched for this project. Your task is to write a guide for those students about the conventions of writing expected in this applied field. Depending on what you have found, you may need to identify what conventions are appropriate for specific genres of writing.

tip sheet

- **The applied fields focus on the practical application of knowledge and career preparation.** Many applied fields also focus on problem-solving as part of the practical application of knowledge.

- **When beginning a writing task in applied fields, carefully analyze the rhetorical situation.** Consider your purpose and your audience carefully, and assess the appropriateness of responding in a particular genre.

- **Much of the writing in applied fields follows conventional expectations for structure, language, and reference appropriate to the fields.** Regardless of your writing task, you should be aware of these conventional expectations.

- **Students and professionals in applied fields often communicate information through field-specific genres.** Nurses, for example, often construct discharge directions, just as students and professionals in the fields of law often compose legal briefs.

Introduction to Documentation Styles

You've likely had some experience with citing sources in academic writing, both as a reader and as a writer. Many students come to writing classes in college with experience only in MLA format, the citation style of the Modern Language Association. The student research paper at the end of Chapter 4 is written in MLA style, which is the most commonly required citation style in English classes. Although MLA is the citation style with which English and writing teachers are usually most familiar, it is not the only one used in academic writing—not by a long shot.

Some students don't realize that other citation styles exist, and they're often surprised when they encounter different styles in other classes. Our goal in this appendix is to help you understand (1) why and when academic writers cite sources and (2) how different citation styles represent the values and conventions of different academic disciplines. This appendix also provides brief guides to MLA, APA (American Psychological Association), and CSE (Council of Science Editors) styles—three styles that are commonly used in the first three chapters in Part Two of this book. These citation styles are discussed in some detail in Chapter 4 as well. Near the end of this appendix, you'll find a table with other citation styles commonly used in different disciplines, including some of the applied fields discussed in Chapter 9.

Why Cite?

There are several reasons why academic writers cite sources that they draw upon. The first is an ethical reason: academic research and writing privilege the discovery of new knowledge, and it is important to give credit to scholars who discover new ideas and establish important claims in their fields of study. Additionally, academic writers cite sources to provide a "breadcrumb trail" to show how they developed their current research projects. Source citations show what prior work writers are building on and how their research contributes to that body of knowledge. If some of the sources are well respected, that ethos helps to support the writers' research as well. It demonstrates that the writers have done their homework; they know what has already been discovered, and they are contributing to an ongoing conversation.

These two values of academic writing—the necessity of crediting the person or persons who discover new knowledge, and the importance of under-standing prior work that has led to a specific research project—shape the choices that academic writers make when citing sources. Anytime you quote, summarize, or paraphrase the work of someone else in academic writing, you must give credit to that person's work. *How* academic writers cite those sources, though, differs according to their academic discipline and writing situation.

Disciplinary Documentation Styles

Citation styles reflect the values of specific disciplines, just like other conven-tions of academic writing that we've discussed in this book. When you compare the similarities and differences in citation styles, you might notice that some conventions of particular citation styles that seemed random before suddenly have meaning. For example, if we compare the ways that authors and pub-lication dates are listed in MLA, APA, and CSE styles, we'll notice some distinctions that reflect the values of those disciplines:

Author's full name

Year of publication listed near the end

MLA

Carter, Michael. "Ways of Knowing, Doing, and Writing in the Disciplines." *College Composition and Communication* 58.3 (2007): 385-418. Print.

Only author's last name included in full

Year included toward the beginning, in a place of importance

APA

Carter, M. (2007). Ways of knowing, doing, and writing in the disciplines. *College Composition and Communication, 58*(3), 385-418.

Only last name given in full, and first and middle initials are not separated from last name by any punctuation

Year also has a place of prominence and isn't distinguished from the name at all, emphasizing that timeliness is as important as the name of the author

CSE

Carter M. 2007. Ways of knowing, doing, and writing in the disciplines. Coll Compos Commun. 58(3):385-418.

MLA lists the author's full name at the beginning of the citation, emphasizing the importance of the author. Date of publication is one of the last items in the citation, reflecting that a publication's currency is often not as important in the humanities as it is in other disciplines. By contrast, APA and CSE list the date of publication near the beginning of the citation in a place of prominence.

Interestingly, CSE does not use any unique punctuation to distinguish the author from the date other than separating them by a period, reflecting that they are of almost equal importance.

Citation styles reflect the values of the respective disciplines. In a very real sense, citation styles are rhetorically constructed: they are developed, revised, updated, and used in ways that reflect the purpose and audience for citing sources in different disciplines. Some rules in documentation styles don't seem to have a clear reason, though, and this is why it's important to know how to verify the rules of a certain system. Our goal is to help you understand, on a rhetorical level, the way three common citation styles work. Memorizing these styles is not always the most productive endeavor, as the styles change over time. Really understanding how they work will be much more useful to you long-term.

Modern Language Association (MLA) Style

WHAT IS UNIQUE ABOUT MLA STYLE?

MLA style is generally followed by researchers in the disciplines of the humanities such as foreign languages and English. One of the unique aspects of MLA style, when compared with other styles, is that the page numbers of quoted, summarized, or paraphrased information are included in in-text citations. While other styles sometimes also include page numbers (especially for exact quotations), the use of page numbers in MLA allows readers to go back to find the original language of the referenced passage. In the disciplines that follow MLA style, the way in which something is phrased is often quite important, and readers might want to review the original source to assess how you are using evidence to support your argument.

We offer some basic guidelines here for using MLA style, but you can learn more about the style guides published by the Modern Language Association, including the *MLA Handbook for Writers of Research Papers* and the *MLA Style Manual and Guide to Scholarly Publishing*, at http://www.mla.org.

IN-TEXT CITATIONS IN MLA STYLE

When sources are cited in the text, MLA style calls for a parenthetical reference at the end of a sentence or at the end of the information being cited (if in the middle of a sentence). The author's name and the page number of the reference appear in parentheses with no other punctuation, and then the end-of-sentence punctuation appears after the parenthetical reference.

> The popularity of crystals and crystallization in chemical research can be traced to the Zantac patent case (Davey 1463).

1. Paraphrase from article
2. Last name of author
3. Page number where paraphrased material can be found

WORKS CITED CITATIONS IN MLA STYLE

The citations list at the end of an academic paper in MLA style is called a Works Cited page. Citations are listed on the Works Cited page in alphabetical order by the authors' last names.

Davey, Roger J. "Pizzas, Polymorphs, and Pills." *Chemical Communications* 13 (2003): 1463-67. Print.

1. Author's name is listed first, with the last name preceding the first name and any middle initials. The first name is spelled out.
2. Article titles and book chapters are given in quotation marks. All words in the title are capitalized except for articles and prepositions (unless they are the first words). Include a period after the title, inside the last quotation mark.
3. Book, journal, magazine, and newspaper titles appear in italics. No punctuation follows the title.
4. For a journal, the volume number follows the title of the journal. If the journal starts new pagination at the beginning of each issue, include a period and the issue number (13.1).
5. The year of publication appears in parentheses, followed by a colon.
6. Inclusive page numbers are provided in the MLA citation of a journal article, followed by a period.
7. Medium of publication (Print, Web, DVD, etc.) comes last, followed by a period.

CITING DIFFERENT TYPES OF SOURCES IN MLA STYLE

Comparison of Different Kinds of Sources in MLA Style

Type of Source	Example of Works Cited Entry	Notes
Book	Davies, Alice, and Kathryn Tollervey. *The Style of Coworking: Contemporary Shared Workspaces.* Munich: Prestel Verlag, 2013. Print.	When more than one author is listed, only the first author's name is reversed in MLA style.
Book chapter	Hochman, Will, and Mike Palmquist. "From Desktop to Laptop: Making Transitions to Wireless Learning in Writing Classrooms." *Going Wireless: A Critical Exploration of Wireless and Mobile Technologies for Composition Teachers and Researchers.* Ed. Amy C. Kimme Hea. Cresskill: Hampton, 2009. 109-31. Print.	Be sure to list both the book chapter and the title of the book when citing a chapter from an edited collection.
Scholarly journal article	Bemer, Amanda Mertz, Ryan M. Moeller, and Cheryl E. Ball. "Designing Collaborative Learning Spaces: Where Material Culture Meets Mobile Writing Processes." *Programmatic Perspectives* 1.2 (2009): 139-66. Print.	If the source is taken electronically from a database, the database is also listed.
Magazine or newspaper article	Goel, Vindu. "Office Space Is Hard to Find for Newcomers." *New York Times* 2 Apr. 2015: F2. Print.	Periodical articles can differ in print and online, so be sure to cite where you found your version of the article.
Website	Arieff, Allison. "Collaborative Workspaces: Not All They're Cracked Up to Be." *CityLab.* Atlantic Monthly Group, 18 Jan. 2012. Web. 2 Apr. 2015.	
Website with no individual author listed	Sage One. "Eight Ideas for Designing a More Collaborative Workspace." *Microsoft for Work.* Microsoft Corporation, 10 Jul. 2014. Web. 2 Apr. 2015.	When no author is listed, you can begin the citation with the title of the article or site. If an organization or some other entity is sponsoring the article (as in this case), that can be listed as the author.

SAMPLE MLA WORKS CITED PAGE

Works Cited

Arieff, Allison. "Collaborative Workspaces: Not All They're Cracked Up to Be." *CityLab*. Atlantic Monthly Group, 18 Jan. 2012. Web. 2 Apr. 2015.

Bemer, Amanda Mertz, Ryan M. Moeller, and Cheryl E. Ball. "Designing Collaborative Learning Spaces: Where Material Culture Meets Mobile Writing Processes." *Programmatic Perspectives* 1.2 (2009): 139-66. Print.

Davies, Alice, and Kathryn Tollervey. *The Style of Coworking: Contemporary Shared Workspaces*. Munich: Prestel Verlag, 2013. Print.

Goel, Vindu. "Office Space Is Hard to Find for Newcomers." *New York Times* 2 Apr. 2015: F2. Print.

Hochman, Will, and Mike Palmquist. "From Desktop to Laptop: Making Transitions to Wireless Learning in Writing Classrooms." *Going Wireless: A Critical Exploration of Wireless and Mobile Technologies for Composition Teachers and Researchers*. Ed. Amy C. Kimme Hea. Cresskill: Hampton, 2009. 109-31. Print.

Sage One. "Eight Ideas for Designing a More Collaborative Workspace." *Microsoft for Work*. Microsoft Corporation, 10 Jul. 2014. Web. 2 Apr. 2015.

American Psychological Association (APA) Style

WHAT IS UNIQUE ABOUT APA STYLE?

Researchers in many areas of the social sciences and related fields generally follow APA documentation procedures. Although you'll encounter page numbers in the in-text citations for direct quotations in APA documents, you're less likely to find direct quotations overall. Generally, researchers in the social sciences are less interested in the specific language or words used to report research findings than they are in the results or conclusions. Therefore, social science researchers are more likely to paraphrase information from sources than to quote information.

Additionally, in-text documentation in the APA system requires that you include the date of publication for research. This is a striking distinction from the MLA system. Social science research that was conducted fifty years ago may not be as useful as research conducted two years ago, so it's important to cite the date of the source in the text of your argument. Imagine how different the results would be for a study of the effects of violence in video games on youth twenty years ago versus a study conducted last year. Findings from twenty years ago probably have very little bearing on the world of today and would not reflect the same video game content as today's games. Including the date of research publication as part of the in-text citation allows readers to quickly evaluate the currency, and therefore the appropriateness, of the research you reference. Learn more about the *Publication Manual of the American Psychological Association* and the APA itself at http://www.apa.org.

IN-TEXT CITATIONS IN APA STYLE

When sources are cited in the text, APA style calls for a parenthetical reference at the end of a sentence or at the end of the information being cited (if in the middle of a sentence). The author's name and the year of publication are included in parentheses, separated by a comma, and then the end-of-sentence punctuation appears after the parenthetical reference. Page numbers are only included for direct quotations.

> The popularity of crystals and crystallization in chemical research can be traced to the Zantac patent case (Davey, 2003).

1. Paraphrase from article
2. Last name of author
3. Year of publication

Often, the author's name is mentioned in the sentence, and then the year is listed in parentheses right after the author's name.

According to Davey (2003), the popularity of crystals and crystallization in chemical research can be traced to the Zantac patent case.

1. Name of author mentioned in the sentence
2. Year of publication listed in parentheses directly following author's name
3. Paraphrase from article

REFERENCE PAGE CITATIONS IN APA STYLE

The citations list at the end of an academic paper in APA style is called a References page. Citations are listed on the References page in alphabetical order by the authors' last names.

Davey, R. J. (2003). Pizzas, polymorphs, and pills. *Chemical Communications, 13*, 1463-1467.

1. The author's name is listed first, with the last name preceding first and middle initials. Only the last name is spelled out.
2. The year directly follows the name, listed in parentheses and followed by a period.
3. Article titles and book chapters are listed with no punctuation other than a period at the end. Only the first word in the title and any proper nouns are capitalized. If there is a colon in the title, the first word after the colon should also be capitalized.
4. Journal titles appear in italics, and all words are capitalized except articles and prepositions (unless they are the first words). A comma follows a journal title.
5. The volume number follows the title, also in italics. If there is an issue number, it is listed in parentheses following the volume number, but not in italics. This is followed by a comma.
6. Inclusive page numbers appear at the end, followed by a period.

CITING DIFFERENT TYPES OF SOURCES IN APA STYLE

Comparison of Different Kinds of Sources in APA Style

Type of Source	Example of Reference Page Entry	Notes
Book	Davies, A., & Tollervey, K. (2013). *The style of coworking: Contemporary shared workspaces.* Munich: Prestel Verlag.	In APA, multiple authors are linked with an ampersand (&).
Book chapter	Hochman, W., & Palmquist, M. (2009). From desktop to laptop: Making transitions to wireless learning in writing classrooms. In A. C. Kimme Hea (Ed.), *Going wireless: A critical exploration of wireless and mobile technologies for composition teachers and researchers* (pp. 109-131). Cresskill, NJ: Hampton Press.	Be sure to list both the book chapter and the title of the book when citing a chapter from an edited collection.
Scholarly journal article	Bemer, A. M., Moeller, R. M., & Ball, C. E. (2009). Designing collaborative learning spaces: Where material culture meets mobile writing processes. *Programmatic Perspectives, 1*(2), 139-166.	In APA, the journal number is italicized with the journal title, but the issue number (in parentheses) is not.
Magazine or newspaper article	Goel, V. (2015, April 2). Office space is hard to find for newcomers. *The New York Times*, p. F2.	Periodical articles can differ in print and online, so be sure to cite where you found your version of the article.
Website	Arieff, A. (2012, January 18). Collaborative workspaces: Not all they're cracked up to be. *CityLab*. Retrieved from http://www.citylab.com/	
Website with no individual author listed	Sage One. (2014, July 10). Eight ideas for designing a more collaborative workspace [Web log post]. Retrieved from http://blogs.microsoft.com/	When no author is listed for a web-based source, you can begin the citation with the title of the article or site. If an organization or some other entity is sponsoring the article (as in this case), that can be listed as author.

SAMPLE APA REFERENCE PAGE

RUNNING HEAD   7

References

Arieff, A. (2012, January 18). Collaborative workspaces: Not
    all they're cracked up to be. *CityLab*. Retrieved from
    http://www.citylab.com/

Bemer, A. M., Moeller, R. M., & Ball, C. E. (2009). Designing
    collaborative learning spaces: Where material culture
    meets mobile writing processes. *Programmatic*
    Perspectives, 1(2), 139-166.

Davies, A., & Tollervey, K. (2013). *The style of coworking:*
    Contemporary shared workspaces. Munich: Prestel
    Verlag.

Goel, V. (2015, April 2). Office space is hard to find for
    newcomers. *The New York Times*, p. F2.

Hochman, W., & Palmquist, M. (2009). From desktop to laptop:
    Making transitions to wireless learning in writing
    classrooms. In A. C. Kimme Hea (Ed.), *Going wireless:*
    A critical exploration of wireless and mobile technologies
    for composition teachers and researchers (pp. 109-131).
    Cresskill, NJ: Hampton Press.

Sage One. (2014, July 10). Eight ideas for designing a more
    collaborative workspace [Web log post]. Retrieved from
    http://blogs.microsoft.com/

Council of Science Editors (CSE) Style

WHAT IS UNIQUE ABOUT CSE STYLE?

As the name suggests, the CSE documentation system is most prevalent among disciplines of the natural sciences, although many of the applied fields of the sciences, like engineering and medicine, rely on their own documentation systems. As with the other systems described here, CSE requires writers to document all materials derived from sources. Unlike MLA or APA, however, CSE allows multiple methods for in-text citations, corresponding to alternative forms of the reference page at the end of research reports. The three styles— **Citation-Sequence**, **Citation-Name**, and **Name-Year**—are used by different publications. In this book, we introduce you to the Name-Year system.

For more detailed information on CSE documentation, you can consult the latest edition of *Scientific Style and Format: The CSE Manual for Authors, Editors, and Publishers,* and you can learn more about the Council of Science Editors at its website: http://www.councilscienceeditors.org.

IN-TEXT CITATIONS IN CSE STYLE

When sources are cited in the text, CSE style calls for a parenthetical reference directly following the relevant information. The author's name and the year of publication are included in parentheses with no other punctuation.

> The popularity of crystals and crystallization in chemical research can be traced to the Zantac patent case (Davey 2003).

1. Paraphrase from article
2. Last name of author
3. Year of publication

REFERENCE PAGE CITATIONS IN CSE STYLE

The citations list at the end of an academic paper in CSE style is called a References page. Citations are listed on the References page in alphabetical order by the authors' last names.

> Davey RJ. 2003. Pizzas, polymorphs, and pills. Chem Comm. 13:1463-1467.

1. The author's name is listed first, with the full last name preceding the first and middle initials. No punctuation separates elements of the name.
2. The year directly follows the name, followed by a period.
3. Article titles and book chapters are listed with no punctuation other than a period at the end. Only the first word in the title and any proper nouns

are capitalized. If there is a colon in the title, the first word after the colon should not be capitalized.

4. Journal titles are often abbreviated, and all words are capitalized. A period follows the journal title.

5. The volume number follows the title. If there is an issue number, it is listed in parentheses following the volume number, but not in italics. This is followed by a colon. No space appears after the colon.

6. Inclusive page numbers appear at the end, followed by a period.

CITING DIFFERENT TYPES OF SOURCES IN CSE STYLE

Comparison of Different Kinds of Sources in CSE Style

Type of Source	Example of Reference Page Entry	Notes
Book	Davies A, Tollervey K. 2013. The style of coworking: contemporary shared workspaces. Munich: Prestel Verlag. 159 p.	Listing the number of pages is optional in CSE, but useful.
Book chapter	Hochman W, Palmquist M. 2009. From desktop to laptop: making transitions to wireless learning in writing classrooms. In: Kimme Hea AH, editor. Going wireless: a critical exploration of wireless and mobile technologies for composition teachers and researchers. Cresskill (NJ): Hampton Press. p. 109-131.	
Scholarly journal article	Bemer AM, Moeller RM, Ball CE. 2009. Designing collaborative learning spaces: where material culture meets mobile writing processes. Prog Persp. 1(2):139-166.	Some journal titles in CSE are abbreviated.
Magazine or newspaper article	Goel V. 2015 Apr 2. Office space is hard to find for newcomers. New York Times (National Ed.). Sect. F:2 (col. 1).	
Website	Arieff A. 2012 Jan 18. Collaborative workspaces: not all they're cracked up to be [Internet]. CityLab; [accessed 2015 Apr 2]. Available from http://www.citylab.com/design/2012/01 /collaborative-workspaces-not-all-theyre -cracked-be/946/	CSE calls for the exact URL and an access date for web-based sources.
Website with no individual author listed	Sage One. 2014. Eight ideas for designing a more collaborative workspace [blog]. Microsoft at Work; [accessed 2015 Apr 2]. Available from http://blogs.microsoft.com/work/2014/07/10 /eight-ideas-for-designing-a-more-collaborative -workspace/	

SAMPLE CSE REFERENCE PAGE

Running head 7

References

Arieff A. 2012 Jan 18. Collaborative workspaces: not all they're cracked up to be [Internet]. CityLab; [accessed 2015 Apr 2]. Available from http://www.citylab.com /design/2012/01/collaborative-workspaces-not-all-theyre -cracked-be/946/

Bemer AM, Moeller RM, Ball CE. 2009. Designing collaborative learning spaces: where material culture meets mobile writing processes. Prog Persp. 1(2):139-166.

Davies A, Tollervey K. 2013. The style of coworking: contemporary shared workspaces. Munich: Prestel Verlag. 159 p.

Goel V. 2015 Apr 2. Office space is hard to find for newcomers. New York Times (National Ed.). Sect. F:2 (col. 1).

Hochman W, Palmquist M. 2009. From desktop to laptop: making transitions to wireless learning in writing classrooms. In: Kimme Hea AH, editor. Going wireless: a critical exploration of wireless and mobile technologies for composition teachers and researchers. Cresskill (NJ): Hampton Press. p. 109-131.

Sage One. 2014. Eight ideas for designing a more collaborative workspace [blog]. Microsoft at Work; [accessed 2015 Apr 2]. Available from http://blogs.microsoft.com /work/2014/07/10/eight-ideas-for-designing-a-more -collaborative-workspace/

Other Common Documentation Styles

Many disciplines have their own documentation styles, and some are used more commonly than others. The following chart lists a few of the most popular.

Name of Citation Style	Disciplines	Website
American Chemical Society (ACS)	Chemistry and Physical Sciences	http://pubs.acs.org/series/styleguide
American Institute of Physics (AIP)	Physics	http://publishing.aip.org/authors
American Mathematical Society (AMS)	Mathematics	http://www.ams.org/publications/authors
American Medical Association (AMA)	Medicine	http://www.amamanualofstyle.com/
American Political Science Association (APSA)	Political Science	http://www.apsanet.org/Portals/54/files/APSAStyleManual2006.pdf
American Sociological Association (ASA)	Sociology	http://www.asanet.org/documents/teaching/pdfs/Quick_Tips_for_ASA_Style.pdf
Associated Press Stylebook (AP Style)	Journalism	https://www.apstylebook.com/
Bluebook style	Law, Legal Studies	https://www.legalbluebook.com/
Chicago Manual of Style (CMoS)	History and other humanities disciplines	http://www.chicagomanualofstyle.org/
Institute of Electrical and Electronics Engineers (IEEE)	Engineering	http://www.ieee.org/documents/ieeecitationref.pdf

Name of Citation Style	Disciplines	Website
Linguistic Society of America (LSA)	Linguistics	http://www.linguisticsociety.org/files/style-sheet.pdf
Modern Humanities Research Association (MHRA)	Humanities	http://www.mhra.org.uk/Publications/Books/StyleGuide/StyleGuideV3.pdf

TRACKING RESEARCH

There are many useful, free digital tools online that can help you track your research and sources. Three of the best are personalized research-tracking tools and social applications that enable you to find additional resources through other users of the application:

- **Diigo (https://www.diigo.com/)** Diigo is a social bookmarking application that solves two dilemmas faced by many writers. First, you can access all of the bookmarks that you save in a browser on multiple devices. Additionally, you can tag your sources and share them with others. That means you can search using tags (not very different from searching with key words in a database) and find other sources that users of Diigo have tagged with the same words and phrases that you have chosen.

- **Zotero (https://www.zotero.org/)** Zotero is a robust research tool that helps you organize, cite, and share sources with others. You can install Zotero into your web browser and quickly save and annotate sources that you're looking at online. Zotero can help you generate citations, annotated bibliographies, and reference lists from the sources that you have saved.

- **Mendeley (http://www.mendeley.com/)** Similar to Zotero, Mendeley is a free reference manager and academic social network that allows you to read and annotate PDFs on any device.

Your school may also have licenses for proprietary tools such as RefWorks and EndNote, which are also very useful research-tracking applications. Most of these applications can help you generate citations and reference lists as well. However, you need to understand how a documentation style works in order to check what is generated from any citation builder. For example, if you save the title of a journal article as "Increased pizza consumption leads to temporary euphoria but higher long-term cholesterol levels," a citation builder will not automatically change the capitalization if you need to generate a citation in MLA format. You have to be smarter than the application you use.

ACKNOWLEDGMENTS

Text Credits

Mike Brotherton. Excerpt from "Hubble Space Telescope Spies Galaxy/Black Hole Evolution in Action." From press release posted on mikebrotherton.com, June 2, 2008. Reproduced with permission of the author.

Mike Brotherton, Wil Van Breugel, S. A. Stanford, R. J. Smith, B. J. Boyle, Lance Miller, T. Shanks, S. M. Croom, and Alexei V. Filippenko. Excerpt from "A Spectacular Poststarburst Quasar." From *The Astrophysical Journal*, August 1, 1999. Copyright © 1999 The American Astronomical Society. Reproduced with permission of the authors.

Wanda Cassidy, Karen Brown, and Margaret Jackson. "'Under the Radar': Educators and Cyberbullying in Schools." From *School Psychology International*, October 2012, Vol. 33, No. 5, pp. 520–32. Copyright © 2012 Psychology International. Reproduced with permission of SAGE.

EBSCO Health. "Sample Discharge Orders." From www.ebscohost.com. Reproduced with permission from EBSCO Information Services.

Arthur L. Greil, Kathleen Slauson-Blevins, and Julia McQuillan. "The Experience of Infertility: A Review of Recent Literature." From *Sociology of Health & Illness*, Vol. 32, Issue 1. Copyright © 2010 by Blackwell Publishing Ltd. Reproduced with permission of Blackwell Publishing Ltd. in the format Book via Copyright Clearance Center.

Dale Jacobs. "More Than Words: Comics as a Means of Teaching Multiple Literacies." From *English Journal*, Vol. 96, No. 3, January 2007. Copyright © 2007 National Council of Teachers of English. Reproduced with permission.

Charles Kerns and Kenneth Ko. "Exploring Happiness at Work." From *Leadership & Organizational Management Journal*. Copyright © 2009. Reproduced with permission of the authors.

Carolyn W. Keys. "Revitalizing Instruction in Scientific Genres: Connection Knowledge Production with Writing to Learn in Science." From *Science Education*, Vol. 83. Copyright © 1999 John Wiley & Sons. Reproduced with permission.

Margaret Shandor Miles, Diane Holditch-Davis, Suzanne Thoyre, and Linda Beeber. "Rural African-American Mothers Parenting Prematurely Born Infants: An Ecological Systems Perspective." From *Newborn and Infant Nursing Reviews*, Vol. 5, Issue 3, September 2005, pp. 142–48. Copyright © 2005 Elsevier. Reproduced with permission from Elsevier.

Myra Moses. "Lesson Plan" and "IEP." Reproduced with permission of the author.

Kalervo Oberg. Excerpt from "Cultural Shock: Adjustments to New Cultural Environments." From *Practical Anthropology*, 1960, Vol. 7. Copyright © 1960 American Association of Missiology. Reproduced with permission.

Kevin Rathunde and Mihaly Csikszentmihalyi. "Middle School Students' Motivation and Quality of Experience: A Comparison of Montessori and Traditional School Environments." From *American Journal of Education*, 2005, Vol. 111, Issue 3. Copyright © 2005 University of Chicago Press. Reproduced with permission.

Gary Ritchison. "Hunting Behavior, Territory Quality, and Individual Quality of American Kestrels (*Falco sparverius*)." From Eastern Kentucky University Web page. Reproduced with permission of author.

Jack Solomon. Excerpt from "Masters of Desire: The Culture of American Advertising." From *The Signs of Our Time: Semiotics — the Hidden Messages of Environments, Objects, and Cultural Images*, by Jack Fisher Solomon. Copyright © 1988 by Jack Solomon. Reproduced with permission of Tarcher, an imprint of Penguin Publishing Group, a division of Penguin Random House LLC.

Index

LaunchPadSolo Additional video material may be found online in LaunchPad Solo when the ⊙ icon appears.

A

abstracts, 174–75
academic disciplines
  conventions of writing in, 90
  defined, 7–8
  genres in, 90
  number of, 8–9
  research in, 89–90
academic journals, 69
academic literacy, 14
academic presses, books published by, 69
academic research, 59–85
  avoiding plagiarism in, 75–76
  choosing primary and secondary sources in, 60–62
  conducting, 59
  developing a supported argument on a controversial issue in, 79–84
  developing research question in, 59–60
  documentation systems in, 76–77
  evaluating sources in, 69–71
  generating search terms in, 65
  paraphrasing in, 72–73
  quoting in, 74

searching for journal articles by discipline in, 67–68
searching for sources in, 62–68
summarizing in, 71–72
using journal databases in, 66–67
writing an annotated bibliography in, 77–79
academic writers
  reasons for citing sources, 307–8
  reasons for writing, 10–13
academic writing
  analyzing genres and conventions in, 91–92
  using structure, language, and reference (SLR) to analyze, 94–96
  values of, 307–8
acknowledgments, 175
active voice, 136–37, 176–77
advertisement
  rhetorical analysis of, 48–52
  student analysis of, 52–57
American Chemical Society (ACS), 320
American Institute of Physics (AIP), 320
American Mathematical Society (AMS), 320

American Medical Association (AMA), 320
American Political Science Association (APSA), 320
American Psychological Association (APA), 77, 97, 307, 308–9
  citing different types of sources in, 315
  in-text citations in, 313–14
  reference page citations in, 314
  sample reference page in, 316
  uniqueness of, 313
American Sociological Association (ASA), 320
annotated bibliography, 77
  writing an, 77–79
appeals, rhetorical, 38
appendixes, 175–76
applied fields, 261–303
  business as, 282–94
  defined, 261
  education as, 272–94
  genres in selected, 264–304
  law as, 294–304
  nursing as, 264–72
  research in, 262
  rhetoric and, 263–64
  scholars in, 9

arguments, 37–58
    analysis of, 48
    assumptions in, 45–46
    audience expectations in, 45
    claims in, 37, 39–40
    counterarguments and, 47–48
    defined, 37
    developing reasons in, 41–42
    developing supported, on a
        controversial issue, 79–84
    expert testimony in, 44
    personal experience in, 43
    proofs and appeals in, 38–39
    statistical data and research
        findings in, 44–45
    supporting reasons with evidence
        in, 43–45
    thesis versus hypothesis in,
        40–41
artistic proofs, 38
artistic texts, 149
Associated Press Stylebook (AP
    Style), 320
assumptions, 45–46
audience, 24
    analyzing expectations of, 45
    for a lab report, 263–64
    primary, 21
    secondary, 21
authors, 24

B

Bahls, Patrick (mathematics), 29,
    219, 225
    on genres ◉
    on research contexts ◉
    on research questions ◉
Baumgartner, Jody (political
    science), 28, 60
    on using evidence ◉
    on writing process ◉
Beeber, Linda. *See* Miles, Margaret
    Shandor; Holditch-Davis,
    Diane; Thoyre, Suzanne;
    and Beeber, Linda; "Rural
    African-American Mothers
    Parenting Prematurely Born
    Infants: An Ecological Systems
    Perspective," 266–68
bias, addressing, 164
Bluebook style, 320

Boyle, B. J., "A Spectacular
    Poststarburst Quasar," 98–99
Brotherton, Mike (astronomy), 47,
    93, 96, 97, 100
    "A Spectacular Poststarburst
        Quasar," 98–99
    on developing arguments ◉
    "Hubble Space Telescope Spies
        Galaxy/Black Hole Evolution in
        Action," 94–95
    on qualifiers ◉
Bruegel, Wil Van, "A Spectacular
    Poststarburst Quasar," 98–99
Bush, George H. W., "Letter to
    Saddam Hussein," 31–32
business, 282–94
    business plan in, 285–94
    memorandum in, 282–84
business plan, 285–94

C

Chicago Manual of Style, 139–40,
    320
Chopin, Kate, "The Story of an
    Hour," 124–25, 126–28
citations, reasons for making,
    307–8
claims, 37, 39–40
    in arguments, 37
close reading
    in the humanities, 113–23
    strategies for, 123–28
collaboration, cooperation and, in
    natural sciences, 226
college(s)
    choosing, 5
    comparing writing in, with writing
        in other contexts, 12–13
    differences between universities
        and, 4–5
    purpose of, 5–6
    writing about, 7
community colleges, 4
comparative experiments, 219
"Comparing the Efficiency of
    Various Batteries Being
    Used over Time" (Lemon),
    230–39
complex thesis statement, 41
content/form-response grid, 123
control groups, 219

controversial issue, developing
    supported arguments on a,
    79–84
conventions, 10
    language
        active and passive voice,
            136–37, 176–77
        description and rhetorical
            language, 136
        hedging, 137, 177
    reference
        in the humanities, 138–39
        in-text documentation, 178
        paraphrase, 179
        summary, 179
    structural, 130
        abstracts as, 174–75
        in the humanities, 135
        IMRAD (Introduction,
            Methods, Results, and
            Discussion) format and,
            166–74
        titles as, 174
    of writing
        in humanities, 129
        in the natural sciences, 221–26
        in the social sciences, 165–74
cooperation, collaboration and, in
    natural science, 226
Council of Science Editors (CSE),
    77, 307, 308–9
    citing different types of sources
        in, 318
    in-text citations in, 317
    reference page citations in,
        317–18
    sample reference page, 319
    uniqueness of, 317
Council of Writing Program
    Administrators (CWPA), 13
counterarguments, 47
    anticipating, 47–48
    dealing with, 48
Croom, S. M., "A Spectacular
    Poststarburst Quasar," 98–99
Csikszentmihalyi, Mihaly,
    "Happiness in Everyday Life:
    The Uses of Experience
    Sampling," 181–82
"Cultural Shock: Adjustments to
    New Cultural Environments"
    (Oberg), 155–58